PRAISE FOR
MOTHER KNOWS BEST

"Pamula Floyd's memoir, *Mother Knows Best*, is a must-read for parents, educators, and medical professionals! Pamula tells her gripping story about a preventable medical trauma with honesty and integrity. Against all odds, Pamula fought and advocated for her son, Chaz, every step of the way. Mother did indeed know best."

—**Jenni Basch,** MEd, MS, Author of *Children and Disability: A Survival Guide for Parents, Educators, and Caregivers*

"Mother Knows Best: A Memoir is a touching, brave story of a mother's love and her journey through a medical communication crisis that left her elder son dependent on a wheelchair. It will make you cry. It will make you laugh. It will help you understand the consequences of failure within the American medical system and the resilience of a family facing life's most painful challenges."

—**Janine Latus,** Author of *If I Am Missing or Dead: A Sister's Story of Love, Murder and Liberation*

"Pam describes the harrowing experience of a parent who witnesses the starvation and dehydration of a previously healthy baby, her son Chaz, while exclusively breastfeeding. Tragedies like these now occur commonly as a result of the current campaign to promote exclusive breastfeeding for all mothers and infants promoted by the World Health Organization, UNICEF, and multiple supporting organizations. Exclusive-breastfeeding education commonly teaches parents that insufficient breast milk is rare, that signs of infant hunger are normal, and that all that is required to feed a hungry breastfed baby is to 'just keep breastfeeding.' For parents with true low milk supply who follow this advice, their infants can become jaundiced, dehydrated, and hypoglycemic, which causes brain injury and permanent disability. Breastfeeding books commonly normalize and minimize the signs and serious consequences of insufficient feeding of breastfed infants in order to promote compliance with global exclusive-breastfeeding targets, to the detriment of the least-fed infants. Chaz is one of millions of infants who have been harmed by the WHO/UNICEF Baby Friendly Hospital Initiative and the Ten Steps to Successful Breastfeeding. Lessons that Pam learns as a breastfeeding parent who becomes a special-needs parent is vital information for every parent who wants to provide their infant safe and optimal infant feeding."

—**Christie del Castillo-Hegyi,** MD, Emergency Physician, Fed Is Best Foundation

"In *Mother Knows Best*, Pam Floyd shares her compelling journey from joyous mother of a healthy newborn to, days later, facing the catastrophic near death of her previously healthy baby, and the radical adjustment to a new life she and her husband, Frank, never anticipated. In her captivating story, Pam recounts how she learned to choose hope and possibility over despair and remorse, and convinces readers that loving unconditionally, advocating fiercely, and accepting and celebrating the child we have can mold us into the person we were meant to be. I enthusiastically recommend this compelling book, not only for every parent of a child with special health care needs, but for every parent. I also commend Pam's memoir as a must-read for all lactation care providers, who always must make a baby's welfare their paramount priority."

—**Marianne Neifert,** MD, MTS, FAAP, Pediatrician, Academy of Breastfeeding Medicine Co-Founder, Author, Colorado Women's Hall of Fame 2020 Inductee

"*Mother Knows Best: A Memoir* is a heartbreaking story of unintended starvation-induced brain damage from insufficient milk intake while exclusively breastfeeding. Mothers like Pam and her son Chaz are the reason I co-founded the Fed Is Best Foundation—where we provide education to parents about how to recognize insufficient breastfeeding. Unfortunately, breastfeeding education often does not teach parents how common low milk supply really is or how to supplement to protect their babies from needless suffering. It's a modern-day tragedy."

—**Jody Segrave-Daly,** MS, RN, IBCLC

"Pamula Floyd writes from her gut, the same gut that told her she knew better than any pediatrician or expert what her newborn baby needed. *Mother Knows Best* reminds new mothers to always trust their gut instincts and warns of the dangers of not trusting new mothers. Her writing is raw and deep hearted and unflinching, much like the side of motherhood we're too afraid to discuss."

—**Kelly Sokol,** Author of *The Unprotected*

"Pamula is willing to open up her heart to readers and share her truth with rawness and vulnerability that engages you from the first page. Her words are a salve to fellow mothers who have said early goodbyes and a reminder to all mothers to trust their instincts."

—**Alyssa DeRose,** Author of *Momoir: A New Mom's Journey to Embracing Her Not-So-Perfect Motherhood*

". . . The ending of the book will surprise the reader when they realize all that had happened to this precious baby at the beginning of the story. The suspense of the narrative makes the book very hard to put down. It stirs up feelings of anger, laughter, tears of joy and sorrow, along with praying and thanking God. AN AWESOME READ."

—**Anne H. Harrell,** coauthor of *Cyndy's Blessed Assurance*

Mother Knows Best: A Memoir
by Pamula Floyd

ISBN 978-1-64663-356-2

Published by

◤ köehlerbooks™

3705 Shore Drive
Virginia Beach, VA 23455
800-435-4811
www.koehlerbooks.com

Mother Knows Best

A MEMOIR

PAMULA FLOYD

VIRGINIA BEACH
CAPE CHARLES

Some names and identifying features of individuals in this book have been changed, but the events depicted are true to the best of my memory.

DEDICATION

Where to begin? I will begin by thanking my family, my husband Frank, and my sons Dustin and Chaz. And the man that has been there since Chaz was six days old, Dr. Larry White. And though we have a complicated relationship, I have to thank God. I thank my parents, Robert and Alease, for putting up with me as I vented about all the things that had to be done on Chaz's behalf. And I have to thank Frank's mom Dot and his sister Linda for coming to every surgery they could get to. Even when it snowed.

TABLE OF CONTENTS

INTRODUCTION

efore you put this book down, read the first paragraph . . . Thank you very much. Time to learn about life. Ready?

Whether you like it or not, the only two certainties in this life are *change **and** adaptation*. Minor and major changes in the world occur multiple times daily. Subsequent decisions are required that often affect our lives. Perspective often dictates the outcome. When one person makes a decision for others, notably in school, the military, or other settings, the result often has mixed outcomes. We, or designated others who make adaptive decisions, can react instinctively or rationally, as individuals or groups, quickly or slowly. They can be forgotten in an instant or remembered for a lifetime.

Read this book or not. I encourage you to learn about the Floyd family. All Pam Floyd ever wanted was to be a good mom. A sick pregnancy, a rough delivery, early separation from her son, and money issues were bad enough. But a decision based on bad advice while she was having problems breastfeeding caused a severe brain injury in her son.

For twenty-seven years, I have helped Pam and her family, the Floyd family, with the fallout: motor delays, cognitive challenges, seizures, surgeries, lawsuits, and especially family PTSD leading to ongoing anger and lack of trust.

So why a book?

Because people don't learn, that's why. Over twenty-seven years, I have marveled at the improvements in treating brain injury, recognizing families at risk, overall management of newborn care, especially in the areas of nutrition. And yet I still keep meeting moms with similar stories. One baby is three now, another is two, and one died. We are not there yet. Repeat after me:

BABIES NEED WATER!

BABIES NEED WATER!

Whether you are mixing formula incorrectly or not giving enough formula or breast milk, either by decreased supply or miscalculation, you are putting your baby at risk. Pam's story was on TV and in the papers in the 1990s. Chaz and his mom Pam, his dad Frank, and his brother Dustin are good people facing adversity, showing as much resilience as any family I have met in thirty years of Child Neurology practice. Just a brief glimpse:

Pam is a great mom. She always sought the greater good for Chaz, whether involving medications, therapeutic devices, computer technologies, adaptive wheelchairs, and accessible vans. She was vilified by writers, healthcare workers, and TV "journalists" without losing her focus or her mind.

Chaz has suffered almost every neurological nightmare you can imagine, including coma, seizures, spastic limbs, surgical misadventures, infections, and many types of pain. He never complained—no matter what. Tough as rawhide. Hard as nails. John Wayne in a wheelchair!

Chaz became dehydrated in the first days of life despite Pam's calls daily for medical advice with healthcare professionals. His mom sensed something was terribly wrong. It turned out that Chaz needed more water, but that advice never came. It cost him and his family dearly.

You will feel her frustration, her guilt, and finally, the sad realization that his lack of water could have ended his life. Reader, turn the page and read the rest of the story.

This mom did, indeed, know best!

Larry E. White M.D.
As Pam described me, "The balding little man with glasses."

PART 1

TEN CRUSHING DAYS
IN JUNE

COULDA, WOULDA, SHOULDA

*L*eaving the hospital, I kept replaying the words over and over in my head: *Tonight will determine if Chaz lives or dies.* And yet I was unable to grasp the severity of the situation.

My brain and body began to shut down. I stopped crying. I stopped thinking. And I was numb. I was in my *don't touch me, hold me, or talk to me* phase. I just wanted to be left alone.

On the ride home, neither Frank nor I spoke. From the outside looking in, you could say that we were in shock. A few hours earlier, we had a baby boy who was crying, sleeping, and moving his arms and legs. And now? Now we didn't know if our son would live to see tomorrow. And if he did, what kind of life would he have?

I was confused and scared. I knew what the doctors said: *We're not sure. We'll have to see how tonight goes.* But I didn't know what those words meant. I brought a child into the doctor's office that was perfectly healthy. What happened? I didn't understand. It didn't make sense.

Besides, according to the home health nurse that examined us a few days earlier, we both checked out fine. Wasn't that enough? What changed?

As I rode along in the car, I put my face in my hands and tried to scream. I couldn't. I tried to cry. I couldn't. It was just too much. It was all too much. All of a sudden, I noticed that my body ached tremendously. Every muscle from my head to my toes was screaming for relief. I hurt just riding in the car. And my brain had failed me. I could no longer process simple sentences. Every time I tried to speak, the words couldn't form. There was no signal from my brain to my mouth. All I could do was stare into the darkness as we made our way home.

When we pulled up to the house, it was dark. We forgot to turn on the porch light. Then again, we thought we were going for a quick doctor's visit, with plans to return home in a couple of hours. That was almost ten hours earlier.

Frank and I got out of the car without speaking. It wasn't that we were angry. There just wasn't anything to say.

When Frank opened the front door, Shaggy and Wolf made their way outside. Though they were glad to see us, I could tell they sensed something was wrong. They even sniffed around the porch, looking for the little person that was no longer with us. It was almost midnight, and they needed time outside.

I volunteered to stay outside with them. They were my babies. I always worried about their safety and never let them out alone. I had failed at keeping my son safe—maybe it wasn't too late for my fur babies.

Although we lived in a beautiful little cottage on the beach, it was located in a not-so-wonderful part of town that was once the crown jewel of Norfolk. Not that many years before, the air had been filled with the smell of popcorn, hotdogs, Doumar's famous ice cream cones, and salt air. Now it looked like a beach that time had forgotten. The happy screams that had once filled the area from people enjoying the park rides at the Ocean View Amusement Park were replaced with gunshots and screeching tires. The ground was once strewn with flying wrappers from cotton candy, popcorn, corn dogs, and other treats. Now it was littered with cigarette wrappers, used condoms, syringes, and beer cans.

Our little cottage represented what once stood there. A time of innocence and happiness. Of laughter and fun. Even in daylight, I kept an eye on my surroundings. It was only inside that I felt safe and secure. As long as my curtains were closed and the sun was shining and Shaggy and Wolf were with me.

I finally noticed that the dogs had finished their business and were anxiously waiting for me to let them in. I guess my mind drifted off somewhere, though I'm not sure where, as I was pretty sure I didn't have a single thought in my head.

I stood frozen in my kitchen, like someone who was trying to remember what it was they had intended to do. I could hear the clock ticking and was surprised by how loud it sounded. It must have been going bad, because I'd never heard it ticking before. The refrigerator was also humming rather loudly as if it was competing with the clock.

Frank was finishing up a bowl of cereal when he said, "I'm going to soak in the tub before I go to bed." And with that, he put his bowl in the dishwasher, turned it on, and left.

With all the noise in the kitchen, I wandered into the living room and sat on the couch. Both dogs jumped up, wanting me to pet them. And without consciously thinking about it, I began to do so. My hands reflexively found their fur. These poor things. There'd been a lot of changes around here this past year. And they'd gone with the flow without hesitation.

After a few minutes of petting, I stopped and reached for one of the dark blue pillows, pressing it to my mouth and screaming. With the scream came tears. My faithful furry friends snuggled in closer to me, knowing something wasn't right. Like all dogs, they wanted to make their human feel better. They nudged my hands. Petting must have been the answer. Petting a dog would solve anything that's wrong, right? *Not this time, guys*, I thought. *This isn't something you can fix.*

Frank was at least trying to sleep. I was too tired and emotional to even think about it. I stared into Chaz's room from my place on the couch, hoping to make sense of things. But I couldn't. My brain wouldn't let me.

Even if it did, I don't think I would have understood.

Everyone handles grief differently. When it comes to me, I shut down. From a young age, I was taught to put my feelings aside. To not show too much emotion. To live in denial. Even in that moment, I was silent, but deep down, I was hurting. I felt as if my heart had been ripped out, with only the arteries left dangling and alone.

In my twenty-eight years on the earth, I had never felt that kind of pain. It felt as if something inside of me was missing. I touched my stomach, which was still swollen from birth six days ago. Six.

Growing up with an overly Southern Baptist mother, I knew all about the number six. From a child, I was taught that six was a bad number and that one should stay away from it no matter what. Six. I was brought up to ignore the number six under any and all terms. If the DMV gave you tags with a six on it, you gave them back. If you were sixth in line at the movies, which by the way you shouldn't be seeing, you let someone go in front of you. Heaven forbid I had a grade with a six in it. Six was to be avoided at all costs. Six. The number of the beast.

Let's see: Chaz had his stroke on his sixth day of life. I made six calls to the pediatrician's office with concerns. Six. They tended to come in threes. *So where is the third one?* I wondered. I stopped there. I didn't want to find it. I wanted to live in denial. Denial was my friend. With denial, I could avoid feeling anything. Yet here I was, crying silently.

As I began to stand up, my muscles ached with a heaviness that felt like I was buried in cement, and I hoped a hot shower would help. I didn't want to wake Frank, so I decided to use the bathroom connected to Chaz's bedroom. His bathroom was huge, especially for such a small cottage. Not only did it come with all the necessities, but it had shelves on two walls. The shelves were filled with diapers, diaper cream, and formula sent to me by some of the ads that I had filled out in my OB/GYN's office months earlier. There was a diaper changing table, his infant bathtub, the dirty diaper bin, a wicker rocking chair, and various other items I had bought during my pregnancy.

As I stood in the shower with the warm water running down my body, I couldn't help but relive the past few days. So many healthcare professionals. So many phone calls. So many things said.

He's a big baby. He'll eat when he's ready.

Don't give him a bottle; it will cause nipple confusion.

Formula is sweeter than breast milk, so don't offer it.

You're a new mother; you don't realize how much he is getting.

Everyone can breastfeed.

Don't supplement breastfeeding with formula because it will confuse the baby and reduce your supply.

The wonderful thing about breastfeeding is you don't have to worry about how much or how little he's getting. Because he'll always get what he needs.

A baby's eyes aren't well developed yet, so they can often wander.

Breast is best.

I hated them all.

I kept saying that I felt like he wasn't getting enough milk from me. I kept saying that I felt like something was wrong. I watched the videos and did what they said. I read and reread the baby books and did what they said. Not one of them mentioned dehydration. Not one of them warned me.

Why didn't I listen to myself?

Why didn't I listen to that motherly voice in my head?

Why didn't I trust my gut?

They said he should have six or seven wet diapers a day. He did—just not *wringing* wet. Wringing was the key word, as I found out later.

They said he should eat every two to three hours, ten to fifteen minutes on each breast. He did.

They said he should have one or two bowel movements a day. He did.

They told me my milk should come in around the third or fourth day. It didn't. They said until my milk came in that the colostrum he was getting was good enough. It wasn't.

I hated them all for not trusting my motherly intuition. I hated Frank for not believing me. Most of all, I hated myself for ignoring my own feelings and for not trusting my gut instincts.

When I finally finished my shower, I opened the curtain to find Shaggy and Wolf sitting there patiently waiting for me. They appeared to be as confused as I was. They knew that a little person lived there now. Only he was nowhere to be found. They knew; they had looked. When we were outside earlier, they had walked up to the car and sniffed around it. We had left as three and came home as two. They were confused, and so was I.

I got dressed then sat down on the spare bed in Chaz's room. As I looked at Chaz's empty crib, I began crying again, that silent cry where your mouth is trying to scream, but the pain is so intense that no sound comes out. That's how I was feeling at that moment. In part, I was angry, and in another part, I felt as if my soul had been ripped from my body, and I was left there to try and find it. My body started to ache again. Even my muscles were turning against me.

I stood up and folded his little blue bear blanket. I straightened up the bumper in his crib and changed the sheet. This wasn't right. His crib shouldn't be empty. He should be here with us.

When I was finished, I sat down in the wicker rocker by the window. Yes, it was late, and I didn't dare open the curtains, but I did peek through them. I needed to see the moon. Even if I couldn't be with my son tonight, I knew that the moon I was seeing was above him too. We could share the moon. It would keep us together. I knew that I was being silly, and yet I couldn't help it. It was late, and I was tired, and I was grasping onto anything that I could. Even if it didn't make sense.

After a few moments, I bent to pet the dogs and do the only thing that made sense to me. I headed into the living room and put a breastfeeding video into the VCR. I watched it again. It didn't make sense. I did everything the video showed, so why didn't it work? Why was I the exception to the rule?

After an hour of torturing myself with *coulda, woulda, shoulda*, I went to bed.

I'M EITHER PREGNANT
OR DYING

It's hard to believe that a year before, we were just starting to talk about getting pregnant. Everything I read said it would take several months to get pregnant after going off birth control pills. So I had taken my last one the previous summer. We decided to keep it to ourselves because we wanted it to be a surprise.

Plus, I wasn't one of those girls that sat around dreaming of her wedding day and starting a family. Yes, I played with dolls but never as the mommy. I didn't cradle my doll, nor did I push it in a stroller. I didn't change its diaper or try to give it a plastic bottle. Babies were not something I envisioned for my future.

At twenty-eight years old, I had only babysat a handful of times, and that was for a toddler that lived in my neighborhood. I'd never held a baby. I'd never been particularly fond of that baby smell. Nor did I think they were all that cute.

But where I'm from, babies are the natural next step in our relationship. Frank and I had been married for three years, and as I approached thirty,

I knew time was knocking on my door—I needed to answer.

After chucking my birth control pills in the trash, I'd made a mental note to visit some secondhand bookstores for books on pregnancy and having a baby. The summer moved on as usual. Both of us were working, and whenever we had time, we'd walk out to the beach for a swim. Our dogs, Shaggy and Wolfgang (aka Wolf), loved the water. Well, Shaggy loved the water. Wolf would stand in the water if you insisted. Otherwise, she was just fine on the sand.

Toward the end of fall, the vibe in our house had changed drastically. Our two cats, Snowball and Gizmo, started acting strange around me. Gizmo refused to come anywhere near me. She would come to Frank, which she had never done before. And Snowball stopped coming to either of us.

I wasn't sure what changed, but I did notice a difference in their actions. They even started sleeping in our spare bedroom. Each morning, I'd wake up and try to entice them to come closer to me, but they weren't having it. Shaggy and Wolf didn't have any problems with me. They'd let me pet them, and they didn't mind sitting beside me on the couch or even the floor.

One day, in late August, I was sitting on the couch watching television, and my cats appeared in the doorway of the spare bedroom. They looked at me and hissed. Then they each made a run for it, speeding past me to get to the kitchen to eat. I didn't know what to do. I was starting to become a little afraid of them. They both still had their claws, and I'd been unintentionally scratched before. I could only imagine what damage they could do to me if they meant to scratch me.

A few days later, while I was on the phone with my grandmother, I mentioned the change in my cats' demeanor. She suggested that I might be pregnant, telling me that animals can sense that kind of thing. I laughed and half-jokingly agreed with her.

When I hung up, I thought about her suggestion a little more. I had been off the pill for about three months then, so it was definitely a possibility. I couldn't really rely on the state of my period since they had always been very irregular. Anything was possible. But I didn't feel any different, so I shrugged it off.

When the weekend hit, it was time to clean the litter box and scrub down my two bathrooms, so I gathered up some sponges and Clorox. After about five minutes of smelling Clorox fumes, I got nauseated. I even ran to the toilet and leaned over it, just in case. But nothing. Instead, I decided to let the fumes settle, so I laid down for a little while.

When I woke up, Gizmo was lying on my stomach, staring at me. Once we made eye contact, she hissed at me. I covered my face because I was afraid that she was going to attack me. Instead, she scurried out of the room. My heart was racing. It was official. I was scared of my two cats. As for the Clorox, I went back to cleaning and was fine.

Later that evening, as I let Shaggy and Wolf out for a potty break, Snowball slipped past me and ran out into the darkness. I called after her, but she just kept running. She'd never done anything like that before. My cats liked looking out the patio doors, but they never tried to sneak out when I let the dogs out to potty. Her running away made me sad. I also felt betrayed. Was life at home with us so bad that she'd be willing to chance life out in the unknown?

The absence of Snowball made Gizmo even more skittish, and she would hiss and meow in a different tone than I'd ever heard before. So Frank and I decided to take her to the SPCA on his next day off, in the hopes of them finding her a home where she would be happy. I cried on the way to the SPCA and when I had to hand her over to them. I knew it was the best thing for her, but it was still hard.

Once we were home, there was a different vibe in the house. My dogs were super chill, and I could relax a bit, even with a broken heart.

As summer ended and fall began, I was getting tired quite easily. I found myself not being able to eat as well as I usually did. Smells really bugged me. This was not the usual annoyance that I had with my migraines, which I had suffered from for years. This felt different. The more I thought about it, the more I wondered if I could be pregnant. I thought about buying a pregnancy test, but it would be the same cost as a visit to my primary care doctor, so why not just see him? That way, if I wasn't pregnant, maybe he could find out why I felt so sluggish and nauseated.

Two days later, he confirmed what I should have known all along: I was pregnant. He referred me to an OB/GYN for more information and proper care.

When Frank got home, I told him the good news. I reminded him that the pregnancy books said not to tell everyone until after the first twelve weeks. So, for now, it would remain between the dogs and us.

As I lay my head down on my pillow that night, I realized that I was excited. I found myself rubbing my belly as I thought about life with a child. I was going to have a baby. The truth is I was probably happier about being pregnant than I was about getting married. The only thing that could come close to that feeling might be winning the lottery. Not that I would compare having a baby with winning the lottery . . . but winning the lottery would help pay for the kid.

So I was going to have a little person that I could love and take care of. And that little person would be there for me, and I for him, until God decided it was time for one of us to go.

The first time I got nauseated, really nauseated, I felt like I was dying. After bouts of nausea, a part of me really *wanted* to die. It was utterly horrible. Throwing up has to be one of the worst things you can go through, especially when you are pregnant for the first time.

They say that nausea is worse in the mornings, but for me, it was bad all day long. I would wake up suddenly, barely able to walk. Then I'd have to run to the toilet. My porcelain friend and I became close during those nine months. My hugs turned into a caress. His body was the cleanest part of the house.

And let me state for the record that the whole *nine-month* thing is something I want to call bullshit on. Forty weeks is ten months, not nine.

And during those *ten* months of pregnancy, I got severely dehydrated and had to have home IVs. Twice. I did have more nausea than I did actual vomiting—but that doesn't change anything.

I tried saltine crackers. That didn't help. I tried water and bread, and neither of those worked. I couldn't stand the smell of chicken or broccoli. And that threw my husband into a tailspin. "What," he would ask, "we can't have chicken ever again?" as if it was the end of the world.

I was able to keep watermelon and strawberries down, but they were not in season and were costly.

I signed up for Lamaze classes at the hospital. I learned a little about formula feeding and breastfeeding. I found out that cloth diapers were better than plastic. We learned how to feed and burp a baby and how to hold and change a baby. It was informative, and I hoped it would later be beneficial. But I honestly didn't see how learning to breathe a certain way was going to help me push a human being out of my vagina.

By the time forty weeks came, my stomach was bigger than a beach ball. I waddled when I walked. I wasn't working, because I lost my job when I missed too much time due to my pregnancy nausea.

A visit to my doctor on that fortieth week showed that I was not dilated to a point where delivery was close. My OB/GYN said that if I didn't go into labor on my own in two weeks, he would have to induce me, so we scheduled an induction for June 2nd.

SOMETHING'S GOTTA GIVE

*J*une 1st started like any other day. I woke up, still very much pregnant. I looked like a beached whale that was never going to make it back out to sea. And just like a beached whale, I had pretty much given up on the idea of ever being rescued. I had started to believe that I would never give birth to this kid. I felt that he and I were destined to remain attached for the rest of our natural lives. I was convinced that this kid was happy where he was at. He had no desire to be out in the world without the safety of my stomach protecting him. It was that or he was having fun kicking the crap out of me. I had been diagnosed with bruised ribs two weeks earlier, so each kick brought a mist to my eyes. He obviously needed room to kick his legs. So I couldn't help but wonder why he didn't want to come on out. He definitely needed some walking-around room, and he wasn't going to get it encased in my belly.

My ritual for the past two weeks had involved a delicious breakfast of toast and fruit then a leisurely stroll to the front porch, where a chaise lounge awaited me and my big belly. My trusted canine friends took the chaise lounge beside me.

I laid the phone on my belly. I was ready for the call. The one that I'd received every day for the past two weeks. And sure enough, my phone rang.

"Well . . ." my mom asked from her end of the phone.

"Nope," I replied.

We had gone from having conversations to speaking in code. Some days I would add, "I think he's happy where he's at." I believed he loved me so much that he didn't ever want to be born and that meant he never wanted to be separated from me.

She, in turn, would joke that I was holding the baby hostage. That he was content where he was at. And other little jabbing banters.

And by this point, I agreed with her on all of it, whereas normally, I would have gotten mad and taken everything she said as a personal jab.

Have you ever noticed that ten people could say the same line to you and depending upon your relationship with them, whether past or present, you tend to take things the wrong way? Yeah, well, that is my mom and me. Only she always means what she says. Honest to a fault. I don't think she ever learned the art of holding her tongue to make someone feel comfortable. But enough about her.

I reminded my mom that it would be tomorrow whether we wanted it to be or not. Tomorrow was the deadline for delivery. If the baby didn't start making its way out of me by tomorrow morning, then it's inducing time. Apparently, it's common for first-time babies to be two weeks late. Though I couldn't help but feel that this had nothing to do with a first-time pregnancy and everything to do with the fact that he felt safe and content where he's at. Either way, my bag had been packed and sitting by the door for a month now. All of those practice runs sort of kick-started Frank and me to be ready. The snacks that I had packed disappeared out of the bag two days after I put them in there. Chocolate was one of the few things that I could eat without wanting to hurl. Add a little mint to that, and you had a wonderful snack for someone who wanted to eat but couldn't. I should have purchased stock in Andes Creme De Menthe Thins because I'd been eating enough for two. No, make that three.

With no money to shop, no appetite to eat out, and no job to go to, I spent my final day of freedom with my furry best friends. They knew that something was about to change; they'd seen a few changes already. Beginning with my getting big as a whale. My hugging the porcelain God quite frequently. The redo of the spare bedroom. My constant complaining of cramp-like pains, sometimes to the point that I had to bend over just to catch my breath. My instincts told me that they knew a little person was coming. After all, Gizmo knew the day that I conceived, so you can't tell me that my doggie pals didn't know what's up. Strangely, I felt like they knew more than me when it came to this child. I wished they could talk so they could tell me everything they knew. It would be nice to have some insight as to what was going on with my body. It would be nice if they were psychics and could tell me what I was having and when.

Tomorrow, everything would change for us. Frank worked today, but come tomorrow, he would be off for a few days. But that didn't prevent me from worrying about our doggies while I would be in the hospital. Frank had planned on rooming in with me, but he was also responsible for letting them out every eight hours or so. I hated the thought of leaving them alone. At least they'd have a quiet night or two. I would be in the hospital with a screaming baby and a picky husband. But tomorrow would be my day. At least for a little while. They say that the wedding is the bride's day. Maybe so. But I felt like the day you give birth was your day. After all, you'd managed to keep not only yourself but your child alive for ten months. And you were going to walk into the hospital as one and come out as two. Okay, three if you count your significant other. But let's face it: he or she did not carry the extra baggage.

For the past few months, I'd felt kind of special. Wherever I went, people wanted to help me. They would open doors for me. They'd help me unload my groceries or pick up large, bulky items or items that were up high. They would do all of this without me asking. It was amazing to see how the public reacted to a pregnant woman. Especially one that looked like she was carrying an extra fifty pounds in her belly. And that's where most of my extra weight was. Yes, my boobs were big. My hair was long, thick, and gorgeous. I had literally been awestruck by the growth of my hair. It was so beautiful right then that even I took the time to look at it in the mirror and play with it constantly. Suppose scientists could bottle a formula that would give women pregnancy hair. In that case, they'd never go bankrupt because pregnancy hair grows fast and is long, thick, and beautiful. I just hoped that the beautiful hair lasted for at least a few more months.

My nails were another thing that changed. They were growing without becoming brittle and cracked—something I wasn't used to. I hadn't used polish or even a nail hardener since I found out that I was pregnant. I didn't want anything that could be harmful to the baby. Honestly, I'd stayed away from everything that could potentially be harmful to the baby. I hadn't colored my already blond hair blonder. Or gotten a perm, which I had to have for my wavy, thick, gorgeous locks. I'd been careful not to put anything in my body or on it that was not necessary. And I'd found that *none* of it was really necessary. Pregnancy had made me naturally beautiful in every way. Maybe that's why people had been rushing to open doors for me.

So, after Mom called, Frank called. He'd gotten a break at work and was wondering if anything was happening. I sadly told him no. He reminded me that he had the pager that we rented two months ago so I could get in touch with him if I needed to. Here it was noon, but there didn't appear to be anything percolating down there.

When I leaned back and closed my eyes, I heard the crashing of the waves. Our end of the beach was deserted. Beside us was an empty lot, and next to that was one of the city's best seafood restaurants. The building complex across the street was boarded up and waiting on developers to raze it. There was a house to the left side of me and one in front of me, but other than that, there was no one around. So, when I was still and resting, all I could hear was the ocean. And it brought a sound of tranquility. The breeze helped, of course, because my body had been running hot the whole pregnancy. Sadly, our winter was mild. Not that it bothered me much.

The week before, we had gone four-wheeling, hoping that the bumpy ride would jostle something loose down there and the baby would come wiggling out. But nope. He wasn't ready. I had sex—with an orgasm—and that didn't work, either. I tried nipple stimulation, and that didn't do anything. I had been walking on the beach, hoping that would help. And all that did was cause my back to hurt.

I admit that I was starting to get a tad depressed. I had been pregnant for forty-two weeks. Forty-two. That's ten and a half months. My OB/GYN laughed every time I disputed the nine months thing, which was during every visit. I'm a realist here when I point out that forty-two weeks was ten and a half months.

After falling asleep on the chaise, I awakened to the dogs barking at the mailman. They didn't get up from their chaise, and neither did I. It was a long walk to the mailbox—a good hundred feet or so. I waited until the mailman had gone on down the road before I headed out to the mailbox with my furry friends by my side.

Lunchtime consisted of watermelon and strawberries. After all that time, I still couldn't eat a lot of the food that I was used to. With some fruit in my belly, I decided to have a peanut butter sandwich and sit on the couch and watch some television. Of course, it didn't take long before I stretched out. That meant my furry friends had to lie on the love seat—not enough room for a whale and two dogs on the couch. Even though it was sunny out, I kept the curtains to the patio door closed. For some strange reason, I felt vulnerable when they were open. I know it doesn't make sense, considering the blinds on the windows were open. But I kept the curtains that hung over that double glass door closed as if they were armor. Some days I wondered if it was the pregnancy that made me feel that way. Or if it was the vulnerability of living on an empty beach across the street from a boarded-up apartment complex frequented by drug addicts and cops that scared me.

When Frank got off work, he smartly thought to bring home some fried chicken and biscuits from the deli. He'd been missing chicken, and he knew I wasn't going to cook it. I wasn't in the mood for much of anything myself. I was sad. I honestly didn't believe I'd ever have this child. It had gone from being a joke to reality.

Tomorrow was D-day. There would be a baby one way or another. Right after Frank went to bed, the baby decided to make a sneak attack. I started having horrible, cramp-like pains. Not like the ones before. Over time, they got so bad that I'd double over. At first, I thought it was those horrid cramps that one gets with diarrhea. So I kept running to the toilet.

After about three hours, it hit me that I must be in labor, so I woke Frank up. I needed him to keep track of how far apart my contractions were. Besides, it was only fair that if I was awake that he be awake too. And it was nice having a hand to squeeze.

Over the past month, I'd already made a couple of practice runs to the hospital. So this time I didn't rush to the hospital. I waited for a few hours. I waited until the pain got so bad that I really wanted to strangle someone. And if I couldn't do that, then I wanted someone to feel the same exact, intense pain that I was experiencing. Someone needed to feel the depth of the aggravation that comes with that pain, the inability to not be able to control the pain. There was no amount of mediation or mantras that was going to control it. And the longer I waited, the worse it got.

When the contractions started taking my breath away, Frank said, "I'm calling the doctor."

There was no comment from me. I was too busy trying to visualize happy thoughts while I controlled my breathing.

WEDNESDAY, JUNE 2, 1993

THEY DON'T CALL IT LABOR FOR NOTHING

I t was officially June 2nd, and I had been having labor pains for about five hours. The doctor called us back within a few minutes. Frank answered the phone and began telling him how long I'd been having pains and how far apart my contractions were, which were around eight to ten minutes.

The doctor asked to speak to me. I was sitting on the toilet, doubled over in pain. Plus, I felt like I was getting ready to take the biggest poop of my life.

So Frank handed me the phone, and the doctor said, "Well," and a contraction hit me about that time, so I couldn't form words. Instead, I doubled over even more and dropped the phone on the floor as I screamed a little. It wasn't the kind of scream that you hear in horror movies. It was closer to the kind of scream you have when you drop something really heavy on your foot and break it. It was part pain and part "Oh fuck! Make it stop!"

Honestly, I think if you recorded mothers during labor, you'd hear things like "shit," "fuck," "damn," and "bastard" a lot.

It was now a little past five in the morning, and the doctor gave us the okay to head to the hospital. I guess when a mom can no longer speak without the desire to use expletives, then it's time to get the baby out.

My trusty bag was sitting by the front door. It was empty of snacks, but at that moment, I didn't care. I waved to Shaggy and Wolf because speaking wasn't an option. Frank tried to carry me to the car, only he half carried me. So I pushed him away and told him to leave me alone. I'm glad my neighbors weren't awake because I'm sure I was a sight—walking hunched over, stopping every few feet gasping in pain, and cussing like a sailor. I looked like someone with a back problem that had to go poop. Seriously, that's what I looked like. I felt like everything inside of me was going to drop at any moment.

Although we only lived fifteen minutes from the hospital, my husband decided to take advantage of the situation and drive fast. As I glanced over at him, I wasn't sure who looked more crazed—him or me. My contractions were getting shorter by the minute. Ten minutes later, we pulled up to the hospital. I rocked back and forth to get out of the car. And Frank carried my bag. At the door of the maternity floor, nurses were waiting for me. My doctor notified them that I was on the way.

One of the nurses smiled as she said, "Looks like it's real this time." Only I think she really smirked, and I'm sure I heard sarcasm in her voice. I had made so many trial runs that I had become a little popular. Or maybe I had become a joke. Either way, I was what they called anxious.

They ushered me back to my little pink room and instructed me to put on my little pink gown. My nurse asked if I wanted pain medication. I replied, "No. I want a natural birth. No medication."

She laughed and said, "Honey, with or without pain medication, it's still a natural birth."

I wasn't sure what she meant. But I was too preoccupied to ask her to clarify.

After I got onto my little pink bed and put my feet in the stirrups, the nurse checked to see if I was dilated enough to have this baby. I was. But my doctor was nowhere to be seen. My nurse excused herself to see what the holdup was.

Then about every ten to fifteen minutes, another nurse would pop her head in to tell me that they were calling him. But he was still stuck in traffic.

Within less than an hour of my arrival, my pain got to the point that it was aggravating the hell out of me and taking my breath away. So I finally asked for pain medication. A moment or two later, a doctor waltzed in to inform me that I was too far along for him to give me an epidural. Good thing he stood three feet from my bed because if I could have grabbed him by his coat, his leg, or his balls, I would have. Then my next contraction hit, and I understood why he told my husband I was too far along to sit still for an epidural.

I had gotten my wish. I was going to give birth naturally, with no medication. The contractions were coming so hard and fast that I didn't have a real chance to process the thought of no pain medication. Not being able to catch my breath was scaring me, and I was beginning to panic. The nurse suggested that I practice the breathing I learned in Lamaze class. I looked at her as if she had lost her damn mind. Then again, at this point, what choice did I have? So I reached back into my mind and pulled out what I learned about breathing.

"Hee, hee, hoo. Hee, hee, hoo." *Hee hee bullshit.*

The inability to make the contractions slow down also bothered me. Usually, you can breathe your way through something. If you cut yourself, you usually have that moment where you stifle a scream, if only for just a few fleeting seconds, and you feel no pain. That shit doesn't work with labor. You cannot breathe through it to get it to stop. It keeps coming at you. It comes at you fast and hard, and you can't wish it away or make it stop. It's right there at one hundred mph, and there's not a damn thing you can do about it.

To envision it properly, let me explain it this way. Let's say you totally despise rollercoasters. Someone knocks you out and puts you on a rollercoaster. And you wake up just as the coaster tips over that first hill.

That feeling is kind of how labor is. You're fucked, and you know it. For them to tell me that I was beyond the stage for an epidural was like waking up at the top of that first hill.

My nurse checked my cervix again. She had been doing this pretty regularly, and I was slowly, emphasis on slowly, dilating to a ten. This time I noticed that the look on her face changed. Something was different. She called one of the other nurses over and quietly told her that she had just broken my water. She knew the doctor would be mad and wanted to know how far out he was.

A few moments after the other nurse went to check on the doctor's estimated time of arrival, a team came in. They walked in there like something out of a movie. But not a medical show. More like a detective show, when the team walks in at attention, and you know they're there to take care of business. That's how they came in.

Next thing I knew, one of the OB/GYNs from my doctor's office rushed in the room. He was putting on his gown as he walked toward me. He apologized for being late. My preferred doctor was still stuck in traffic. I guess that's what happens when someone lives on an island and has to drive through a tunnel to get anywhere.

Before I could blink, he was at the foot of my bed, saying, "Let's get this baby out."

In unison, everyone in the room yelled, "Push!"

Their collective yelling startled me. I had only closed my eyes for a second. Okay, for a minute, while I had a contraction. And somehow the room had filled with even more people.

The pressure in my stomach was so strong that I felt like I didn't need to push. But I was wrong.

I pushed, and the doctor struggled to get the baby out. I pushed, and the doctor used forceps. I pushed, and he tried suction. I pushed, and he said, "We probably should have pushed the baby back up the birth canal."

Next thing I knew, a nurse was patting me on the shoulder as she said, "Honey, he's going to have to cut you."

I was so tired I had no idea what that meant. I had learned about episiotomies in Lamaze class, but that knowledge escaped me now.

I was lying there, looking up at the ceiling, when all of a sudden, I saw blood splatter on the ceiling. Confused, I turned my head in the direction of my feet in the stirrups. I saw blood splattered on my doctor's face. I looked to my left to see my husband, and he was going down like a rag doll when a nurse cracked something open and put it under his nose. He immediately stood back up, saying, "I'm all right."

The doctor informed us that he had to break the baby's collarbone to get him out. It turns out my baby was larger than my birth canal. Who knew? That one they didn't tell us about in Lamaze class.

When my baby was finally pulled from my body, the doctor held him up and said, "Look. You have a one-year-old."

Natural childbirth, I get it now.

At 11:51 a.m. on June 2, 1993, I became the proud mama of a beautiful, blond-haired, blue-eyed, dimple-cheeked little boy. Only he wasn't so little. He weighed ten pounds four ounces and was twenty-two and a half inches long.

It was a boy! My husband was so excited that he started crying. We had had a boy! And his name was Chaz.

When I was younger, I had a dream that stuck with me for years. I eventually wrote a screenplay based on that dream. I called it *P.S. I Love You*. My main character had blond hair and blue eyes and was named Chaz.

I watched as my husband cut the umbilical cord, and I mouthed, "Chaz."

That moment in time seemed to stand still. It was like watching a movie in slow motion. After the cord was cut, the hospital's on-call pediatrician walked in, suited up, and grabbed my son. She had been called in because Chaz had, unfortunately, had a bowel movement while he was still inside my womb.

She proceeded to check his Apgar scores. She also checked to see if he had inhaled any of the meconium—a fancy word for feces. It turns out this can be a huge concern. Inhaled meconium, known as meconium aspiration, can cause severe respiratory symptoms in a newborn. Something else we didn't learn about in Lamaze class. It was even more important than the broken right clavicle that Chaz suffered when the forceps failed to assist the doctor in getting him out of my womb.

During this time, Chaz had not made a sound. Not a peep. There was no loud cry like you saw in the movies. For those first three minutes, time stood still. Everyone in the room was focused on watching the pediatrician examining Chaz. She announced that he hadn't gotten any of the meconium in his mouth or lungs. Finally, as if on cue, Chaz cried. You could feel the relief in the room. It was like everyone let out a collective sigh.

Chaz was feverish. His temperature was a little over 100.4. The doctor called this a febrile temperature. With my gestational diabetes and Chaz being so big, they were going to keep a check on his glucose levels.

The pediatrician wiped him off and swaddled him. She left his right arm inside the blanket so he could only move his left side.

Chaz was handed to my husband, and he brought him over to me. He had a bruised head and red marks that extended to the left side of his head due to the suction. He had several red splotches over his left eye, which a nurse called stork bites. Chaz ended up bumped, bruised, and broken, and I ended up with a fourth-degree episiotomy that required fifty-two stitches.

Yes, it is as disgusting as it sounds. I was cut from one end to the other. Luckily, I didn't feel a thing. My doctor said that he had given me anesthesia in that area while I had been pushing and cringing.

Though I don't remember being told not to lift him under the arms, I made sure not to put any pressure on his right side when I lifted him. Then again, with him being almost eleven pounds and having such a big head, I was careful to lift him with a hand under the middle of his back and one under his head.

After Chaz and I were repaired and cleaned, everyone left the room to give us some time alone. The problem was I was still on my hospital bed and Chaz was in his baby bed, on the other side of the room. I couldn't get up. And Frank had left for lunch.

The nursing staff knew that I was going to breastfeed. That was one of the first things they asked me upon arrival. It's also one of the things they kind of coax you into doing—telling you how wonderful it is for the baby and everything. So everyone left as quickly as they had come in and no one said anything to me. Nothing.

A while later, Chaz started crying. Before I could get out of the bed, a nurse came walking into the room. She carefully picked Chaz up, laid him upon my chest, and said, "I think he's hungry."

I pulled my hospital gown down, turned his little face toward my breasts, guided his mouth to my nipple, and began breastfeeding. I don't think the nurse liked my technique. She came over and lifted my breasts and lifted his little chin and kept making his lips touch my nipple and grab on. She even got up on the bed with me to show me how to do it. This went on for at least fifteen minutes. Then she was called out of the room because another mom was coming in for delivery.

I did what she had shown me, and I continued doing so about every two hours, up until that night, when my son started sleeping in three-hour stretches.

PART 1: BABY'S HERE

little after midnight, I was awakened to the sounds of a baby crying. It sounded like my son, so I got out of bed to check. Chaz wasn't in his crib. My heart skipped a few beats, and I started to freak out a little. I had to wake my husband up because he was sound asleep. And all he said was, "That's him crying. Isn't it?"

"Yes," I said. "Where do you think he is?"

My husband never got up. He just rolled back over as he said, "Probably the nursery."

Quietly, I walked over to the door and cracked it. I could still hear a baby crying, and I was positive it was Chaz. I looked down the hall toward the nursery, saw no one, and began slowly walking that direction. Suddenly, a nurse peeked her head out of the nursery door and asked me, "Do you need something?"

"I was just wondering where my baby is," I stuttered quietly.

She smiled so sweetly as she said, "Oh, he's in here. We had to check his blood, and we didn't want to wake you."

I thanked her and walked back to my room.

As I closed the door, and without turning over, Frank asked, "Did you find him?"

"Yes," I said. "He's in the nursery. They're checking his blood sugar," I volunteered sharply.

I was grateful for their consideration. But a part of me was still freaking out a bit. Especially since the media had covered several stories in the past few months about babies being stolen from hospitals. And since I didn't know these ladies from Adam, I was a little scared. They may have had their security bracelets to sound alarms if someone tried to take the baby out of the maternity unit. But this was new technology I didn't have a lot of faith in.

Besides, some of the babies that were stolen were taken from hospitals by nurses. Or people pretending to be nurses. So who was to say there wasn't someone there right then that wanted a baby so badly they would steal Chaz? After all, they could remove the bracelets. And I wasn't that trusting.

My only choice was to lay back and wait for someone to bring him back to me. I started watching every minute of the clock ticking by. My eyes grew heavy, and I fell asleep. Then this high-strung, over-caffeinated, assertive nurse walked in holding Chaz. She rushed over to my bedside and laid him upon my chest for a breastfeeding session. She pulled my gown down and worked with both of us on proper positioning. After about five minutes, she got a little agitated with me and told me to work on my positioning, make sure I could feel the sucking motion, and if not, try this way or that way, and she demonstrated. And then she left, and Chaz and I were left to figure out breastfeeding on our own.

I spent the next four hours with him lying on my chest and me offering him my nipple in various positions. Sometimes he would suck. Other times he would just push me away. He would cry a little between feeds. But he would never scream at the top of his lungs. I took that to mean I must be doing something well.

As Chaz and I pushed throughout breastfeeding escapades, Frank remained on his bed, sleeping away. In a way, I resented him. After all, I just gave birth. Vaginally. Fifty-two stitches' worth because I delivered a huge baby, dubbed a one-year-old. And now I was expected to breastfeed too. When was it my turn to rest? I needed to sleep too.

The nurses kind of ticked me off because they would come in to ask if I needed anything then remind me to get some rest because once I got home, there would be no rest. I think I already had a taste of what that was going to feel like. Where was the paternal help? Shouldn't both of us not be sleeping? Shouldn't I be waited on hand and foot? Actually, I had to go to the bathroom. How the hell was I going to do that? I looked to my left, and Frank was sound asleep with his back to me. I looked for the call button. I decided to use both. Frank mumbled, "I'm coming," as I told the nurse that I need someone to walk with me to the bathroom and to take Chaz.

Well, that place must have gotten busy quick because no one showed up. After about ten minutes, Frank finally got up, took Chaz from me, and placed him in his crib. Then he helped me off the bed by holding my arm and waist as he walked me to the bathroom. Once there, I debated peeing because I was afraid. I hadn't peed since I left the house the day before. But that couldn't be right, could it? I gently sat on the toilet as I tried to remember, and then I began to pee.

Before getting back in bed, I told Frank I was hungry. It's was a little past five in the morning, and breakfast wasn't expected for a few more hours. As Frank got in bed, he reminded me about the sandwiches and drinks in the kitchenette down the hall. So even though I could barely walk to the bathroom, I walked down the deserted hall to the kitchenette. I opened the fridge, and the angels sang.

I greedily grabbed a turkey and cheese croissant sandwich and a cold can of Coke and hustled back down the hall. I was unintentionally walking like a woman whose kimono was too tight. They were baby steps. But they were fast, shuffled, determined baby steps.

I got back in bed and ate, my first food in nearly twenty-four hours. Speaking of which, my twenty-four hours was almost up. That's how long hospitals would let you stay after pushing a baby out of your lady parts. Twenty-four hours. I should have at least been allowed to stay for one hour per stitch. Fifty-two hours should have been my time limit. That twenty-four rule needed a swift overhaul.

As I finished the sandwich, my OB/GYN walked in. I was praying he would tell me I could stay another day. Instead, he was there to ask if we wanted to circumcise Chaz. Of course, we both said yes. I was yes with a caveat. I wanted to know about pain meds. I had read story after story about OB/GYNs not using pain medication during circumcisions. He reassured me that he did, so I sent them away with my blessing.

As for me, I was still hungry. I didn't recall ever being that hungry in my life. I told Frank I was headed off for another sandwich. There was finally some activity in the hallway. I made sure to smile as I stole a second sandwich and Coke. As I made my way back down the hall, I did notice a very old man coming out of my room, and I just thought he was a visiting grandpa that had the wrong room.

I closed the door to my room and began to munch down that second turkey croissant and Coke. Frank came out of the bathroom and told me that I had just missed the pediatrician.

"Oh, the lady from yesterday," I said. "What did she want?"

"No," he said. "He was from the pediatrician's office that we had written down as the one to contact once you gave birth."

"Oh," I said, slightly disappointed. That first pediatrician's office didn't impress me much after our pre-baby visit, so we had met with someone else.

"He seemed rather old." Frank handed me their brochure. "He had to be one of the founding physicians."

Chomping away on my croissant, I said, "I think I saw him in the hall as I was walking back."

I looked over the pamphlet as I asked Frank what he said.

"All he said is that he had a rough delivery. And he won't be going home today," he said.

"No?" I asked.

"No," Frank repeated.

"Did he say why?" I asked as I bit into my sandwich.

"Only that he'd had a rough delivery."

Really?! So did I! Who's out there fighting for me to stay?

And before I could say anything, the OB/GYN walked in with Chaz. "He did great," he said. "He may be a little cranky later, but it will pass."

"So when am I going home?" I asked.

"Soon," my doctor said.

"Well, the pediatrician came by and said that Chaz would be staying one more day," Frank said. "So shouldn't she be too? Especially with all of those stitches in her?"

As he nodded his head, the OB/GYN said, "Unfortunately, with vaginal delivery, health insurance only allows for twenty-fours."

Say what?!

I scratched my head as I calmly said, "But I have fifty-two stitches down there."

"Sorry. Twenty-four hours only," he said as he made his way out of the door backwards.

I wasn't sure if he was afraid that I was going to jump him or what. I looked at Frank and shrugged my shoulders. This was one of those *what the fuck?* moments.

Did he even try to get me some extra time? Did he inform them that I had a fourth-degree episiotomy and fifty-two stitches? Something told me he hadn't—that would explain why he left backwards.

JUNE 3

PART 2:
GOING HOME WITH BABY
ISN'T SO EASY

I t was getting closer to noon, and things were beginning to pick up in my little room. A discharge nurse came in with her rolling table sidekick to help us with my discharge.

Chaz was beginning to stir a little. And this very nice, elderly lady came in to see if we wanted a picture. We did. But first, we put him in this baby blue outfit that my husband had worn home thirty years earlier. She also was there to do the birth certificate paperwork.

She pointed to Chaz's dimples, which I had yet to notice. I thought she was seeing things. It turned out she wasn't seeing things. Then she pointed to the stork bites. So that's what those red splotches were on his face.

When we got to the name, I said, "Chaz." Then I immediately began to spell it, because it wasn't common. "C-H-A-Z," I said.

"Oh, Chaz, not Chad," the nice lady said.

"Yes." I smiled at the name that I had so cleverly thought of ages ago.

"Is that your name, too?" she asked Frank.

"No. My name is Coleman, and I wouldn't wish that on anybody. Then you add the Floyd to it, and people want to call me Floyd Coleman," he animatedly explained. "No child should have to go through that."

"Well, where did the name come from?" she asked. "Another family member?"

"No," I softly said. My voice dropped a little more, as I didn't want the world to hear me. "I had a dream years ago about a boy named Chaz. And he had blond hair and blue eyes and was popular." By now I was every shade of red one could possibly turn—and then some. "So, I wrote a screenplay about the dream and decided that if I ever had a boy, I would name him Chaz. And my other boy name is Dusty, after another character from the screenplay."

"That's a good story. You shouldn't be ashamed of that," she said. I guess my voice lowering to a whisper gave me away. But I'd always been one of those people that never really liked to talk about themselves, and if I did, then I was as quiet as possible. And if it was something really personal, like this, then I was super quiet.

"Middle name," she asked. "You don't have to have one if you don't want to." I loved her. She really was a new age kind of thinker. I always hated my middle name and never really found a use for it. It didn't serve any purpose that I was aware of. And my husband had a middle name worse than mine. His could be a first name or the last name. So he had three first names and three last names. No wonder he hated his name.

"Michael," I said. Frank and I had agreed upon Michael the night before. I'm not sure which one of us thought of it first or for sure what the reasoning was behind it. But I can say this much. There's a *Batman* movie poster in Chaz's room. I love movie posters. And it has Michael Keaton on it. Then again, we might have thought of it for another reason. At this point, I was so tired and overwhelmed that it didn't really matter.

The rest of the process was pretty simple. Then she left.

So I asked the nurse what would happen to Chaz since I wouldn't be there. "He'll stay in the nursery," she said.

"And what will they do?" I asked.

"Feed him, change him, keep an eye on him," she said.

"Anything else?" I questioned.

She glanced at the chart in front of her then shook her head. "No. That's all. There are no special instructions."

"Then why can't I take him home and do that?" I asked. "And can't I stay here with him?"

She glanced at her chart again. Shaking her head, she says, "No. It looks like your doctor has you going home, and the baby is staying here."

"How much will it cost for him to stay here?" Frank asked.

"I'm not sure," our poor nurse said. "Excuse me for a moment." And she rolled away with her cart.

Frank pulled me aside. "You know we're probably going to have to pay for him to stay here since they're sending you home. And we don't have five hundred dollars to do that."

I nod in agreement. *But what the hell am I supposed to do about it?* I wondered. To show that I understood where he was coming from, I even asked him, "So what do you want me to do about it?"

"I don't know. Talk to the doctor or something," he pleaded.

When the nurse came back in, I asked her if she could get my doctor in here so I could ask him some questions. And I asked her if she knew where the pediatrician was.

"Well, he left here before the sun came up," she said with no animosity.

"Okay. So what can I do?" I asked.

Fidgeting with her ink pen, she said, "You could call them. They might be able to tell you something."

"Can you get Pam's doctor back in here," Frank spoke up, "so we can talk to him?"

"I can try," she said, and she rolled her traveling desk with her as she left.

Frank handed me the pamphlet the pediatrician had left earlier. This meant I was supposed to call them, which I did. I explained to the lady on the phone that I had just given birth a few hours ago, one of their pediatricians had been in to see us earlier, and now I needed to speak with him. She kindly asked who stopped by, and I told her. And then I told her what he said about it being a rough delivery and that Chaz wouldn't be going home today. She kindly told me that the doctor would not be calling me back and would not be changing his mind. I thanked her for her time and hung up.

As I relayed the message to Frank, the only thing that kept bugging me was when she said that the doctor would not be calling me back. What kind of doctor didn't call their patients back? Or at least have someone from their office call for them?

My discharge nurse came back in and let me know that my doctor would be in to see me the next chance he got. I, in turn, told her what the pediatrician's office said. She took notes as I talked.

We didn't buy any baby pictures because we were broke. I had insurance but had no idea what it covered or how it worked. I was silently embarrassed by this lack of knowledge. If I had known this information, then I'd be able to contribute to this discussion. But to be honest, I was tired, in pain, and a little delirious. I hadn't slept. I was either trying to breastfeed Chaz or watching him sleep. And my trusty nurse kept an eye on every move we made. I began to feel as if she was afraid we were going to steal the gowns, the phone, and the bed. Other than that, there wasn't really much in the room besides Chaz's crib and my own private bath.

The circumcision doctor finally showed back up, and he was in an obvious hurry. "Do you see any reason that Chaz can't go home?" Frank asked him.

He took a quick peek at Chaz and said, "No."

Then Frank told him what the pediatrician said about the rough delivery. Still, he said that he didn't see any reason why he couldn't go home.

So Frank asked me to call the pediatrician's office again. I did, but it was a no go. Baby Chaz had to stay.

Frank and I discussed what little we knew about the insurance, which was nothing really. I called them to see if they would cover Chaz's stay. The lady on the phone said that they wouldn't cover mine but they might cover his. So I called the insurance company. I got switched around a few times before I found someone that sounded like they knew at least as much as I did. She couldn't promise that the insurance would pay. They would not know the answer to that until they got the bill with accompanying doctor's paperwork. And for the hell of it, I asked about me and my fifty-two stitches. She gave me the same answer that she had given me about Chaz's stay.

I looked at my discharge nurse and sighed. The tension in the room was so thick it was as if there was an impermeable wall between us. I looked from Frank to Chaz, to the nurse, and felt the weight of the world on my shoulders. What were we going to do? I asked the nurse, "What are my options?"

On a piece of paper, she wrote each one down as she explained them. One, Chaz stayed there, and I stayed in the waiting room (which was actually a broom closet with an OB/GYN bed in it, sort of). Two, Chaz stayed there and I went home. Three, we could take the baby home AMA.

"What is AMA?" I asked.

"Against medical advice," she said.

"What does that mean?" I questioned.

"That you take the baby home, acknowledging that the doctor is against it, but you have chosen to do so anyway."

Wow. Who knew?

Before I had a chance to process items one through three, Frank pulled me aside. "We have to do AMA," he explained in a lowered voice. "Or we're going to owe a whole lot of money for a visit that insurance probably won't cover." He barely took a breath. "And you can't stay here in a chair all night with your stitches. Plus, you can't breastfeed him if you're not here."

Sounds like the decision had been made.

"I guess we're doing AMA," I said, so quietly that the nurse asked me to repeat it.

"Okay. Let me get the paperwork," she replied, and off with her cart she went.

We gathered up our belongings. I signed the AMA paperwork. They gave me a bunch of instructions, and off we went. People were not as friendly going out as they were when we were coming in. I guess now we were known as the family that took their baby out AMA.

* * *

Once we arrived home, Frank walked ahead to let the dogs out. He set the carrier down for them to see our little person. Meanwhile, I waddled up the sidewalk. I was still holding my stomach, even though there was nothing left to hold. But with each step, my lady parts were screaming.

We were home barely an hour when the phone rang, and I picked it up.

"Well," I said, after the brief call, "apparently my insurance covers a home health visit."

"And yet they wouldn't let you stay for an extra day," Frank spurted. "I wonder how much that's going to cost them," he added sarcastically.

"Well, she will be here tomorrow at noon," I noted. "So you can ask her then."

I knew he wouldn't ask her, but it was worth putting it out there. Especially since the insurance wouldn't let me stay an extra day. Even though I had a fourth-degree episiotomy.

The nurse on the phone had told me to write down any questions I may have for her, and that's exactly what I did. By the time I finished, I had ten.

I wanted to know if pacifiers were a good idea or not. Especially since Chaz was taking advantage of his strong vocal abilities. It was hard to tell which he was doing the most, screaming or crying. It didn't really matter because I never bought any pacifiers because my Lamaze instructor had spoken negatively about them. She felt that parents used them a little too much. And now, I was beginning to second guess that decision.

I wanted to know what to do about chapped lips since his were lightly chapped and flaking.

  Chaz had not been cooperating during our breastfeedings, so I wanted to know how I was supposed to go about waking him up.

  There were just so many little things to think about when you had a newborn. It's mind-boggling when you think about it.

  I went over my list with Frank to see if he had anything to add. But he felt that I covered everything.

WHY CAN'T I NURSE MY SON?

We were up early if you can call never going to bed early. I think this was our new definition of up.

I breastfed Chaz. Frank let the dogs out, and I made breakfast. Chaz was still fussy, so I tried to breastfeed him at the table while I ate. He would suck. Stop. Make a smudged-up face. Grump a little. Then suck again. This too had become our routine since we got home from the hospital yesterday.

Frank volunteered to go to the grocery store after the home health nurse left, but I said that I wanted to go too. I was going a little stir crazy. Honestly, I was drowning a little. There was crying and screaming, which I was not used to. I'd never babysat before in my life. And I'd never been around babies growing up. So Chaz's vocals were challenging my head, causing my migraine to rear its ugly head. And that was not good for any of us.

So as we waited for the home health nurse, I replayed my breastfeeding videos and fed Chaz while Frank witnessed him give me a hard time. But it was more than that. It was like I either didn't taste good or he didn't like me. Maybe it was both. How the hell did I know?

Frustrated, I moved from the floor to the couch. As I did, I saw a car pull into our driveway. It really wasn't a driveway. It was a concrete spot big enough for two cars, three if you pulled them in really close together. But that's about it. The rest was an empty yard with splotches of grassy areas. But it was mostly sand and horrible prickly things that hurt like hell if you got one stuck to you. That's why we never stepped off the concrete sidewalk leading up to our house if we could help it. Poor old Shaggy and Wolf always tried so hard to watch where they stepped when they went to potty. But we still had to check their feet when they came back in. I waited a few moments before I told Frank someone was in the driveway because more people use that spot to turn around in than we have actual visitors.

About twenty years ago, Ocean View was a hopping area, complete with its own amusement park. In 1977, the movie *Rollercoaster* featured The Rocket, a big, wooden rollercoaster in Ocean View Amusement Park. And in 1979, another movie was made called *The Death of Ocean View Park*, where they blew up The Rocket, making it the official end of Ocean View Amusement Park. But in full disclosure, I have to tell you that The Rocket did not go easily. The film crew set explosives twice, and the coaster didn't budge. The third time they cheated and used a bulldozer and tie cables to pull it down, off camera of course. I think it was a sign.

And even though I lived on the water side of Ocean View, we were far from pristine living conditions. When it got dark, I made sure that my windows and doors were locked and all curtains closed tightly. I didn't like a sliver of an opening in them. As irrational as that was, I felt that as long as no one could see in, then no one could get in.

So when a lady stepped out of the vehicle and proceeded to open her trunk and began loading herself up with bags, I told Frank she was here. As the home health nurse made her way down our sidewalk, she carried a scale and several bags. My husband held the front door open for her as they introduced themselves. Frank escorted her to Chaz's room, where I was now sitting and waiting.

We made our introductions. She began by informing me that we had a lot of paperwork to get out of the way before we started. So I sat beside her on the double bed by Chaz's crib.

"It's just a few routine things," she said as she pulled out a bunch of papers in all sorts of colors.

Routine things like insurance, employer, date of birth. All the things that had not changed in the past twenty-four hours. But I played along and answered them as if it was the first time.

We made small talk as I signed her various papers. She said, "It must be fun to live on the water." *It can be hit or miss.*

She mentioned that she was a La Leche member and a lactation nurse. Simultaneously, we replied, "Great!"

Because we needed someone with breastfeeding experience since Chaz and I were battling back and forth with the whole breastfeeding thing.

Frank told her that I was in pain and having trouble walking and sitting. She mentioned that she was there to examine both of us. I liked this, since I felt like someone had cut me open from back to front. Oh, wait. They did.

She picked up her scale and said, "Let's begin." As she glanced at him in his crib, she added, "My, he's a big one." Frank mentioned that he was born ten pounds four ounces. Surprised, she said, "But I only brought a ten-pound scale." While holding the scale, she said that she would check her car for another one. When she returned, her hands were empty.

As she reentered the room, I retrieved my list of questions. She noticed and said, "Oh good. You have some questions."

She began her examination of Chaz, and I asked my first question. "What can I do about his chapped lips?"

"Rub a little Vaseline on them with your fingertip," she demonstrated the movement, "but not a lot." I noticed that she changed his poop using only one diaper wipe.

I immediately said, "I couldn't have done that with only one." This made me wonder if I might be doing something wrong. *How come it takes me six or seven wipes, and she did it with one?*

She smiled as she said, "Lots of practice." She motioned to us about where to put the diaper, because it was a cloth one.

Frank took it from her and placed it in the special container our cloth diaper service had provided us. She asked me to continue with my questions.

"How do you know if you are breastfeeding correctly?" I asked. She mentioned that he had just had a good stool, so I must be doing something right. Stools meant that he was getting what he needed.

"The colostrum that he gets now is enough for him until your milk comes in, which should be four to five days," she said. "And sometimes as late as six or seven days. But the colostrum is all he needs until then."

She recommended that I feed him at least ten minutes on each side. Look for one stool a day until my milk comes in. Then he should have four to five stools a day and he should always have six to eight wet diapers a day. But whatever I do, do not supplement until after the first two weeks. No bottle. No formula.

I mentioned that he was falling asleep at the feedings. She said that I needed to wake him by placing a cold, wet rag to his face or taking his clothes off of him. "Babies hate that, and they wake right up," she added.

As she examined him, checking his eyes and ears, I continued with my questions. "What are the pros and cons of pacifiers?" I asked. And she suggested the same thing that the Lamaze instructor had, and that was not use one. Because once I tried to get him off of it, it would be hard.

"What about baby powder during diaper changes?" I asked as she looked at his belly button.

"It's best not to use baby powder in the summer," she said. "But if you do use it, use the one with cornstarch." She said that his belly button looked fine and to just wait for the rest of it to fall off. Then she continued, "But if he gets a diaper rash, we are to make sure to use a vitamin A & D ointment."

Chaz began to fuss a little as she poked around his broken clavicle. I tried not to watch, knowing this had to be unpleasant for him. So I spoke a little louder as I shifted in my seat and scrunched my eyes closed. "So how long do you try to burp and what if he doesn't?"

Wrapping him back up so that he couldn't move his little arm around much, she said, "Try for at least five minutes, and when all else fails, try on the right side of his spine."

When Chaz was awake, he was grumpy. He would scream and cry at the top of his lungs and would only rest for a few minutes at a time. If he slept an hour or two, I would worry. And yet I asked, "How many hours should I keep him up during the day so he'll sleep at night?" Obviously, I was referring to as he got older. She said that it all depended upon him and me but to make sure I fed him every three to four hours and pumped if I did not breastfeed so I wouldn't become engorged.

I told her that my pump didn't work. I tried it and nothing came out. She took a look at it and said, "The electric ones work better than the hand pumps." So we said we would see about getting one.

Chaz always felt warm to me, so I felt the need to ask about fevers. "Anything between ninety-seven and one hundred degrees is normal," she said. "And his whole body will be hot if he has a fever." And she suggested that a dropper full of Tylenol infant drops would be the best thing to give him.

After looking him over head to toe and writing notes in her chart, she said, "Now let's see how you're doing."

Since I was sitting on Chaz's spare bed, I pushed my sweatpants down and laid back on the edge of the bed. I saw Frank wince as if he was in pain when I did this. I hadn't taken a mirror and looked at myself. I was actually afraid to. I had no idea how bad or good everything looked. As she proceeded to check out my incision area, overseeing my stitches, she suggested that I watch out for hemorrhoids. She asked if I was taking the stool softener that the doctor recommended, and I said, "Yes."

She motioned for me to pull my pants back up as she went back to writing her notes. She then pulled a donut pillow out of her bag and gave it to me to sit on. Then she pulled out this tub-looking thing and recommended that I use a sitz bath to help alleviate the pain.

Then she went over the discharge instructions for us both. Basically, it was to follow up with our doctors as needed. She then gave me her card and said to call if I had any questions.

The bottom line was Chaz and I were given the medical A-okay, in her opinion.

Shortly after she left, our little family headed to the grocery store. Then the strangest thing happened. This black bird came flying through the opening of our backseat window. Thank God he hit me instead of little Chaz. Then he landed on the floorboard. He was dead but I didn't know that at the time. I just know I started screaming at Frank that there was a bird in the car. He freaked out and pulled over as soon as he could. It wasn't until then that we found out the bird was dead.

So it was a hundred degrees outside, we had no air conditioning, and we'd just had a bird fly into the backseat. But we still rode with the windows down. We grocery shopped a little bit shakily. But not Chaz. He was actually sleeping pretty good. Several people stopped us to comment on how big he was and to ask how old he was. They freaked out when we told them he was only a few days old.

And once we were home, it began again. Suck. Smush. Grump. Only now there was a little whine added to it. So I called the pediatrician's office. I asked to speak to someone. I was transferred to a nurse. I had to give her the basics like when I gave birth. I explained the home health visit and what that covered but added that something was off. A part of me wondered if this child hated me. Okay, I didn't say that, but I wanted to. I did keep saying that something wasn't right but I wasn't sure what. I needed someone to tell me what was wrong. What was I doing wrong?

BEING ALONE
COMPOUNDS STRESS

I woke up to the sad fact that Frank had gone back to work. He had taken as much time off as we felt he could afford. After all, he was the only one working right then. And we needed every penny that we could get. However, I did plan on going back to work after my six-week checkup. So I was going to have to start looking not only for a job but for daycare as well, which from what I'd seen in my local baby magazines wasn't cheap. And like most families, we were a two-income family, so I had no choice but to go back to work.

I was up at the crack of dawn to feed Chaz and let the dogs out. That morning, the dogs were sleepy, and Chaz was still asleep. So I took that as a sign and went back to bed. I figured one or the other would wake me when they're ready. Not that I would call what I did sleep. It was more like I lay down and eventually passed out. I wasn't actually sleeping. Never have, really. I've had insomnia for as long as I can remember. In high school and college, it was really bad. I'd go to bed at a decent hour then spend hours upon hours thinking about everything and nothing at the same time. Then I'd get up and do homework or read. And just about an hour before I was due to get up, I'd fall asleep. Then the next day I was tired, grumpy, not at my peak mentally, and my body would ache and my muscles would get all tight. Well, nothing had changed in the following decade. I still had trouble sleeping.

Honestly, I'd probably gotten more sleep during my pregnancy than I had in the previous decade. Now, all I wanted to do was sleep. I laid down a lot. I'd drift off while reading a book, watching television, or listening to the ocean. But I never really slept.

Not an hour later, Chaz woke up crying, and that woke the dogs up. The first thing I did was change Chaz. He was wet. Not super wet, but wet. I placed his dirty diaper into the container. Cloth diapers were the way to go, they said, so that's what we did. We then sat down in the wicker rocker to begin breastfeeding. After a minute or two, he squished up his little face and turned his head away from my boob as if I'd poisoned him. So I tried on the other side. And this time he lasted twice as long but again squished his little face up. We went at this for about thirty minutes. I could feel his lips on my nipples sucking. I could feel something moving in my breasts. But my gut was screaming, "Something is not right! Something is not right!" I just wished I knew what the hell what. I couldn't shake the feeling that he wasn't getting enough.

After thirty minutes, I gave up and let the dogs out. Then it was time to clean my incision area with a peri bottle. I squished up my face because it hurt like hell down there. I grabbed my hand mirror and lay down on the spare bed in Chaz's room so I could look at myself. I was bruised, swollen, and ugly. Of course, I couldn't see most of the stitching, but I didn't need to. I knew what I felt. Strangely, I couldn't help but wonder if this was how a female looked after being raped. You always heard doctors and police on television say, "There are signs of rape. There's vaginal tearing." Was it because they looked like I did right now? I shook my head, hoping to make the thought disappear. When I returned the mirror to the bathroom, I saw the case of formula sitting on the shelf. It'd never been opened. I stared at it for a moment, wondering who I could give it to. I had a friend in mind, but I wasn't sure if that's her baby's brand. I shook the thought out of my head.

Even though I wasn't pregnant anymore, I still didn't have the love for food that I did before. My stomach still wasn't cooperating with me on which foods I could and couldn't eat. So it was a bowl of fruit and some bacon. I was just not feeling the eggs this morning. Toast, yes. I fed the dogs and sat on the couch. Chaz was in his crib in the next room, making gurgling noises, so I checked on him. He was lying there sucking on his little fist and kicking his legs, just like he did when he was in my belly. This child was definitely a kicker.

There were no phone calls that morning. My mom wasn't checking on me. Frank wasn't checking on me. It was now just me. Me and Chaz. Me and the dogs. Just me.

After I finished my breakfast, I picked Chaz up and fed him again. Again, he fussed with my breasts. Sucking. Squishing. Sucking. Squishing. Then fussing.

I picked up my *What to Expect* book and re-read the list of foods that make breast milk unappealing for babies. I saw that I had not had any of them. So I followed some of the other advice and gently stroked the side of Chaz's face. Yes, he came back to my breast, but not before he fussed some more. *Today is going to be a long day.*

Frank got home around three. He said his brother would be by a little bit later to see the baby. I told him that I needed to go out and pick up my prescription. My OB/GYN had been kind enough to call me in some pain reliever for my incision area. Not the kind of pain reliever I wanted. He claimed that since I was breastfeeding, he could only recommend over-the-counter pain relievers. But he could prescribe me a cream to put on the swollen, bruised area. At that point, I'd take whatever I could get. So I headed out. He said he'd have dinner ready when I get back. His brother should be there by then, too.

Even though it hurt to move around, I was happy and a little relieved to get out of the house for a bit. Even if it was only for a quick trip to the pharmacy.

I'd been caught up in my own world so much that I hadn't realized Harborfest was going on that weekend. It's the city's big land and sea party. Since the event is free, I try not to miss it, as do the thousands of other people that live here. Not to mention the thousands of others from all other the eastern seaboard. Including my OB/GYN. He had a hard time understanding me when he returned my call. Funny thing was I could hear everyone around him clearer than I could him.

When I got to the pharmacy, they were still in the process of filling my prescription, so I looked around. I was hoping to find something else to help ease the pain. I didn't care if it was pills or cream, I just needed something. After finding nothing, I sat down and waited for my prescription. I looked down and saw that my stomach had gone down a good ninety-five percent. Honestly, you wouldn't know I had just given birth. I smiled. Content. I successfully gave birth. And now I was starting to look normal again. At least on the outside. Another part of me was looking kind of hideous right now. I wrapped my hair around my fingers, wondering how long it would remain thick and beautiful. I did see some pills on the shelf for hair and nails, but I was afraid of trying it since I was breastfeeding. From what I'd read, new moms couldn't put anything in their bodies for fear that it would harm the baby. While I was pregnant, I had to watch what I ate, drank, and did so as not to harm the baby. And now I had to watch myself even more because I was breastfeeding. I was beginning to think that I'd never get my life back.

As soon as I walked through the door, Frank's brother complimented me on having a beautiful baby. And a boy at that. Now, there was someone to carry on the male name. I smiled.

On the inside, I was rolling my eyes. *What is it with males and the need to carry on a name? Is it really that big of a deal?* I said thank you then sat down to eat. As soon as my butt hit the chair, Chaz started crying. So I went into his room and breastfed him while Frank and his brother caught up. It was the same old song and dance that we'd been doing all day. Fuss, suck, squish. Fuss, suck, squish. This time my gut screamed again, "Wake up, will you? Something isn't right here." I ignored that guttural voice.

It was just my own insecurities coming out. I'd always had a love-hate relationship with my self-esteem. And now, with my son rejecting me, it was sinking even lower. I thought that we had built up a bond the past ten months. Maybe I was wrong.

I took Chaz into the living room so the men could hold him while I ate my cold dinner. Then I fed the dogs. Afterward, I told Frank that I was going to lay down for a while since he was home. He stretched out on the couch with Chaz on top of him. Shaggy and Wolf were confused. They stood in the doorway, trying to decide if they should follow me or stay with the baby. Doorway it was.

When I woke up, it was dark out, and Chaz was crying uncontrollably. Frank said he'd been like that for ten minutes. I yelled, "Why didn't you wake me?"

He responded with, "I thought for sure you'd hear him crying." Good Lord. So I picked him up and put him to my breast. The same old song and dance had now changed. We'd gone from fuss, suck, and squish to scream, suck, and squish.

Frank asked if he could help. I looked at him like he was stupid. *Sure. Pull up a chair, pull out a breast, and begin feeding.* But I didn't say that because I was tired and aggravated. My migraine was still rearing its head, and the tear between my legs was bringing tears to my eyes. Besides, sarcasm was not going to be my friend right now. I spent almost an hour feeding Chaz. He was becoming crankier, and I didn't know why. I repeated those words. *I don't know why. I don't know why. Something isn't right. Something isn't right. He's not getting enough. He's not getting enough.*

Frank went to bed because he had to be up early for work. I re-read the *What to Expect* book and watched one of my breastfeeding videos again. I tried the various breastfeeding positions on Chaz, and the football hold seemed to be the winner. I could feel movement inside my breast. And it appeared to be moving in the direction of the sucking. And Chaz was burping quite nicely after each feed without my having to pat him on the back. Fortunately, he didn't spit anything out like some babies that I'd seen.

HE WON'T STOP SCREAMING! WHERE IS MY BONDING?

It was a little past midnight, and I guess I'd passed out because I woke up in my bed and had absolutely no recollection of how I'd gotten there. I didn't even bother to go to the bathroom; I ran to the other room to check on Chaz because I could hear him crying.

I peeked around the corner and saw Frank was rocking Chaz in his rocker. When Frank saw me, he said, "He won't stop crying. He just keeps crying." And from the looks of it, Frank had done some crying, too.

"Hand him here," I said as I took Chaz from him. He let me have the rocker to sit in. I opened my gown, exposing my breasts to offer to him, and he screamed even louder. I was going to try to not take that personally. So for the next couple of hours, we went through a continuation of crying, sucking, squishing, and screaming.

That was our pattern for most of the night. I rocked Chaz, holding him to my breasts while I re-watched my breastfeeding videos again and again and again. At a little past three, I had to lay down.

So I lay on the spare bed in Chaz's room, laying Chaz beside me. I built a barrier on his side with pillows.

A few minutes before four, I was jarred awake by the sound of Chaz crying. My first thought was that he'd fallen off the bed or I'd rolled over onto him. But it was neither. He was lying right where I left him, on his right side, facing me. So I opened my top and offered him my breasts. The woman in the breastfeeding video made this position look easy. So why not try it? Well, that time, he squished his face, turned his head, and let out a sigh followed by a crying face that just broke my heart. He was asking me for something, and I had no idea what he wanted. I didn't know what else to try. I was failing as a mother.

I must have fallen asleep again, because I woke up to the sound of breathing in my ears. I rolled over and saw Shaggy and Wolf looking at me. It was time for them to go out. Chaz was finally sleeping, so I gently rolled out of bed, laid more pillows beside him, and let the dogs out for a quick potty.

This was one of those days where I wished I drank coffee. I needed something to keep me awake. I let the dogs in and then laid down on the couch. I needed just a little bit of sleep. Just a little.

But Chaz had other things in mind. He started crying and screaming. It was more like listening to someone screaming and crying at the same time. But he was only a baby. Not quite a week old. How on earth could he be screaming? Crying, yes. Screaming, no.

WHY WON'T ANYBODY
HELP ME?

I'd been up half the night with Chaz. He was grumpy, agitated, and not happy with me at all. I laid him in the crib, he screamed. I picked him up, he screamed. I tried to breastfeed him, and he turned his head away from my breasts and screamed.

I was at my wit's end, and it was barely dawn. Frank was about to leave for work, and he looked even worse than I did. I fed Chaz to the best of my ability. I changed Chaz. I lay on the bed with Chaz. And nothing seemed to work. He flat-out hated me. This was so not how I expected motherhood to be.

Everyone made it sound so wonderful. Bonding with your baby was supposed to be so joyous that it felt like you'd touched heaven. Where was this joyous, happy moment for Chaz and me?

I placed him in his crib and headed for the kitchen. I needed to eat and drink. At least that was what the baby books said to do to keep my breast milk supply going.

When it was finally operating hours for most doctors, I began calling everyone I could think of. I gave Betty a call because I was concerned about how my breastfeeding had been going over the weekend. She wasn't in. But the lady I spoke to said she was Betty's supervisor.

So I told her that Betty had been at my house on Friday and we had had a discussion about my breastfeeding and she had said I could call her if I had any questions.

The lady asked what was wrong. I told her that even though I was breastfeeding, it just didn't seem like it was going right. He just didn't appear to be interested. She asked if I had been giving him formula; I said no. She asked if I had given him a bottle; I said no. She then said, "All babies are born with the natural instinct to breastfeed, so keep trying."

I wasn't quite satisfied with her answer, so I called the pediatrician's office again. I told the lady that answered that I had spoken with someone on Friday regarding my son Chaz and had some concerns over breastfeeding. I said I wasn't quite sure if he was getting enough and I'd like to see the doctor.

I was put on hold. Then someone else came to the phone and asked how they could help me. I said that I had called on Friday and spoken with someone about some concerns I was having with breastfeeding. The nurse told me, "Don't worry, he will eat when he gets hungry. Breastfeeding takes time."

I explained that I worked with him all weekend and it seemed like I was constantly breastfeeding him. I'd tried every position that I could possibly try. He was latching on, but it didn't seem like it was enough. I really felt like he hadn't gotten anything from me at all since yesterday afternoon. He only wanted to suck for a few minutes at a time, and then he turned his head away.

She interrupted me and asked if I had given him formula. I said no. She said good because formula was sweeter than breast milk and I might have a hard time getting him to breastfeed if I had given him formula. She made it sound like it was one of the worst things in the world to do. I had nothing to worry about because I hadn't given him any formula. But if I had, I honestly didn't think it would cause the kind of trouble she had implied.

I then told her that all he wanted to do was sleep. But when he was awake, all he wanted to do was cry. She wanted to know what he was doing then because she could not hear him crying. I said sleeping. She asked me to wake him, feed him, and call her back in two hours. I said okay.

I did my best to breastfeed him. I woke him. Undressed him. Placed a cold rag over his naked body. Still, he wasn't interested. I felt like I was forcing him to do something he didn't want to do. I found myself crying while I breastfed him because he made me feel as if I was torturing him.

When two hours rolled around, I called again. I stated that I had spoken to the nurse earlier and that she had asked me to call her back. When I was finally switched over to the nurse, I told her that things seemed to have gone as well as possible. But I had a very hard time waking him. I had to place a cold rag on his head, face, and chest and continuously do so because all he wanted to do was sleep. He latched on twice, but I still felt as if he was hungry. I told her that the bottom line was I just felt like something was wrong. What, I didn't know. She said that since he got two good feedings, everything seemed fine, so don't worry.

She told me that I was a new mother and it was normal to feel that way. All moms could breastfeed. She said that she'd call me tomorrow morning to see how we're doing. Until then, she wanted me to keep a count of feedings and diapers because he should have a minimum of six wet diapers a day and should go no more than four hours without eating. I said okay.

PART 1:
FROM BAD TO WORSE

It was morning, and I was so tired that I was hearing and seeing things. I was stumbling around like a drunk. Chaz wouldn't stop crying. Or I guess it was fairer to say that Chaz hadn't stopped crying. I hadn't slept, but I had passed out a few times.

I spoke with Betty and told her I wasn't sure if Chaz was getting enough from my breasts. He just didn't seem interested. I told her I was having a hard time keeping him awake. I had to use cold rags on his face and body. I had to strip him in order to wake him. But he just lay there uninterested.

She asked about his stools and voids. I walked over to the diaper container and counted them. I'd gotten the required amount.

She repeated to me what she said on Friday, reminding me about no bottle giving. She did say I could give him a cup of water, that they sometimes did that. But other than that, all sounded okay.

I then called the pediatrician back. I asked to speak with the nurse. I had to tell them my whole story all over again. I was placed on hold.

Someone came to the phone and said, "Hi, Ms. Floyd, how are things going?"

I said, "When he sees my breasts, he screams."

She asked if I had kept a diary like she asked. I said yes. She asked how many diapers he had. I said three stools and four pees. She said that this seemed fine, that he must be getting something. She said my breast milk was probably just coming in and to keep at it. It would be okay.

Less than an hour later, I called her back, crying hysterically. I screamed into the phone, "My son is having a seizure!"

I was immediately transferred to a nurse. A female answered the phone, and I told her who I was and shouted that my son was having a seizure. I explained that his eyes were zig-zagging back and forth rapidly. She told me that a newborn's eyes sometimes did that, as they tend to be unfocused. She told me to calm down. Crying, I told her that I knew he was having a seizure. I shouted that I had had friends who'd had seizures; I knew what they looked like. She continued to tell me it was not a seizure but I should call back if his eyes did that again. And she hung up.

I called Frank at work, which I rarely did, and hysterically, between tears, explained to him what was going on. He didn't need to see what was happening to understand the severity of the situation. He knew I wasn't crying hysterically for nothing.

He told me to call the pediatrician's office and tell them we were coming over now. He said that what they told me over the phone was pure bullshit, especially with me crying. Then he added that he was leaving work immediately.

So I called the pediatrician's office back and told them that his eyes were still zig-zagging rapidly and I wanted to see someone. I was placed on hold for who knew how long, then finally someone came back and gave me an appointment time for a couple of hours later. But with Frank on his way home, we hoped to be seen once we arrived.

BACK TO THE HOSPITAL – REALLY SICK NOW

When we got to the pediatrician's office, we sat in the waiting room for what felt like forever. Oddly, we were the only ones there. Even the girl sitting at the front desk began to sense the awkwardness between us.

As we waited, Frank looked down at Chaz, in his little carrier, and said, "He's not crying now." And just like that, we were finally called back.

The nurse that took us back must have been having a bad day because she didn't say a word to us. She barely even looked at us. So I had no way of knowing if she was the one that I'd been talking to or not.

Once in our room, she asked that we undress our son so they could weigh him. This was done rather quickly. Then we were left alone in our room. We debated putting his clothes back on him because the air conditioning was on.

The doctor came in without introducing herself, making her way between Frank and me. She grabbed little Chaz, held him up, and looked at his entire body. Then she listened to his little heartbeat.

"He's lost twenty percent of his birth weight," she said in a tone that I didn't like.

I immediately spat back, "I've made five calls to this office in two days!" And out the door she went.

She was not about to blame this on me. I called and called them for advice. I did exactly what they said. I was the one that should be mad. Hell! I was the one that was mad!

As soon as that door closed, I looked at Frank and started crying. I was crying in part for Chaz and partly in the anger I felt at their office staff. Pretty soon, I was blubbering. I looked at Chaz, who was fast asleep in his carrier. He looked so peaceful at that moment. So gentle. He could have passed for one of those Anne Geddes babies. Just lying there, not making a sound, with his right little fist in a ball. He looked so fragile. So tiny. Not the little over eight pounds that the pediatrician said he was.

Before I could say anything, she came back in and said, "Follow me."

Follow her. Where were we going to? Why didn't we talk about the interview that we had with her before I gave birth? When we showed up that day, she was disheveled and off her game, complaining about needing a new babysitter, nanny, gorilla, or anything at that point. She gave us five minutes of her time, of which we talked more about her crisis than her practice. But we went with them anyway because they were supposedly the best. Then today she didn't even know who we were. And let's talk about that old pediatrician showing up after the birth, not even waiting to speak with me at the hospital then refusing to speak to me on the phone. Oh, and my favorite, then he went as far as having the receptionist tell me that he would not be calling me back, that that was the end of the conversation. Oh yes, this was a very friendly practice. But I'd follow her. As long as it was somewhere else but there.

When the pediatrician said that we were going to the emergency room straight away, I assumed that we would drive there. Frank carried Chaz, and I gathered up the carrier, diaper bag, and blanket as we quickly followed her through the back of the office.

A nurse opened the door for us as she hurriedly said, "They're waiting for you."

I was completely in the dark and didn't know what she meant. This was all going too fast. A huge part of me was mad as hell, and another part was frightened and shaking. The past thirteen minutes had whisked me away to a place of anger, fear, and desperation.

We made our way down the barely lit stairway that surprisingly led us directly into the emergency room.

4:08 p.m.

As soon as we reached the bottom of the last step, a tall, young, lanky-looking doctor with sandy blond hair immediately took Chaz from Frank and placed him on a stretcher. He began spitting out instructions, numbers, and terminology that I did not understand. And a flurry of nurses began carrying out his instructions. Then he turned to us and introduced himself as Dr. Hurst, the pediatric resident.

The other two nurses were attaching electrodes to Chaz from various machines. He was hooked up to a pulse ox machine, that little red thing that makes you want to say, "*ET, phone home.*"

Dr. Hurst removed Chaz's diaper, and Chaz peed on him. "At least he's still wetting," he said. One of the nurses grabbed a specimen cup and gathered up the salvageable urine for the lab. I moved toward the stretcher to change Chaz's diaper. One of the nurses had the same idea. But one look from me and she moved back and let me change him. He was still my baby, and I felt the need to intervene as best as I could. Frank touched my arm as he suggested that I move back.

After all, the medical team was not finished. They were still attaching wires, starting equipment. Taking blood samples. A urine sample.

I stepped back and watched the medical team. They reminded me of an orchestra that had practiced many times before, and Dr. Hurst was their conductor.

They each took a turn at getting an IV in Chaz. They wanted to start an IV to replenish his lost fluids, but they weren't having any luck. After several failed attempts, Dr. Hurst asked one of the nurses to call up to the nursery and have them send one of their nurses down since they had experience with inserting IVs into preemies.

4:15 p.m.
IV initiated in anterior scalp vein by NICU nurse.

I watched as Dr. Hurst was scribbling on the bedsheet. Most of it was numbers. He appeared to be lost in his own world. I wanted to ask what he was doing. But before I could, a rather chubby nurse with brown wavy hair appeared at the head of Chaz's bed. She took his little arms in her hands and looked for a place to put the IV. She checked out his little legs and feet. Finally, she gave up and grabbed the razor that had been put on Chaz's bed by one of the other ER nurses.

Then she began shaving the left side of his little head. I couldn't help but cry. Only it came out more like a wail. I was crying over the loss of his blond, curly hair. He had been born with a great head full of hair. Looking up at me, the nurse that was shaving his head assured me that it would grow back. But in my heart, I knew that it was more than that. I was mourning the loss of my son. He was only six days old. He shouldn't have been in a place like this. He shouldn't have been lying on a stretcher getting poked by needles.

Crying, I turned to Frank. "Do you think he feels it?" I asked.

He shook his head no. He had no more of an answer to that than I did. But I knew we were both praying that he couldn't.

After shaving a two-inch patch of hair from Chaz's head, the nursery nurse proceeded to insert the IV into Chaz's head. I couldn't help but cry even more.

I glanced over at the pediatrician, who was huddled in the corner of the room whispering to the nurse from the pediatrician's office. I didn't understand why she was still there. She wasn't contributing anything. And the more I watched her over in the corner whispering, the more I wanted to whisper too. So I did.

I grabbed Frank by the arm and pulled him aside. "Why do you think she's still here?" I asked.

He glanced over at them. "I don't know."

"She shouldn't be here," I said.

"I know," he said. "They made us sit in the waiting room for a long time."

"That's because their nurse insisted we make an appointment."

"And what about all of those phone calls?"

"I don't want her here," I said as I began to cry even more.

4:20 p.m.

Labs drawn from the left arm, no bleeding noted from the site.

Anyone that's ever had blood drawn knows that afterward a piece of gauze bandage is applied to the site with gentle pressure. Then a Band-Aid is applied over that. This is to stop the bleeding from the site. Chaz's labs were drawn from his left arm. But no bleeding was noted from the site.

When I asked why that was significant, one of the nurses said, "It means he's dehydrated."

Hearing another negative thing about Chaz's condition caused my tears to flow again.

Dr. Hurst quickly added, "It's nothing to worry about."

Worrying was all I could do. I couldn't get close enough to Chaz to hold his hand or his little feet. I couldn't even stand at the head of his bed. Too many people.

As the lab lady finished her collection of Chaz's blood and started gathering up her things, Dr. Hurst reminded her, "We need that STAT."

STAT. What a funny word. We hear it on television all the time. We know that it means to hurry. But like many people, I'd never really thought about what it meant. No time like the present to ask. So I did.

"It just means urgent," Dr. Hurst replied.

Urgent. Okay. But what does it mean? What does it stand for? More so, why do I even care? It's not going to change anything. It isn't going to make a difference in the care Chaz is receiving. It's not going to make him all well again. So why do I care?

But I guess that's what you do in situations like this. You find something to fill the time. You stop and notice that the walls are painted ecru instead of snow white. You notice the fly that has miraculously made its way inside. The smell of chicken whisks by from an undisclosed location. You notice that there are two chairs in the bay next to you instead of one. And you wonder who was there last. Then you look at the doorway and you notice all of the scratches. This makes you wonder what emergency caused that. Did someone die in this room? Will your child die in this room?

Then you shake your head in disbelief. Because you know better. He was just crying an hour ago. He was moving his little hands and feet. You know that you shouldn't be here. He shouldn't be here. But here you are. You look to your left and notice that the pediatrician and her nurse is gone. You breathe a sigh of relief. You didn't want her here anyway. It is her fault that you are here. It is the fault of her office. That nurse. The one with the "what me, holier than thou" attitude.

I told you something was wrong. I told you over and over again. I told you something didn't feel right. I told you I couldn't explain it. I told you. I told you. I told you! I told you something didn't feel right! I knew something was wrong! And that was a damn seizure that he was having!

4:40 p.m.
Moved via stretcher to the cubicle.

4:45 p.m.
IV infusion, Pedialyte offered – child not sucking – sleeping off and on.
Finally, after all of those needle sticks, Chaz was finally given an IV. He was getting fluid and phenobarbital to help with the seizures. One of the nurses offered him some Pedialyte, but he refused. When the nurse offered him a bottle, he just squished his little face up and tried to turn his head. Just as he had done when I offered him my breasts in the past few days. He couldn't turn it as much as he wanted because of the IV that was in his little head. But he was so sleepy that he didn't even cry. There wasn't even a little grumpiness. No gurgling sounds. No signs of protest. Just a little squished-up face. The nurse wrote, "child not sucking."

That's kind of what got us into this mess. He had sucked and sucked so much over the past six days he was tired of sucking. He was miserable. I could feel it. He deserved a break. A little rest. Good for him. He was taking this time to rest. He could sleep while the fluids nursed his little body.

When I overheard Dr. Hurst tell Frank that the phenobarbital would make Chaz sleepy, I couldn't help but wonder how the nurse had expected him to suck on a bottle to get Pedialyte in his system if he was drowsy.

He looked peaceful. Curled up in a little ball. I wanted to offer him a blanket. But there was nowhere to put it. He had electrodes on his chest to detect his chest movements as he breathed. He had a line that they used to draw blood. There was a little cuff on his arm detecting his blood pressure. A pulse oximeter was on his foot. Then there was the IV on his head. I looked at the shaved area of his little head and wondered if it would ever grow back. And if it did, would it still be curly? Thinking about this caused me to cry even more.

4:50 p.m.
Parents at the bedside – mom crying – mom comforted.
Frank put his arm around me. This time he didn't say anything. There were no words of encouragement. No reassurance. It was only the reality of a bad situation.

Dr. Hurst took a step back from Chaz's bed and turned, just slightly, so he could see us as he talked. Only he wasn't really seeing us. His eyes were still focused on Chaz lying on the bed. He was only pretending to be looking at us.

"We are going to transfer him to children's hospital," he said. "Their PICU will take care of him."

I started crying again. This time, Frank pulled me to the side.

"I think we should call everybody," he said. I nodded in agreement.

Quietly, Frank asked no one in particular, "Do you have a phone we can use?"

Dr. Hurst shook his head yes. Then he nodded to one of the nurses. I never heard him say anything, but somehow he was understood, and we were taken to a cubicle and left on our own. Only this one had dim lighting and a comfortable chair with a desk to sit at. From here, we could still see Chaz. Frank called first.

When Frank's mom answered his collect call, I was sure her imagination ran wild.

"Chaz is in the hospital," he said. "We're in the emergency room, and they're going to transfer him to children's hospital." I could hear her let out a scream, followed by a cry.

She wanted to know what happened. Frank told her about Chaz's eyes and the seizure. He told her that we really didn't know anything just yet because the doctor didn't. He told her that we were waiting on lab work and that a nurse from the nursery upstairs had to come down and put an IV in his head. And that they shaved his hair. And as he relayed these details to her, I could hear her crying. And each shriek was followed by a "how did it happen?"

How, indeed.

I did what the videos said. I put Chaz to my breasts every two to four hours at least five to ten minutes on each breast. And sometimes more. He was wetting at least six diapers a day. I still had those diapers. The diaper service hadn't picked them up yet. It wasn't time. I spoke with one of the nurses that was present during Chaz's delivery, and she insisted that I keep doing what I was doing. *He would eat when he got hungry.* I spoke with one of the home health nurses. *She said not to supplement. It causes nipple confusion.* I spoke with one of the nurses in the pediatrician's office, six times in two days. And she said, *Newborn eyes do that.* I told them something was wrong. Something didn't feel right. *You're a first-time mom. You don't appreciate how much he's getting.*

This might be a good time to tell you that I never got engorged and I never leaked. Never. Never. N-e-v-e-r!

So what else was I supposed to do? Ignore all of the medical professionals' advice? That's where Frank and I disagreed. He felt that they knew better than me. Them with their fancy degrees and their experience, they were supposed to know what they were talking about. Wrong! Dead wrong.

5:05 p.m.

Glucose finger stick.

Frank rehashed the past few days with his mom and promised to call her as soon as he knew something more.

Now it was my turn to call my parents. Oh, how I wanted to be someone else right now. My parents, especially my mom, are not that great in an emergency. Calling them would not be easy.

When my mom answered, she appeared to be a little agitated. She was probably thinking about the collect call charge. "Hi, Pam," she said. "What do you want?"

I always wanted something. It was either money, advice, or both. Sniffling from my tears, I said, "Chaz is in the hospital."

"Why?" she demanded.

As I went through my story of the past few days, I didn't sense any sympathy from her. It was more of a "what did you do" attitude coming from the other end of the phone. With only my story of the past few days bundled with no real answers from Dr. Hurst, I had no way of telling her what was going on where it made any sense. There were too many unanswered questions. And the more I talked, the more agitated she became. The more agitated she became, the more upset I got. Finally, my dad got on the phone. Of course, that meant rehashing my narrative all over again.

With every one of my sentences, my dad would reply with an astonished, "How?" And I had no answers for that. All I could do was relay the events of the past few days. Not even I understood what had happened. None of it made sense to me.

My dad ended our call on a good note, telling me to call back once I knew something more. As I hung up, I couldn't help but wonder how I could do all this crying. Where were the tears coming from?

JUNE 8

PART 3: DEHYDRATION
IS KILLING HIM

5:08 p.m.

L ab here to recollect blood – states values were off. Dr. Hurst holding restick for now pending printed results.

    You've got to be kidding me. After all those people did all of those sticks into Chaz as if he was a pin cushion.

5:10 p.m.

Dr. Sheffield here at the bedside – COBRA form initiated and signed by mom.

Right when I started studying the panels in the ceiling and the tiles on the floor, the pediatrician walked over to me, holding a clipboard. She had a nurse with her. There were twelve tiles. Three vertical and four horizontals. And each had fifty popcorn-like holes in them. So I was trying to figure out if I was looking at a twelve or a six hundred. But then I looked at the floor, and there were even more tiles. But my counting was interrupted by a voice.

"Mrs. Floyd. Mrs. Floyd," she said, with much authority. I looked up, in a trance-like state, which I sometimes get into when I get anxious and "go away" by counting and grouping things around me. I gave her a quizzical look since I only half heard her. "We need you to sign this form. It's a COBRA form, not only for the emergency room treatment but for the children's hospital transport that will be here shortly."

Frank stood by me as I signed the paper. I had no idea what I was signing. I just knew that whatever it was, it was supposed to help Chaz.

The fact that I was able to contain my disgust for the pediatrician, I thought, showed remarkable restraint. As much as I wanted to scream at her and that horrible nurse of hers, I didn't. I couldn't. I was not one to rock the boat. I was raised to be quiet, even when I disagreed with something or someone. And especially when I was disgusted with something.

5:20 p.m.
Dr. Hurst on the phone arranging children's hospital transport.
I signed the form, and the pediatrician and the nurse walked away without so much as a thank-you or a good luck. But it didn't matter because we were leaving here soon. Frank and I listened as Dr. Hurst was on the phone with children's hospital arranging medical transport for Chaz. I heard the words "dehydrated," "seizures," "no fluids," "intake," "for at least twenty hours," and "parents by the bedside." Then there were a bunch of numbers and medical terminology that I didn't understand and had never heard before. Because I had never been in this kind of situation before.

One of the nurses called out to Dr. Hurst to come here. He wasted no time in discontinuing his call. He walked swiftly to Chaz's bedside. Frank and I watched from our little area of the emergency room.

5:25 p.m.
Eyes deviating to the left – seizure disorder per Dr. Hurst – placed on the cardiac monitor.
I wanted to scream, finally. They were finally seeing what I had been

telling everyone about. Dr. Hurst took his ink pen out of his pocket and started scribbling on the bedsheet again. None of the numbers made sense to me. Once he was sure of his calculations, he asked the nurse to increase Chaz's phenobarbital. Then he turned and explained to us that the phenobarbital was there to stop any seizure activity.

He also informed us that the transport team from children's hospital was on the way. Then he walked back over to the phone and called them to tell them about Chaz's seizure activity and what he had just observed, along with what he had just prescribed.

I cried more. In a perfect world, I would have never wanted anyone other than me to see Chaz's seizure activity. Because that would mean it wasn't true. That I imagined things. Unfortunately, I did know what a seizure was.

And the more I thought about my conversation with Dr. Sheffield's nurse about Chaz's seizures, the madder I got. She accosted me with:

How do you know he's having a seizure?

What's your medical background to say it's a seizure?

5:35 p.m.

Few attempts at starting second bigger IV – access by Dr. Paul, Dr. Sheffield, and Nurse Jackson, all unsuccessful.

Dr. Hurst stressed to the nurses that we needed to get more fluids into Chaz's system. His little body was in need of nourishment. Nourishment that he obviously didn't get from me. My mother always said that I was a failure. I guessed I just proved her right. I succeeded in having a natural childbirth. No meds for me. Yet I couldn't do something as simple and as natural as breastfeeding.

Dr. Hurst suggested that a second larger IV be started. So I watched as Dr. Paul tried and failed. Then Dr. Sheffield tried and failed. Nurse Jackson tried and failed. All three were unsuccessful. Chaz suffered even more needle pricks. He was just too dehydrated. His veins kept popping. That was if they could find them to try. So they did a lot of "fishing" for a vein. Watching this and knowing that I couldn't do anything about it was killing me.

Every time I saw one of them stick a needle in Chaz, I would breathe in deeply. So deep that it sounded like I was gasping for air. And the tears. Oh my Lord, the tears would not stop. And that meant that my nose was running. And all of this was causing me to have a headache. And I hurt down below. With all of my stitches, I was supposed to be taking it easy. Ha! I was participating in the Mt. Everest of movement. And despite how badly my body ached and despite the swelling and bleeding I was having from the episiotomy, I couldn't stop. I had to be by Chaz's bedside. I had to watch these people poking my son, in hopes that they could give him the fluids and medicines that he needed. I was just thankful to God that none of it seemed to bother him much. Though he would squish up his little face, cry, and try to roll himself into a ball, he wasn't screaming. I really didn't know if that made it all better or not. At least if he cried, I would know that he was still okay. You'd have to be okay to feel pain. Right?

PART 4: NEEDS A SPECIALIST, HOSPITAL, AND CARE

6:00 p.m.

*C*hildren's hospital transport personnel taking over.

After multiple attempts, Dr. Paul, who appeared to have taken over for Dr. Hurst, announced that the children's hospital transport team was there for Chaz. Frank and I peeked through the sea of bodies that had formed around our son.

The transport team consisted of a man and a woman. I had no idea what their titles were. I just knew that they came rolling in with this incubator-bed-like thing. It was the kind you see in the movies, where people put their hands through these huge gloves that are attached to the side of it so you can touch the person without really touching them.

The transport team conversed with Dr. Paul and the nurses for a few moments. Then they exchanged paperwork.

First, the wires attached to Chaz were disconnected. Then he was carefully placed on the incubator-bed-like thing.

As they rolled Chaz out of the emergency room and outdoors to the pediatric mobile intensive care transport vehicle, we watched and waited for almost an hour before they took off. It took them about thirty minutes of messing with wires and IVs before they loaded Chaz. Then they took another fifteen minutes or so getting him ready to move.

While we stood there watching, my brother-in-law showed up. I had forgotten that Frank had called Jay in the midst of all of this. We needed money to eat dinner. Though I wasn't really hungry, my headache said otherwise. I have gotten headaches from not eating for as long as I can remember. That explains why I've never been supermodel thin. It was nice to have at least one relative with us.

They waved to us as they drove away. We didn't know where to go, so we followed Jay. But first, we stopped off for some fast food. And we relayed the story of the past few days.

Then we rushed over to children's hospital.

When we got there, we walked up to the check-in desk where badges were being given out. We were told to head over to registration, that the PICU was still admitting him. What was a PICU and what else could they possibly be doing to him? And didn't I sign a bunch of papers when the transport unit showed up and then took him away?

So Frank and I headed into registration while Jay called their other brother. He had just gotten home from work, but due to the seriousness of the situation, he said he'd head right over. Though he lived nearby, he did have a rather long drive, yet he got there just as we finished registering Chaz into the PICU, which I finally found out meant pediatric intensive care unit. We were provided with so many booklets, sheets, cards, and manuals that we were given a bag for them all.

Once we finished registering Chaz, we met back up with Frank's brothers, got our check-in passes, and headed up to the PICU. It was already near the end of visiting hours, but I think they gave us a break due to the situation. After all, he'd just gotten registered. I had the papers to prove it. Literally.

When we got off the elevator, it was a little bit darker than it was downstairs. The lights on this floor were already dimmed for the evening.

It was a little after eight p.m. As we turned the corner, there were all of these warning signs. Of course, I had to read them all. And count them all. I picked up the phone and let the PICU know that we were there, that we had just finished registering Chaz. I was surprised when these two giant doors opened, and I was grateful we were allowed back because the nurse said that one, they were still getting him settled and two, they were getting him registered for some tests.

Once we were back in the PICU, we were instructed to wash our hands before we came near Chaz. When we saw him, he didn't look much different than he did in the transport unit, but this time it looked more real, and I began to cry. Of course, doctors and nurses were introducing themselves and asking me questions, and I was answering them without much thought. It was like I was on autopilot. Which I guess in a way I kind of was.

Frank asked the nurse if his brothers could see Chaz really quick since they had both come with us and one had driven a little ways to get there. She said yes, so he took turns bringing them in. And I spent my time over in the corner answering questions. Basically, I went over the past six days.

When it finally came time to send Chaz for a test, we were told to go home and get some sleep because it was going to be a long night for Chaz and there was nothing that we could do for him tonight.

In the back of my mind, I couldn't help but say, "Pray." We could pray for him. But a lot of good that had done so far. Then again, I wasn't sure I had prayed for Chaz up until that point. I was too tired to really know.

Frank told the nurses about my fourth-degree episiotomy and numerous stitches, so he said that it would be good to get me home. I think it was more that he could feel that I was getting agitated about answering the same questions I'd already answered about ten times that day and going on ten more now. Each doctor, nurse, and technician that walked in asked me what happened. And each asked specific questions. Basically, it was a recap of the past six days. I'm one of those people that hates to repeat a story. I don't like to hear myself talk. That's never been one of my things. Frank, though, Frank likes to talk. And I understood that most of the past six days he couldn't answer because he wasn't there. But there's a lot he could tell them. So we answered questions until we were excused for the night. I kissed Chaz goodnight. I dropped a few tears on his head, feeling like the worst parent in the world. Much deserved, I'd say.

PART 1: ICU – THE INTENSITY OF THINGS AND HOW IT HAPPENED

"Hello," I answered the phone.

"Mrs. Floyd," said an unfamiliar voice. "This is Doc Pam, with children's hospital. Chaz had a few pauses in breathing, a couple of episodes of sleep-like apnea, so we decided to intubate him."

Oxygen.

A respirator.

Another device.

More tubes.

She paused. I said nothing. What was I going to say? What was I supposed to say?

"The intubation appears to be working. So we hope it's temporary," she continued.

"Yes," I said softly. "I understand. Thank you for letting us know."

"Of course. Get some sleep," she suggested. "We'll see you later on today."

Later.

Get some sleep.

Now, my son had a tube inserted in his trachea that's attached to a breathing machine. Yes, I'll sleep soundly now. I know she meant well but it's hard to go back to sleep after hearing that about your seven-day-old son.

He was in good hands.

At least better than he was here. With me.

Last night I was told to go home when I didn't really want to. I wanted to be there with my son. Even though all of this had happened while he was in my care, I couldn't help but feel like I was the only one looking out for his best interests. After all, I was his mother. But by Doc Pam calling me to let me know what Chaz had hit a bump in the road, I felt like I could trust them to watch over Chaz while I was away.

I hung up and told Frank what the hospital said. Frank got out of bed and said, "I'm going to call my mom and sister."

He went into the kitchen and began to make coffee. Then he called his mom. I laid in bed as I listened to him recant the events of the evening to her. Then he hung up and called his sister, Linda.

I laid in bed looking at my poor doggies. They had joined me. The poor babies were going to feel like orphans today.

I must have dozed off as he talked to Linda because the next thing I knew, he was poking me with the phone. "They're coming down," he said. "They'll be here in a few hours. You might want to call your parents."

Shaggy and Wolf jumped off the bed when they noticed my struggle to do so. We had a water bed, and to be honest, it had been tough getting off of it while I was pregnant. Now that I was hurting from my stitches, it was even harder to get off the bed. And Shaggy had been my helper for the past few months. He would come to the side of the bed so I could grab his collar to help pull me up. God, I loved that dog.

Grabbing the phone, I opened the front door to let the dogs out. Shaggy and Wolf stopped in the doorway. It was still dark out. They were not used to going out in the dark. So I walked out first. Then they followed.

Before I had Chaz, the only lives I'd come close to loving as much as I did him was my dogs. They were my world. And I treated them like they were my children. And I loved them in the same way.

Once we were outside, I plopped down on my lounge chair. It had been my daily companion for those two overdue weeks of my pregnancy. Then I did what I dreaded most. I called my parents to give them an update. I already felt like a failure. Not only as a mother but a person. And yesterday's phone call to my parents hadn't gone so well. I was bombarded with the typical accusatory "how could that happen" questions. Only they had come out as implied statements more than questions.

That's how it had been all of my life. Everything was negative. Accusational. If I lost something, it was followed with, "Why did you lose it?" Once, I ended up in the emergency room from a car wreck. My parents went to see the car before they came to see me. Some might look at that and think, *Wow, these people don't love her.* But deep down, I know that they did in the only way they knew how. And considering I couldn't keep a child alive and healthy for a week meant I had no grounds for judgment.

Taking a deep breath, I dialed my parents. My dad answered the phone; he was already up. He'd always had this weird obsession for getting up at like four or five in the morning. At least my grandmother, his mom, waited till five or six before she got up. I told him what Doc Pam said about putting Chaz on oxygen, and he told me that they would be coming down later since things were that serious.

"This might be the only time we get to see him," my dad pointed out. It was obvious that what he really meant was the only time that we might get to see him alive.

I let him know that Dot and Linda were coming down, too. I suggested that he call them so they could all ride down together. Then I hung up.

Could things get any worse?

That was a question I swore I would never ask. At least not out loud. So I tried to think of something else. Anything else. I'd count sheep. No, that was for sleeping. I'd recite the Pledge of Allegiance. Did I even remember how that went? How about counting the waves as they crashed? Okay, never mind. I'd gotten my mind off the thing that I didn't want to think of, so let's move on.

My doggies had joined me on the lounge chair. And I could see in their eyes that they too were tired. They felt our stress, and that made them stressed, too. I petted them as I explained that I would be gone most of the day. I promised them that I would come back around five to let them out. And with that, we went inside.

I made breakfast. Our favorite, bacon and eggs. Turned out neither Frank nor I was hungry. Shaggy and Wolf, on the other hand, loved it.

I then decided to clean out Chaz's diaper bag from the day before. Frank asked what I was doing. I told him I wanted to take a few of Chaz's favorite things to the hospital. They were things that I assumed he'd love. I gathered up his little blue bear blanket. A toy bear that had come with the Enfamil formula I had gotten for free. Oh, the irony. And that was it. He hadn't been home long enough to have any favorite things yet. And the hospital appeared to be supplying everything else.

It had been four hours since the hospital called to tell me that Chaz had to be intubated, and it felt like a week. My mind and body felt as if I hadn't slept for days. Which when you really stopped to think about it, I hadn't. My body ached from head to toe. Yet somehow I had pretty much forgotten that I was walking around with a gigantic incision between my legs.

When Frank and I arrived at the hospital, we had to check in at an information desk. We told the woman at the desk that we were there to see our son. She asked us to wait a moment while she checked to see if we were on the list. The list. What list? No one told us about a list. We were the parents; shouldn't we know about a list? She told us that the only way to get up to the PICU was to be on the list. We were. Thankfully. Apparently, parents were automatically.

As we walked along the first floor, the smell of bacon filled the air. The elevators were right in front of the cafeteria, and while waiting, I started to get hungry. I was beginning to wonder why I hadn't eaten my bacon and eggs at home. That was a dumb move. The smells coming from the cafeteria were divine. And here I thought hospital food was supposed to be awful. Maybe it was. But the smell was enticing.

Once upstairs, we came face-to-face with the huge double doors from last night. I hadn't really paid much attention to them last night, but today they had my undivided attention. I turned to Frank and asked him what PICU meant. He had no clue. I picked up the phone and told the voice on the other end that I was there to see my son. I was relieved when we were immediately buzzed through.

Once we were inside the magic doors, we began making our way over to Chaz. A nurse reminded us to wash our hands before we touched him, so we stopped by the sink first. I looked over at Chaz, and he had even more tubing than he did last night. It hadn't been twelve hours since I last saw him, and he looked even more vulnerable than he had then. The nurse standing by his bed noticed my concerned look and informed me that he was not in any pain despite all of the tubing, tape, and machines.

Before the nurse could introduce herself, Dr. Kawaguchi walked over. He asked if anyone had called us about the oxygen. We said yes. He shook his head and said, "Good. Very good."

Then he told us that things had been pretty uneventful for the rest of the night. However, today was going to be a busy day for Chaz. He was going to have multiple tests and a bunch of lab work. As I listened to him talk, I couldn't take my eyes off of Chaz. He looked so vulnerable. He had a tube in his mouth that was taped to his face. And it looked like even more of his body was covered now.

"Your son is in here for dehydration," Dr. Kawaguchi said. In layman's terms, his sodium level got so high that his blood thickened, and as it tried to make its way through the brain, blood vessels started popping, causing the seizures. This was the hell that my son was going through.

Dr. Kawaguchi asked us to repeat the same story that we had related to Doc Pam the night before. Hearing about my concerns about breastfeeding, he told one of the nurses at the main desk to give me some tubing and containers, and he had them direct me up to the NICU, the neonatal intensive care unit. The NICU had a large breastfeeding room with state-of-the-art electric breastfeeding pumps.

We waved to Chaz's nurse to let her know that we'd be back in a few minutes. Then Frank and I headed upstairs to the NICU. It took Frank and me a few minutes to figure out how to attach everything. Once we did, I sat in the rocker that was provided, and Frank turned the pump on. With it hooked up to both breasts, I started to feel like a cow being milked. Their pumps had forceful suction. At least that meant it was working. After about fifteen minutes, I noticed that there were only a few drops in one of the containers and nothing in the other one. Thirty minutes later, both containers had less than one cc of fluid.

So Frank tracked down one of the NICU nurses and asked for her help. He explained how long I had pumped and how little milk was obtained and asked her to tell us what we were doing wrong. She checked everything over and assured me that I was hooked up properly. She suggested that I give it a few more minutes. Her thinking was that I had not actively breastfed in the past day or so, so things might be dried up.

After she left, I sat there for another thirty minutes. By time the hour was over, I had successfully accomplished suctioning a grand total of three cc's from both breasts, combined. I took my containers down to the PICU. When I gave them to the nurse that had provided me with the supplies initially, she said that she would store it in the fridge for Chaz to have later. She also suggested that I try again in a couple of hours. I had no idea how much three cc's was in ounces, but all I knew wass that it sure didn't look like a lot.

Frank and I washed our hands and went to stand by Chaz's bedside. We relayed our pumping experience with his nurse. She reassured me that something was better than nothing. She informed me that Chaz was getting ready to go for some more tests, so it was a good time for her to go over a few things with us. She grabbed one of the empty rockers and pulled it over to Chaz's bedside. Frank let me sit, explaining to the nurse that I had a fourth-degree episiotomy.

The nurse gave us a "Welcome to the PICU" packet. In it was the rules of the PICU and the hospital in general.

Parents were welcome any time, day or night. But we were not allowed to sleep by the child's bedside.

We were asked to compile a list of people that were allowed to visit our child. That list was limited to six. Frank and I were included in those six.

Only two visitors at a time were allowed by the child's bedside.

We were not allowed to remain by the child's bedside during the nurses' shift change.

We would not be allowed to remain by the child's bedside during procedures.

We were given a number that we could call anytime day or night to see how our child was doing.

All of these made me feel as if I no longer mattered. And was no longer needed.

Since our relatives were arriving in a couple of hours, I put them on the visitor's list. I knew that no one locally would be visiting. I had no relatives in the area, and Frank knew his brothers would not visit again. Taking the list with her, she went back to her station in the middle of the room.

There was a new nurse by Chaz's bedside now. She smiled. "Good morning. I am Eileen." Then she bent to the side and said, "You know, I lean." I really needed that laugh this morning.

She went back to busying herself with all of Chaz's wires and things. As she began to adjust the wires and tape, there were several noticeable red patches surrounding the taped areas. She called Dr. Kawaguchi over. After a short discussion, they determined that he was allergic to the plastic tape that they were using.

From that moment on, Chaz was going to need cloth tape.

We were asked to take a step back as Eileen and Dr. Kawaguchi began removing all of the tape, cleaning the various areas, and replacing it with the cloth tape. As they finished up, the nurse told us that Chaz was getting phenobarbital for his seizures and they hoped that would help. Another nurse placed a sign above Chaz's bed that showed that he was allergic to plastic tape, so please use cloth tape.

As Dr. Kawaguchi walked away, Dr. Jack came over and asked us to leave; they were going to run some more tests on Chaz. "Blood work and a spinal tap," she said unemotionally.

I wasn't sure what a spinal tap was, but it didn't sound pleasant. So Frank and I headed back to our dreary little cave called the PICU waiting room, where we would wait for our relatives.

PART 2: BRAIN DAMAGE –
IT'S REAL, AND IT'S
NOT GOOD

The little PICU waiting room appeared to be an afterthought. It was as if someone walked out of the PICU, turned right, and said, "Oh. We need somewhere for the parents to go instead of sending them downstairs every time they're asked to leave their child's bedside."

And I'm pretty sure that at one time it was a supply closet of some kind. It was that small.

We sat down in the dull, gloomy room and waited. We were not there long when a man with thick glasses entered the room. He introduced himself as Dr. White, the neurologist in charge of our son's care. He appeared to be in a hurry and rattled off some information that I honestly didn't understand.

After reading Chaz's EEG from last night, they had decided to put Chaz in a drug-induced coma in order to control his seizures. Frank and I looked at him as if he was speaking another language. Which, when you think about it, he kind of was. Because neither of us went to med school.

"I don't understand," I said.

"Your son has suffered severe brain damage," he said. "Because of dehydration. Can you tell me what happened?"

Here I went telling the same story. Again. Frank filled him in on the pregnancy and the birth. I told him what happened after we got home.

"Will he be okay?" I asked.

"We don't know," Dr. White said solemnly. This seemed to be the motto of the day in the PICU.

I was shocked. Weren't doctors supposed to know everything?

"What do you mean you don't know?" I said a little louder than I intended to.

Unfazed by my outburst, he said, "With the kind of damage that Chaz has received, we just don't know."

My tears started flowing, and my eyes started burning. I felt like someone had punched me in the stomach, and I bent over a bit, feeling a tad nauseous.

"It doesn't look good," he continued. "He's going to have some problems. Some degree of cerebral palsy."

Oh Lord, I thought. I knew what cerebral palsy was. Or at least I thought I did. My mom was related to someone that had a son with cerebral palsy. He was in a wheelchair and had to have assistance with everything, from eating to toileting to transfers.

But I was determined. "When we brought him in here, he was kicking and screaming," I said through my tears. "He was moving his arms and legs," I spat out. "Are you telling me that he won't ever do that again?"

"It's possible," he said.

Well, at least he wasn't sugarcoating anything. He was straightforward with his information regardless of how bad it sounded. I didn't know if I should respect him or despise him. Right then, I just hated him. But I kind of hated everyone, including myself.

I had so many questions, but my mouth had not caught up to my brain. So I remained quiet. I glanced at Frank, who looked like he was about to throw up.

With nothing more to say, Dr. White left us with our thoughts.

I wasn't sure what was gloomier: us or the room we were in.

Dr. White's negativity weighed on me so badly that I had to see my son. I wanted to see him moving his little arms and legs, as he had done earlier in the day yesterday. This couldn't be real. He couldn't no longer move. He had to move. He had to be the little baby that kicked me so hard when I was carrying him in my stomach that he caused my ribs to bruise. He had to still be able to take my breath away and make me bend over, just by a kick. A small baby kick. That's all I wanted now. I longed for that. I wished for that. *God, don't take that away from him. Please don't. Please. Oh, please, oh please, oh please.*

So I went to the dreaded PICU phones and asked to see Chaz. They should have had time to do what they needed to do by now. After all, when I left not too long ago, they were just changing the tape to all of his tubes, electrodes, and gadgets.

"Sorry, Mrs. Floyd. It's going to be just a little bit longer," quacked the nurse. This time she didn't even confer with Eileen. I wanted to ask what was going on, why I couldn't see my son. But I didn't. I was afraid of the answer. These people were in charge of whether I got to see my son and when. I wasn't about to rock the boat. Yet every twenty to thirty minutes I picked up that phone and asked to come back.

It didn't take long for Eileen to become irate with me. If only there had been a little more communication going on. For instance, she could have said, "The doctors are doing their rounds. He's still in x-ray. He's still in radiology and they're backed up." Something besides, "Mrs. Floyd, it's going to be a little longer." Instead, she was leaving me to let my mind wander and fill itself with worse-case scenarios. And as we all know, the mind can be a dangerous thing.

Then, as if on cue, my parents walked in.

Everyone said hi to everyone else, making a point to note that they wished it was under better circumstances. Frank provided updates on Chaz. Then he took my parents back to see Chaz. Yes, they got to go back and see Chaz. He quickly came back since only two people were allowed at the bedside at all times.

He told them to take their time because we were not going anywhere and we had all day. Besides, Frank and I knew that with our relatives traveling four to five hours to get here, they deserved to spend as much time with Chaz as they wanted. And I agreed.

Frank and I took this time to discuss what Dr. White had said. "I don't like him," I blurted out.

"He's not so bad," Frank said. "At least he told us the truth."

"Yeah, maybe. But did he have to be so crude?"

"You've got to remember that he's looking at tests results, so he's got to know what he's talking about."

I chose not to challenge him. Sitting in the drab little waiting room, I was reminded of my role in this place. Even though Chaz was my son, as long as he was in the PICU, he was more theirs than ours or mine. Thirty feet away from those huge double doors, we were required to pick up the phone on the wall and announce ourselves.

Each time, I was required to say, "I am here to see my son, Chaz Floyd. This is his mother, Pam." Then I had to wait for the head nurse to confer with Chaz's personal nurse about whether or not I could enter. To me, this was just another kick in the butt to my inability to care for my child. He was my son, and I shouldn't have to ask for permission to see him. But I did. Several times a day. Every day.

The waiting room was a quiet reminder of how insignificant you were in the world. In this world. The medical community. There, you were just someone that couldn't do anything right. It was like a prison for parents that fail. It was definitely the ugliest room that I had ever been in. And I hated how it made me feel. Incompetent.

The walls seemed to mock me. It was as if they were the mean girls of high school. Sitting in there was a reminder that I couldn't even get the parenting thing right.

PART 3: I HATE EVERYBODY, INCLUDING ME

My parents weren't with Chaz long before they too were asked to leave. My dad explained that a technician had come in with orders to take Chaz for another EEG. So we decided to go downstairs and grab some breakfast.

In the cafeteria, I moved like a sloth. Even though I knew that, in reality, I was amongst the living, I couldn't help but feel like I was watching myself in slow motion. It was still early, so I got some hash browns, bacon, and a plain biscuit. I got a soft drink because I didn't drink coffee. And I sat by one of the windows that looked out onto a small garden area. I watched some birds play chase with one another while I ate. I sat there staring. Lost in thought. Before I knew it, almost an hour had passed. Somehow I had managed to block out the noise of people chattering. Including the people sitting at the table with me. I was alone.

I managed to eat all of my food. If you can call that a lot. I finished my drink, dumped my trash, and then led the way to the gift shop. I wanted to get Chaz a stuffed animal. He deserved one after going through all of this. Even though he couldn't have it in the PICU, he could have it when he returned home.

I walked around and looked at all of the pretty things. I fell in love with the stuffed animals. Especially the doggies. But the cheapest one was twenty-five dollars. There was no way I could afford it. Frank said that we could stop by Wal-Mart on the way home.

Once we got back upstairs, Frank and I went in to see Chaz really quick. Nothing had changed. He had slept through the EEG and the spinal tap, as well as the bloodwork. He was scheduled for an MRI, but Eileen couldn't tell us what time they would come get him to do that. I asked her if Frank and I could step out while my parents visited Chaz, and she said yes. So Frank stayed with Chaz while I went and retrieved my parents. I didn't think I'd ever seen two people move so fast when I told them that they could go on back.

Meanwhile the nurse gave me some containers and tubing and asked that I try to pump again. So I told my parents that I'd be upstairs pumping. The PICU people wanted me to do this at least twice a day. The reason they gave me was so my milk wouldn't dry up. And all I could think about was how disappointing yesterday's pumping situation went. But I did as I was told and headed up to the NICU to pump while Frank made his way back to the grim waiting room to wait for his mom and sister.

Again, I hooked up both of my breasts to the hospital-grade breast pump's collection kits, both breasts, for thirty minutes and came back with an astounding two cc's from breast one and three cc's from breast two. I was pretty sure that mothers were supposed to produce more than this. But what did I know? After all, we were here because I questioned my breastfeeding abilities.

I turned my supplies in to the nurse, waved to my parents, who were still by Chaz's bedside, and returned to the drab waiting room with Frank. No sooner did I sit down than the phone rang. It was Linda and Dot. They were there, but for some reason, they were not on the list yet.

I quickly relayed my breast-pumping experience with Frank, and then I walked back to the phone by the PICU door to let the head nurse know that Linda and Dot were here and that they were from out of town and were anxiously waiting to see Chaz, only they were not allowed up yet since they were not on the list. The nurse said that she would let Eileen know.

I went back to the dungeon and relayed the conversation to Frank. He said that he was going to go downstairs and wait with them. I stayed put. I needed a moment alone.

One would think that I wanted to be alone so I could process everything. That was partly true. The other part was that I just wanted to be alone. I wanted to sit still and not have to think about anything. I wanted to sleep. I wanted to be able to sit on these hard, ugly seats and not feel as if I had been cut open and sewn back up. And I wanted to cry. I needed to cry. Crying was what I was becoming good at.

I cried because I was sad. I cried because I was mad. I cried because my heart was broken, and I cried because I was in physical pain. I was in this horrible cloudy bubble, and I couldn't get out. It was as if I was screaming and no one could hear me. I felt like I was drowning, and each time my head bobbed up out of the water, no one could see me or hear me and back down I'd go.

Before I knew it, an hour had passed since my last phone call to the PICU. I called again, relaying the same message. "This is Pam Floyd, and I have relatives from out of town that are downstairs and want to see Chaz, but they have not been added to the visitor's list."

"Okay, Mrs. Floyd. It's going to be just a little bit longer," quacked the nurse. I asked to come back. She reminded me that only two people were allowed by the bedside. I said that I understood, that we would switch out once I was back.

So when the golden doors opened, I went back and talked to Eileen. I wasn't switching with my parents. I wanted to know why my in-laws were not allowed up yet. Eileen told me that I already had six people on the list. I told her that I was taking Frank's brothers off the list because I knew they would not be back to visit. She was agitated and let me know that she didn't have time for such nonsense. But within a few minutes, she fixed things.

After I left the PICU, I went to the bathroom to see if I was bleeding or if I'd ripped something because it suddenly hurt like hell when I walked. Sitting had not been fun either. I had my donut pillow with me, but let's be honest, when you've been sewed front to back in between your legs versus a pillow, the pillow will lose every time.

I'd been hobbling around since I got there that morning. Between my legs felt as if I had run a marathon. Fortunately, everything looked all right. So I made my way back to the drab, depressing, hopeless PICU waiting room. And there sat Frank and his mom, Dot. Frank had already called back to the PICU to see if one of my parents would switch out with Dot. I walked in just in time to overhear him tell her, "I'll take you back when one of Pam's parents comes back."

My timing couldn't be worse because as soon as I walked in, Frank's mom wanted to know what had happened to bring us all here. We told her everything from the delivery up to now. She just couldn't believe it. She kept shaking her head and muttering, "What a shame."

As I stirred uncomfortably in my seat, my dad walked in, looked at me, and asked, "Uncomfortable?"

Then pleasantries were extended, and Frank walked out with his mom.

Linda was going to be a while because she didn't ride elevators, so she was going to have to walk up to the seventh floor. But this gave us time to talk. My dad expressed how sad the situation was. He was amazed at how tiny Chaz was. And six days ago, when he was delivered, he was referred to as a one-year-old by my delivering OB/GYN. My mom entered the room right on cue, telling my dad that she wanted to buy a camera so she could take some pictures. I screamed, "No! I don't want there to be any pictures. I never want Chaz to know that he was here." I didn't want any reminders. So she let it go for the moment.

After about thirty minutes, Linda showed up. She was out breath but glad to be able to come up to the PICU. She was relatively quiet. This was unusual for her. I couldn't tell if she was heartbroken, confused, mad, or just plain worn out. After all, she had been woken up in the middle of the night, drove for five hours, and walked seven flights of steps. Actually, it was more than that because she said some of them were not listed as floors with numbers.

My dad filled her in on Chaz's condition since he had already gone back to see Chaz. I volunteered to go page the nurse so Frank could switch out with her. The truth was I was beginning to feel a little uncomfortable, so I ran away downstairs. Just to explore.

All morning people had been asking me what happened, and I didn't know what to say. I told them the events of the past six days, and that was it. I didn't know what happened. I sure as hell couldn't explain what happened. All I did know for sure was that this felt like a bad dream that I prayed that I would wake up from eventually. Or so I hoped and prayed.

As I walked past the cafeteria and radiology, I saw, in the corner, a sign that said "chapel." You would have missed it if you blinked. Obviously, I didn't blink. Or maybe God had wanted me to see it.

Sitting in the hallway was a carved wooden scalloped wall table. On it was various pamphlets about grief, God, and prayer. I grabbed one of everything. Not only did I need reading material, but I also needed God. We needed to get back on track in order to save Chaz. I desperately needed his help. The doctors needed his help. And Chaz's relatives needed his help. And Lord knows I was in need of his help. Not only had I failed as a mom but I was in bad pain. And my heart was broken over Chaz. I felt so helpless with him in the PICU. I didn't know what to do. My role here was extremely limited.

To the left of the table was a tiny chapel. Its back wall was made of beautiful stained glass. There were a few short pews, a prayer bench, and a prayer book. First I sat on one of the pews and just stared at the stained glass and the white marble Jesus that stood nearby. I wondered if he was up there. Was he listening? Was he watching?

I had been raised Southern Baptist and had grown up in a church that didn't practice what it preached. Especially at home, by my mother. We were constantly butting heads over the simplest things.

One Sunday after church, my mom came into my bedroom and took down all of my posters. Apparently, I was praising false Gods by having pictures of Donny and Marie Osmond, Shaun and David Cassidy, and

Scott Baio on my wall. She ripped them off the wall as she mumbled on about how I was going to hell for idolizing these figures. I, of course, was walking behind her, crying, as I tried to stop her. They were posters that I had gotten out of *Tiger Beat* magazines that she had bought for me. I wasn't idolizing anyone. Lusting maybe. Idolizing no.

Then on another horrible Sunday, the preacher had gotten all uptight about Elton John's song "Rocky Mountain High" because he swore up and down he was singing the praises of getting high. Then the band KISS came along with their highly devilish costumes and their songs like "I Was Made for Lovin' You." So as far as the adults were concerned, we were going to hell if we listened to "that type" of music. I didn't listen to either of those, so I thought I was in the clear. But with my mom, that answer was an astounding no.

Once we got home from church, my mom started another one of her outdoor fires in the backyard and began to burn my record albums, all while she screamed at me that I was going to hell. I thought she was crazy. Was God really not going to let me into heaven because I was listening to the Osmonds, who by the way were Mormons? And the Partridge Family, and Shaun Cassidy? After all, "Da Doo Run Run" was invented in my parents' teenage years. Let's just say that things got worse after that.

So there I was fifteen years later, and I was sitting in a chapel, looking at a white marble statue of Jesus, wondering. First I had to ask him why he did it. Why did he cause Chaz to suffer? Was he punishing me for leaving the church all those years ago?

Or was he mad because I had sung along to Prince's "1999"? Or maybe it was because I did love Rick Springfield. Or was it because I wanted to be just like Joan Jett and dance to "I Love Rock 'n' Roll"? Could it be because I loved to roller-skate to the J. Geils Band's "Centerfold" or to Clarence Carter's "Strokin'"? Was I really that bad of a sinner that God was now punishing my son and me?

In my heart, I honestly didn't believe that God was that petty. So using telepathy, I cussed him out. I let him have it. How dare he put me through hell for the past ten months and then have the nerve to take it all away? Who the hell did he think he was? This was my child. Not his.

After about thirty minutes of yelling at God for allowing this to happen to Chaz, I walked over to the prayer book and wrote Chaz's name in it. I wrote that he was in the PICU and any prayers would be forever welcome. Then I began to walk out of the chapel. I got to the doorway, and I stopped. I turned around and looked at the stained glass and the statue again, and I quietly said aloud, "Please save him." And I eventually dragged myself back upstairs to the PICU waiting room.

When I walked into the dreaded PICU waiting room, I had expected to see Frank sitting there, alone. Instead, it was Dot.

"How are you?" she asked. She always asked this even if it's only been an hour since she last saw you.

"Okay," I lied.

"Linda's in there with Frankie."

That's what she always called him. Frankie.

Through weepy eyes, Dot told me that Linda couldn't let go of his little foot and that when she talked to him, he responded. "He can hear me," she said.

I told her that was excellent news. It made me wish they could be there all the time. "We have to go back tonight," Dot shared with me. "Linda has to go back to work tomorrow." I shook my head in understanding.

"Where's Mom and Dad?" I asked. But before she could answer, Frank entered the waiting room.

"Where were you at?" he asked me.

"In the chapel," I said quietly. "I didn't even know that they had one." I pulled the pamphlets out of my bag. "I picked these up while I was there."

He didn't look at them. He didn't even ask about them. He told his mom she could come back for a quick visit. He was going to take her back to the PICU before they kicked us all out for lunch. He looked around. "Where are Mr. and Mrs. Goff?"

"They went to find a bathroom," Dot said.

Frank turned to me. "You don't mind if Mom goes back, do you?"

I shook my head no.

"Maybe you can figure out where everyone wants to go for lunch," he said to me.

I shook my head okay.

I knew that with all of the relatives here today that I wouldn't see Chaz that much. And my visit to the chapel had actually helped me. I felt a kind of calm rush over me that was hard to explain. Somehow I knew that things were going to work out the way they were supposed to; whether good or bad, I would find a way to deal with it.

My dad and Linda had to go back to work tomorrow. Dot had to get home. It seemed like everyone had a life to get back to. But me. I was going to be left in this constant state of the unknown. A state of insecurity. A constant state of pain. A state purgatory.

PART 4: DEALING WITH DISASTER IN EVERY WAY

rank was the first one to come back to the waiting room. He said that they were taking Chaz for more tests and that the nurse suggested we go to lunch and if I wanted to see Chaz before then, the nurse would allow me a few moments.

When I walked back into the PICU, Linda was holding Chaz's foot. It was the only thing on him that was uncovered. She was whispering to him. Chaz's nurse whispered to me, "She's wonderful with him." I took that to mean that I wasn't. I told Chaz that we were going to lunch but we would be back soon.

Back in the waiting room, everyone had decided on Shoney's for lunch. Frank volunteered to walk down the stairs with his sister while the rest of us took the elevator.

Once we were back in the lobby, Dot suggested that I ride with my parents and Frankie ride with her and Linda. I didn't care who I rode with as long as I didn't have to talk to anyone. No talking meant no thinking. I had become a master over the years of just allowing my mind to go blank.

I could shut down quicker than a power plant with no electricity. And that's what I hoped to do for the next hour or so. Shut down. I needed that time to reboot. To recharge my batteries. If not, then mentally, I would explode. And that wouldn't be pretty.

I got lucky because my parents weren't in the mood to talk. I did have to tell my dad where to turn as we were driving. He had passed Shoney's when he came in, but he couldn't exactly remember how to get back there. Directions I could do. Huge emotional talking I could not. Though my mom did tell him that she wanted to stop and buy a camera so she could take pictures of Chaz in the PICU. Again, I simply, firmly, and quietly said, "No."

A child should never know that they were near death before they could have their first memory. Was I being naive? Probably. Should I have let her? Yes. Would I regret that decision? We'd see. Maybe one day. Most likely.

When we walked into Shoney's, our family looked like any other touristy family that summer. Problem was we were not there for a joyous occasion. The way the doctors spoke, it might be a funeral in a few days. All any of us could do was wait and see.

After we were seated, everyone had a hard time ordering. I don't think anybody really had an appetite, but we knew we needed to eat something.

After we placed our orders, Dot touched our waitress on the arm and said, "We have a Shoney's, too." It seemed like the whole restaurant got quiet, or at least our table did.

To which Linda replied, "They only let her out once a month." We all burst out laughing.

My dad, the serious one, even though he was smiling, said, "We're from Lynchburg."

Our waitress smiled and said, "That's nice, honey. What brings y'all down here?"

"Our grandson is in children's hospital," my dad said quietly, without smiling.

Our much-needed moment of laughter immediately ended once our ears heard those words said out loud. Yes, we all knew why we were there, but to tell someone else, a stranger, that kind of made it so much more real. At first, it was just a bad dream that we all shared. Now we were sharing it with the world. Or maybe we already had. Because my parents, Linda, and Frank had already shared the news with their employers, and Dot was alerting her friends and neighbors. And then that news would be shared with others. And so it began. The world would slowly but surely know.

After the waitress left, we tried to look like a normal family enjoying lunch together. But we were anything but normal. And there I sat, the pink elephant in the room. At lunch, it was basically the same old song and dance. How did things get this bad? Didn't you see the signs? Didn't you tell them what was wrong? Were you accurate in your description of the events? Why didn't you give him a bottle? Why didn't you take him to the doctor sooner?

Did you know something was wrong? Yes. Why didn't you do something about it? Because all the medical people said nothing was wrong. What made you finally ignore their advice? Because my insides were screaming, "Do something, damn it!!"

I felt like I was being roasted. The only problem was the things that they were saying were things that I, myself, wondered. I thought of myself as a strong, smart woman. I had graduated from high school. I went to college for a while. I at least gave it a try. I had worked since I was sixteen years old. The question was why I chose to ignore my own instincts and accept the advice of others. I had no idea. I could guess. Maybe it was because I was young and anxious. Maybe it was because I was in pain and totally exhausted. Maybe it's because having a child was new territory for me and I needed to trust the experts in this field. I have a feeling that I will ask myself this for the rest of my life.

Frank and I answered their questions as best as we could. Not once did we take offense at them. After all, they had not been here during all of this, so they didn't know any better. And we knew that they were coming from a good place. They didn't want their grandbaby, or nephew, in Linda's case, to die. And since they were slightly removed from the situation, they were able to take in what the doctors said and make more sense of it than I could.

Either way, I felt like a huge failure when they looked at me. After all, I had a track record of things not going my way. I was living proof of Murphy's Law. That seemed to increase three-fold once I met and married Frank. Now it appeared that we had unfortunately passed it along to our son.

Looking at their faces, I could tell that they too thought that I had failed. They knew that I screwed up and there was no one to blame but me. It was more convenient that way. After all, everyone that was attached to this awful event needed someone to blame, so why not me? What none of them were aware of was that no amount of finger pointing was ever going to be equal to what I was doing to myself on a minute-by-minute basis.

Thank God the food arrived, because then came the casual, light conversation. And I was finally not the point of conversation.

My dad was taking a vacation in July, so he could only stay a day. My mom was, well, my mom. Her motto was if it didn't involve her, then it didn't concern her. Dot was retired and spent her days lying out in the sun and working in her garden. Linda was working and taking care of her own kids. Frank was only off for a few more days. As for me, I was in a state of flux. I was on Chaz time. I would be at the hospital with him for as long as he needed me. Or until I ended up in the hospital because right then between my legs was really hurting. I had to pee and I didn't want to. I didn't want to stand up. I didn't want to walk. And I definitely didn't want to crouch down to the toilet seat, pee, and do all that's going to hurt me. Just thinking of it was bringing tears to my eyes. So for now, I'd take another bite of my food.

In my state of flux, I was a mother yet I wasn't. Mothers always knew what's best for their children. They kept them safe. They kept them healthy and alive. They made their children happy. Mothers knew what's best for their children, and no amount of medical school could substitute for that. It didn't matter how many letters were after your name, because motherhood was, after all, natural. Just like giving birth and breastfeeding. Right?

When our waitress came back with the check, she asked if we wanted doggie bags. We all declined. We had to head back to the hospital.

In a few hours, our relatives would be leaving. And that would leave Frank and me to deal with this tragic event. And once he went back to work in a few days, it would all be on me. And I had no idea what kind of mental state I was in. Physical exhaustion compiled with pain and toppled with severe stress would do that to you.

When we got back to the hospital, I had to pee. I didn't want to. I knew it was going to hurt like hell. Dot told me that it was now or never. So I went. Being the only one in the bathroom, I sat down and cried. I had a huge hole in my heart. I was losing something that I so desperately wanted. And now everyone that I was related to knew that I had failed as a mother. Not only could I not do such a natural thing as breastfeed, but I had failed in other ways, by ignoring my motherly instincts. And we still didn't know if Chaz was going to live. And if he did, what kind of life he would have. I couldn't think about that now. It was just too much.

Back at the hospital, everyone agreed that Frank and I would go back first to check on Chaz. Nothing had changed. He had gone for some more tests, and they were waiting for the results. They had taken some more blood and were waiting for those results, too. We went back to the waiting room and let the relatives take turns visiting Chaz.

And I took my containers and tubing that the nurse had given me and headed upstairs to the pump. This time I was only hooked up to the machines for about twenty minutes when I gave up. Two breasts and only two cc's from one of them. My left breast had said, "That's it. I'm done." And breast two said, "I think this is the last time we do this." I carried my measly little amount to the head nurse, and she thanked me for it. She reassured me that every little bit made a difference. Apparently, whatever breast milk I was able to produce was so important that it would heal Chaz. And maybe eventually he'd be able to walk on water because of it.

Those of us that sat in the stale, drab waiting room didn't really talk about much of anything. Instead, the conversation was general. Things like what everyone was up to, how work was going, what the weather was like, things like that. Things that in the course of this tragedy seemed so important to hang onto. Normal, everyday life allowed for the escape from this reality.

Even though I had not complained out loud, the relatives said aloud what I was thinking. The waiting room was depressing.

"It needs some color," replied Dot.

"It needs some light," my mom said. "It's too dark in here."

"Look at this furniture. It looks like something you'd pick up off the side of the street that someone was throwing away," Linda said.

My dad chimed in, "There's no magazines. No water cooler. No coffee maker."

Color. The color was something we all agreed on. And, of course, better-shaped furniture.

Oh, the irony. Furniture that required a death. But it was revitalized. And on the other side of this wall were doctors, nurses, and machines working day and night to make sure that children remained alive. Regardless of the futures they would experience.

The relatives kept taking turns going in and out to see Chaz. I knew that this irked his nurse. But it was an out-of-town family day.

Dot couldn't get over all of the tubes connected to Chaz. There were so many of them that you were never sure where they started and where they ended. He had a tube to help him breathe. He had a feeding tube, an IV for medications, his little ET finger to check his pulse ox.

A little before five o'clock, the doctors and nurses noticed that Chaz was developing a rash on his back, including the back of his arms, legs, and neck. Dr. Kawaguchi decided that Chaz must be allergic to the detergent that the hospital used to wash their linens. He called it contact dermatitis. So they made a note to let us know about this once we returned to the bedside. Until then they would place an underpad under him so his body would not be able to touch the sheet.

My dad came out of the PICU to let me know that he and my mom were getting ready to "shove off," as he called it. And he told me what Dr. Kawaguchi said about the rash and the linens.

Linda and Dot visited Chaz one more time, as they too were "shoving off" around five. They also told me about the rash and the linens.

So I went back to see Chaz and speak with the nurse. She recommended that I bring Chaz's sheets, blankets, and clothes from home to assist in the breakout. I told her that I was going to walk my parents out and that I'd run home after that. She insisted that I take my time.

At five o'clock, when the relatives would normally be calling it a day at work, they all decided to call it a day with us. They wouldn't get home till around nine or ten, and that's if they didn't stop for dinner. Which I doubted they would since no one really ate lunch. Then they had work tomorrow.

So we hugged everyone goodbye and promised to keep them up to date on Chaz. My dad told me to take it easy.

"You don't need to pop any stitches," he said.

Linda called me Wonder Woman for being able to walk around with that many stitches in that area.

Dot told me to make sure that I got some rest and to call her if anything changed.

My mom said goodbye and that she'd have her church pray for Chaz and us. And she jokingly said, "I wish I had some pictures to show them."

I reminded her that I didn't want any record of this day. I never wanted Chaz to see himself like this. Honestly, I was shocked that she had respected my wishes. But a small part of me wondered if she had snuck a camera in there without my knowing it.

So Frank and I left the hospital and went home to pick up linens and stuff for Chaz. I had sheets and his bear blanket. But the clothes that I had purchased at a consignment shop would not fit Chaz. I purchased newborn clothes, and Chaz needed clothes for a 6-week-old baby. It made me wonder how many other mothers made this mistake. Or was I the only lucky one? Another thing that I didn't get right.

I did have plenty of those sleeveless shirts that tied in the front that my grandmother on my mom's side had made for Chaz. She liked to sew and had been making stuff for Chaz all year long. She would give them to my mom to send to me, so I got a package from her at least once a month.

I had shirts, blankets, and booties galore.

I took my stuff back to the consignment shop in hopes that they would exchange them for twelve-month-old baby clothes. It was no problem. So I took them home and washed them.

I tried to lie down and get some sleep, but my mind wouldn't let me. It screamed, "Bitch, you ain't sleeping."

So instead, I took a hot shower and changed my clothes. Then I sat and petted the dogs.

As soon as Chaz's clothes came out of the dryer, Frank and I returned to the hospital with his linens and little front tie shirts from Grandma.

When we arrived, we were told that Chaz also had a latex allergy. The nurse had noticed that every time Chaz's skin made contact with a latex glove, it would leave a red mark that had the look of a power slap behind it. So she informed us that from now on if he was in a hospital we needed to request non-latex items. So now there hung a big red sign above his bed that said "absolutely no latex."

So in the past twenty-four hours, we found out that Chaz was allergic to plastic tape, industrial-strength laundry detergent, and latex. His chart was filling up with notes of what not to do.

As the nurse went to finagle Chaz's wires so that she could change his bedsheet, I finally got to see his breakout. He looked as if he had been burned by scalding hot water. My eyes started tearing because when Chaz first entered the PICU, his skin was unblemished except for the stork bites that appeared over his eyes.

After moving Chaz around to change his sheets, the nurse wiped him down with a wet cloth. She said this was a safety measure. Hopefully, it would make the redness go away. When she flipped him back over onto his back, something strange happened. He had developed a line down the middle of his face and body. One side was violet and dark red and the other side white. One of the nurses called this a harlequin, so no one was too concerned. But everyone rushed over to see it. Apparently, it's one of those things that you read about and hear about in medical school but never actually get to see. As a medical facility that teaches, they loved seeing it.

Dr. Kawaguchi relayed the news to Dr. White, who came running to see it but missed it. It only lasted about a couple of minutes.

Frank asked, "What causes that?"

"Usually the patient is experiencing some sort of upset," replied Dr. Kawaguchi.

Frank smiled. "So kind of like the Incredible Hulk."

Smiling, Dr. Kawaguchi said, "Sort of."

"Can you imagine when he gets older, and somebody messes with him, and he does that?" Frank said happily.

Laughing, he replied, "Yeah. It would be a sight to see."

Chaz's harlequin move kind of put a damper in my thinking. I was hoping that since he was in a coma that he was one hundred percent unaware of everything going on. But the harlequin happening because Chaz was feeling an upset emotion of some sort bothered me. That meant that he did know something was going on. I just wished I knew what. I didn't know if he could hear us or feel us. I didn't know if he was in pain or scared. There was so much I didn't know and probably never would. And this really bothered me.

When the evening started to quiet down and Chaz's redness was almost gone, it was time for Frank and me to head home. Our bodies may have been tired, but our minds were exhausted.

So we kissed our son on the head and rubbed our hands up and down the only visible part of his little legs we could see. And we told him we loved him and that we'd see him and everyone else tomorrow morning. Besides, we had to get home and let Shaggy and Wolf out.

WHAT IF

Back home, Frank had a message from work. Due to Chaz's circumstances, they arranged for him to take a week off. They wanted him to spend time with his son since it was unclear if he was going to live or not. And today's events hadn't changed that possibility one iota.

With Chaz in the hospital, Frank and I were living two separate lives when we were home. He retreated to soaks in the bathtub and time in bed. I spent time with the other sad, furry faces in our home. Shaggy and Wolf had always been happy dogs. They were both rescues, and it was obvious that they loved us as much as we loved them. Yet I could tell that they knew something was terribly wrong. They seemed to be questioning the absence of a little person.

But maybe that was my fault, since I spent my time at home, in Chaz's room, playing the what-if game. With every passing moment, I was quickly rising in the ranks of the what-if game. And I knew that by playing it, it was like playing Russian roulette. It was dangerous and something that you could never take back. But I didn't care. I had to find answers. This had to make sense. Something obvious was missing, and I needed to know what it was. I had to for my sanity's sake. This couldn't have been all for nothing.

In Chaz's room, I'd sit in the wicker rocker, holding his teddy bear, and cry. I would rearrange his stuffed animals over and over and over again.

Being in his room reminded me of how broke we were. We were living off of Frank's salary as a produce clerk and he didn't make a lot of money. I had lost my job when I was pregnant. I had missed too much time from work due to nausea and dehydration. Now a sign. I had to have home IVs several times during my pregnancy.

We couldn't afford new baby things for Chaz's room. And we didn't know if we were having a boy or a girl because I had wanted it to be a surprise. I felt that if I had to go through all of that pain, then I deserved a surprise at the end. So we went with our hopes and chose light blue for everything.

We made a bear carousel to hang over his bed. We bought these little brown bears and decorated each one in a different-colored outfit. We bought a used dresser and crib and painted them white.

I really wanted one of those glider rocking chairs that you could find in all of the baby stores. Only we couldn't afford one. So we found an old wicker rocker, bought it, and painted it white and bought some light blue cushions to match the painted walls and placed them on it.

The only thing we could afford to splurge on was a bear border to match the carousel that we had made. We even made our very own bear lamp that we put on a round coffee table that we had found and painted white. Everything that we bought was used. But we painted and decorated each item to make it special for our baby.

I kept going into the kitchen for some water. It had been drilled into my head that I needed to stay hydrated, to help keep up my breast milk supply. I was beginning to think of all of this breastfeeding-related talk was trickery or witchery. It was all starting to feel like a load of crap. Something so natural was becoming hard work.

I stood in front of the sink as I drank my glass of water and looked out onto the ocean. The waves were up; that meant some sort of weather was coming our way. It didn't really matter to me. I knew that I wouldn't be hitting the water this summer. I felt like I might not ever get into the ocean again.

With each crash of the waves, I could feel my heart crashing as well. As I looked at the vast ocean, I felt like I was lost somewhere inside of it. Drowning. Sinking deeper and deeper. For some reason, I felt that the ocean was calling out to me. It was saying that it felt my pain. Then the tears flowed.

The whole day had felt like such a waste. The relatives got to see Chaz, but they had to see him in such a live or die state. No one knew what his future held. Or if he would even have one.

All day long, whenever I asked a question, it was answered with, "I don't know. We don't know. We'll have to wait and see."

The only thing that we did get confirmed today was that Chaz had suffered a superior sagittal sinus thrombosis. I had to have this repeated to me several times. If anyone asked, that meant that my lack of being able to produce breast milk had caused Chaz to suffer dehydration, which had created blood clots in his brain, causing him to have a stroke, seizures, and irreparable brain damage.

The only good news of the day was that the phenobarbital appeared to be controlling his seizures. And since he was in a drug-induced coma, he wasn't feeling any pain. Thank God for small favors. Right?

With another glass of water in hand, I sat in the living room and watched my breastfeeding videos again. With each new demonstration of how to hold your newborn to breastfeed, I looked at Shaggy and Wolf and said, "I did that. I did exactly that."

So why the fuck didn't it work?

Just like the ocean outside my window, I knew that this was something that I may never know the answer to. It would remain a mystery.

And even though the videos reassured me that I had done everything right, I still had nagging questions in my head.

Why didn't you give him a bottle?

Why didn't you listen to yourself? Your mom instincts were screaming, and you ignored them. You fool.

Why didn't you tell everyone to go fuck themselves and open a can of formula and offer it to your son?

Why didn't you think of taking him to the hospital?

Why didn't you invite Dot or Grandma down to help you out that first week or two?

The more I played the what if, why didn't you game, the closer I felt to the deepening, dark ocean. It was like we had become kindred spirits overnight. Every time the waves crashed, so did my heart.

I was surprised that Frank could sleep. I couldn't. I tried. I spent the rest of the evening going from the couch to the spare bed in Chaz's room and even to my own bed. And not one of them enveloped me in a way that I felt comfortable enough to sleep. I couldn't get comfortable enough to rest, even though my body was screaming for some relaxation and my stitched area was swollen like a huge balloon. I was walking like John Wayne. And whoever said that that damn donut pillow was the answer obviously never had a fourth degree episiotomy stitches in their private area. Then again, most people with fifty-two stitches wouldn't be walking around hospitals day and night, either.

But Shaggy and Wolf cared. They understood. They followed me room to room, making sure that I was always in sight. Making sure that I was at least a little okay.

So I wouldn't wake Frank up, I used the bathroom in Chaz's room to pee. And there, sitting in front of me, was that case of formula that I had gotten in the mail a few months before. I barely even remember filling out the coupon for it. I honestly don't remember my rationale behind it. I had known from day one that I was going to breastfeed. Or at least that's what Frank had talked me into.

That line of thinking didn't help me too much, either. Yes, we were breastfeeding because it was supposed to be the healthiest thing for the baby. And it was supposed to reduce his chances of having seasonal allergies, which Frank and I both had, and let me tell you they're a bitch. But the biggest reason was that we couldn't afford formula. I had to question our rationale behind having a baby at this point in our lives. If we couldn't afford formula, then why did we feel the need to have a child? So why had I turned in that postcard to get that free case of formula? I think Frank had said that we should apply for every free thing we could get because we needed it. Because we were officially broke. Broke people with two dogs. That lived in a cute cottage on the beach. Go figure.

SOMETIMES ANGELS DRESS AS SOCIAL WORKERS

Day three had started out like yesterday. Breakfast, dogs, hospital. Arriving at the PICU was a little heart stopping because you never knew if you'd be allowed back. We weren't. Chaz was out for a test. But the nurse gave me more tubing and containers and sent me upstairs to pump. After thirty minutes on both breasts, I came back empty-handed. The only thing that came from that hospital industrial-strength breast pump and my breasts was a mist. Embarrassed, I walked back to the PICU and gave the nurse my mist.

She told me not to worry, it was just stress. And she suggested that I was probably not eating and drinking enough. So in her eyes, I had stress-induced breast problems. Who knew? I wonder what kind I had up until then.

The day before, several people had stopped by briefly just to introduce themselves. But when they saw that we had relatives visiting from out of town, each one said that they would come back the next day.

Now that it was the next day, we expected to be overwhelmed with hospital visitors. Gail, the hospital social worker, was the first to stop by. She asked a few questions and said that she was there to offer us some assistance. Of course, she was someone else that we had to tell our story to. But she was used to sad stories. That's all she heard all day from other parents like us. Especially parents with a child in the PICU.

We talked to her about our living situation. Our financial situation. And our entire lives, in all of about twenty minutes.

She had a few solutions to some of our problems. Parking at the hospital was like seven to ten dollars a day. We didn't have that kind of money, especially because we were going to be here for quite a while. So she provided us with a free parking card.

Meals at the hospital were also something that we couldn't afford. So she provided us with some free meal vouchers. They didn't cover three meals a day, but they at least provided something to assist us while we were there during the day. At that point, we were grateful for anything.

She asked if Chaz had Medicaid. I said, "No. He did at one time because they sent me a free car seat, but he's not had it since then."

"That's strange," she said. "Usually a pregnant woman gets Medicaid, and the baby is covered automatically."

I told her that I had not received any more Medicaid cards since that first month or two.

She asked if I had signed up for WIC, the Women's, Infants', and Children's program that would provide us with formula for Chaz and some necessary foods and juices for myself. This was definitely something that we were going to need now that I obviously would not be trying to breastfeed again. Hearing that formula would be provided for Chaz was a huge load off my mind.

After hearing our story about Chaz, she recommended early intervention. She said that they would provide necessary therapies for Chaz that would assist him in his delayed development. Delayed development? I wasn't quite sure what that meant. But I had a feeling I was about to find out. And she would give them our information. She stressed how important these supports and services would be not only for Chaz but for us, especially me, as well.

Gail provided us with so much information that I forgot most of it by the time she left. Fortunately, she was going to apply for everything on our behalf. So I didn't have to be burdened with that while we were at the hospital stressing over Chaz.

Who, by the way, was constantly having tests. There were ultrasounds, MRIs, EEGs, CAT scans, and blood tests. Some of these happened daily. I was so glad that Chaz was in a coma so he wouldn't be aware of any of this. And since he was still an infant, he wouldn't remember any of it. This provided me with some comfort. And at this point, I would accept all I could get.

With each EEG and head ultrasound they ran, they were able to keep an eye on his brain activity. Though they really meant the lack thereof. I had no idea what they meant by lack of brain activity, but I believe Frank did. So he was the one that was relaying this information to our parents.

The way I heard him explain it was Chaz did not have blood flowing through certain parts of his brain due to the clotting that the stroke caused. Stroke. That felt weird to say. He was only six days old. Six days old and having a stroke. Didn't make sense. He had to be the only infant to ever have a stroke. Didn't he? I'd known adults that have had strokes but never a child, much less an infant.

Dr. White entered the waiting room, as if on cue to my thoughts. He pointed out that Chaz was still hanging in there. I asked if Chaz would still be able to move around and cry, since he was able to do these things before he entered here. So he should be able to do them when he left. Right?

I didn't understand anything that Dr. White said. So in between the tears that he caused, I demanded to know if my son was going to be all right. To which he simply replied, "We don't know." I despised that short, balding little man with glasses.

As I sat there crying, Dr. White provided us with various outcomes of Chaz's condition. He may need a feeding tube. He may be blind. He may never walk. He may need a shunt. He may be visually impaired. Nothing good came out of that man's mouth. I couldn't wait for him to leave the room.

As soon as he left, this bright, chubby, little old lady entered the room. She introduced herself as Chaplain Daisy. She had heard about Chaz through Gail's brief visit yesterday and wanted to stop by and introduce herself.

She mentioned that she stopped by yesterday, but we were not available. I told her that my dad said that a chaplain had stopped by. She sat down and asked how we were doing. This was the first time that I felt like someone was truly asking about us. Then she asked about Chaz. Talking to her was easy. Words and emotions just flowed through me. Before I knew it, we had been talking for over an hour. And not once did she make me feel rushed. It was an emotional talk, but it left me feeling somewhat lighter. Like a heaviness had been lifted off of my shoulders. And finally, she asked if we wanted to pray. That was a definite yes, from both Frank and me. So we prayed for Chaz. And we prayed for each other. She asked if we wanted to see her again, and we said yes. So she agreed to stop by daily to check in on "little Chaz," as she called him, and us.

Before the day was out, we were visited by several other individuals employed by the hospital. All of them were there to make us feel more comfortable and secure.

Even though we were helpless when it came down to the interactions that we could have with Chaz in the PICU, we could at least work through our emotions with our various visitors. Plus, they were setting up services that he would need in the future.

But basically, people came in and told us what they recommended based on their conversations with the doctors and from reading his chart. And I just agreed to it all. My brain was not able to process any of it. So I just went with the flow, nodding in agreement, as if I understood. Honestly, half of the time people spoke to me, I barely heard them. Sometimes my brain was blank. Nothing. I did not have one thought in my head. This was my defense mechanism. I could shut down when necessary. I had years of experience doing that. Traumatic events in your childhood tend to do that to you. They tend to grant you with the ability to "go away" when necessary. It was the coming back that was hard.

Coming back took a lot out of me. I had to talk myself into doing it. And while that was happening, I couldn't hear a word anyone was saying.

I know that this was the time when I should have been paying attention to everything that was said to me, but I had to distance myself from it all. I just went through hell, and I was mad to the point that I wanted to scream at everyone. I wanted to scream, "Why didn't you listen to me?!"

More so than that, I wanted to scream at myself. Why hadn't I listened to myself?

And I wanted to scream at Frank. How dare he take the word of others over me?

Later that evening, Frank was paged. There was a request that he go to the lobby because he had a visitor. We looked at each other funny because we had no idea who it could be. Our relatives had left, and we didn't have any friends in the area. So we went downstairs to see what was up.

When we got downstairs, we looked around, and Frank saw three of his coworkers. They were there to bring us a card. It had been signed by the people he worked with, including some of the beer and bread vendors. And it included three hundred dollars that they had collected. We were touched by their thoughtfulness.

The funds would go toward our bills since Frank was not getting paid while he was out of work. So they knew that we desperately needed the money. Frank thanked them and gave them an update on Chaz before saying good evening.

Before we went home for the night, I was asked to pump my breasts one more time. This time, there was barely mist in the containers. That's when the rhetoric in my head turned it up a notch. But I could also sense the rhetoric spilling out onto the hospital staff. *Finally!* I thought. They believed me.

She was telling the truth.

Her milk should have been in by now.

There's nothing? There should at least be some remnants of something.

It's stress, pure and simple.

She's not taking care of herself. You know that if she doesn't eat right and drink enough fluids that problems can occur.

She had very little on her first day here. And her second day wasn't any better. I think she just dried up.

But did she have anything to dry up? That's the big question here.

I believe her. That girl should have produced more than six cc's her first day here. But she didn't. I think that says it all.

Wow. Who knew?

PART 2

REAWAKENING

DEATH AVERTED, RECOVERY DOOM AND GLOOM

With each day, Chaz appeared to be getting better and better. He was having EEGs and head ultrasounds every other day. The phenobarbital appeared to be helping with the seizures. Another MRI was performed. He was brought out of his coma, weaned off the incubator, and switched over to feedings by mouth.

But the pink elephant in the room was the question of the amount and type of damage that had been done. Chaz should be dead. But he wasn't. But we were still not sure if he'd be able to move, talk, or feed himself. And Dr. White made a point to tell us that he'd definitely require 24/7 care for the rest of his life.

So the question was why? Chaz's severe dehydration had caused the sodium levels in his blood to get so high that it caused blood vessels in his brain to rupture. All of those popping blood vessels had now left behind nothing. Really. Nothing. The best way to imagine how Chaz's brain now looked was to think of it this way. Take a white 8 1/2 x 11 piece of paper. Color a quarter of it in with a black crayon. Now color the remaining three quarters with a gray crayon. The piece of paper represents the brain itself. Black represents the part of the brain that is functionally properly. And gray is the part of the brain that's so damaged that it's best to consider it dead.

This was what Chaz had to look forward to. All because no one wanted to listen to me. All because they all thought of me as the young mom that didn't know any better. Okay. Maybe I didn't know any better. But the same applied to them. They didn't know any better. With all of their education and training, they too were wrong. The alphabet behind their name had betrayed them. It had betrayed my son. And it had betrayed me. I was never a person huge on hating, but I was beginning to learn.

Each time I saw Dr. Sheffield or one of her colleagues in the PICU, I would have to leave the room. I honestly could not look at them without feeling ill. My body would tense up, and I'd begin to shake. My nerves would get the worse of me, and I'd have no choice but to leave. The problem was they were so popular in the area they were often in the PICU to see other patients. But for me, it didn't matter. The physical illness that I experienced each time was enough for me to get the hell out of there.

Then, Dr. Doom and Gloom, aka Dr. White, informed me that my body's inability to produce sufficient breast milk was not uncommon. In fact, an estimated 5% of US mothers are unable to make enough breast milk to adequately nourish their babies. That places about 200,000 newborns a year at-risk of excessive weight loss after birth. And that's just in the United States. So why the hell was this not in all those damn books, pamphlets, and videos that I accumulated over the past year? That information is vital to mothers. Especially first-time mothers like me. That shit should have been mentioned in all those damn books. Every single damn one of them.

I was honored that he shared that information with me. It kind of felt like a peace offering. An olive branch. And in a small way, I felt better. I thought that I was the only idiot on the planet that this had happened to. I felt a little better knowing that I was not alone. And yet I still couldn't help but be angry. If breastfeeding is so damn magical and natural, then why is it so damn hard?

We've all heard of women that cannot conceive. We've also heard stories of women having babies at the drop of a hat. So why do we think that all women can breastfeed? Maybe some of us are not equipped to. Maybe some of us don't have parts that function properly. Maybe, for some of us, it's just not meant to be. Where motherless women accept their fate and finally adopt, those of us that can't breastfeed need to accept our fate that breastfeeding isn't going to work and formula feed. And do so before it's too late.

I was glad to know that Frank was with me throughout this ordeal. Yet a small part of me still blamed him for insisting that I listen to the alphabet team. I also knew that he was as disappointed as I was. And no amount of blame was going to change that. That's not to say that I didn't share that information with some of the people that visited. People like Chaplain Daisy, our hospital social worker, Gail, and the entire hospital staff. After all, every damn time someone new was introduced to Chaz's care, or as part of the team, I had to go through that same damn story. I was slowly becoming sick of myself and my own story.

Frank, on the other hand, didn't mind talking about it. He would tell everyone that he encountered. He was wired up. But that's how he is. When something is bothering him, he has to tell everyone. He's what I call a nervous talker. The more nervous he is, the more he talks. And he doesn't care to who. As for me, if something is bothering me, really bothering me, then I want to be left the hell alone. The less interaction I have with people, the better I feel. So my having to interact with so many people each day was taking a toll on my body. It was forcing me to retreat back into my shell. So I know that I may have seemed standoffish and uncaring. And yes, I probably had a little attitude, too. But not only was I having to deal with an abundance of strangers on a daily basis, I was being asked to trust them as well. And with the first set of medical professionals failing me, I was somewhat skeptical of this set. After all, I was only human. A human ready to have a nervous breakdown.

Though all it took was one look around the PICU and one look at

Dr. Kawaguchi and Dr. White talking to know that these people had their shit together. And having one nurse per patient was a step in the right direction. But I would give anything not to be here. No one should have to be here. And with all of the damn medical professional follow-up that Chaz had, he definitely shouldn't have to be here.

ANOTHER ICU AND
A WHOLE NEW
PERSPECTIVE

Chaz had now been weaned out of his coma. Though he was still on phenobarbital, it was time to move on. But it was not the kind of moving on that I expected. Instead, we were moving to the NICU, the neonatal intensive care unit, where all of the preemies were.

I asked Dr. Kawaguchi what this move meant, and he said that it meant that Chaz was "out of the woods." We no longer had to fear him dying. "But he still has a long road ahead of him," he added.

So the proper step-down unit for Chaz was the NICU. In that unit, there were four babies to one nurse. We were told that the nurse would be present at all times. Chaz would be given his phenobarbital and watched over for his intake. It was just until they felt like he had gained enough weight. They also preferred that he have at least one semi-normal EEG or head ultrasound. And they were going to try for another MRI. And he reassured me that Dr. White would continue to follow Chaz's care.

Dr. White was the little man that I didn't like. But this was something that I needed to get over rather quickly. At least we would have one doctor that was there from the beginning overseeing his care. In my eyes, Chaz has had two beginnings: his birth and then the reawakening from his near-death experience. I wasn't sure if I wanted any more beginnings. I didn't think I was cut out for them. But we'd see.

At least in the NICU Chaz would be able to have some of his own things. He could have the stuffed mouse that I had bought him at Wal-Mart. He could have his blue blanket. He could even have a Mylar balloon. His feet could have little socks. His body, all of the clothing that it wanted. I was excited. This was going to be as close to home as we could get at this point.

The PICU recommended that we go home and take a nap, get some lunch, or go for a walk because it was going to take a while for them to transfer Chaz down to the NICU. And then the floor doctor and nurse would have to get him situated and read up on his record and get acquainted with his care. Since Frank and I had a couple of hours to kill, we did just that.

When we returned to the hospital and made our way up to the NICU, I felt a little relief. This move meant that Chaz was doing better. But as I made my way down the corridor, I couldn't help but notice how quiet it was. It was a kind of eerie, spooky silence that you often hear in horror movies. Imagine this young, innocent woman walking down a long hall and with each step she makes she can't help but feel that there is someone behind her, watching her. But when she turns around, there's no one there. That's kind of how I felt. Each time I looked behind me, there was no one there, but there were lots of closed doors. In the PICU, I understood the silence, since most of the patients were in comas, like Chaz.

As I turned left, I came upon a room with three little incubators in it. The nurse referred to those three babies as long-stay preemies. Looking at Chaz's body compared to theirs was something I don't think I'll ever forget. He looked like a one-year-old compared to these teeny tiny little babies that you could hold in one hand. If their fragile little bodies could survive the trauma that they'd endured, then Chaz should be able to. And even though he looked enormously big compared to them, he was still, in fact, my baby. My little almost month-old baby.

Chaz was in the room next to theirs. The only thing that separated them was glass so the nurse could see him at all times. He was in a small crib with metal bars that could be moved up and down for feedings and diaper changes. The nurse appeared nice and was glad to hear that I would be staying with Chaz as long as he was there so she didn't have to worry about feeding him and changing him. She let me know that when I did change him, I needed to place the diaper on the edge of the sink, by the door, so she could weigh it. They would weigh every diaper that Chaz had. And she would bring me the doctor-recommended amount of infant formula, and I had to let her know how much he drank and how much he spit out. So began my journey of writing down dates, times, intake, and explanations.

For the next few hours, Frank fed Chaz and changed him while I laid on the pullout chair and tried to get some rest. But there was no rest. Between my mind racing and the uncomfortable bed-like furniture, I couldn't sleep. Frank pointed out the area on Chaz's head where they cut his hair to insert an IV. In other areas, he appeared bruised and red. When I looked at him, I saw a baby that had gone through hell. Another reason I couldn't rest.

As evening came, Frank left; he had to let Shaggy and Wolf out, and he had to work the next morning. My evening started out like the ones I previously had at home. Chaz would cry, only it wasn't a distressful cry, it was more of an *I'm not satisfied* cry. The nurse would bring me tiny bottles of infant formula, and I would give them to Chaz, only it went more like this: He'd cry, so I'd offer him a bottle, he'd suck a little, then turn his head away while squinting up his little face. Then he'd cry a little and we'd go through the whole thing again. Each feeding lasted an hour because he was doing all he could not to cooperate. We're giving him the so-called recommended amount at each feeding. And we did this until each bottle was empty. So why was he still crying? As the medication from the PICU wore off, the more agitated he became. And it reminded me of his behavior at home. I couldn't help but doubt his love for me. At this point, I would have been happy if he would have just tolerated me.

After a few hours, the nurse popped her pretty little head in and said that if he didn't quiet down, she'd need to give him something to sleep. I didn't like that. He'd just gotten out of a medication-induced coma. So he didn't really need anything that would knock him out.

As the night dragged on, Chaz didn't let up. He would be lying in his crib, eyes closed, either making grumpy noises or crying. Sometimes I would just hold him and rock him, but it didn't matter. He just wasn't happy. I feared he was having nightmares about his experience in the PICU. Or maybe he was having nightmares from the fiasco at home when I was feeding him. Or maybe it was me. I couldn't rule that out because right now, sitting with him at four in the morning, the only common denominator that I saw was me.

As Chaz's grumpiness continued, so did the nurse's agitation. I totally understood her concern, but I still couldn't let go of the fact that he was just weaned out of a coma. I really had a hard time justifying making him sleep. Shouldn't this time be for the hospital to observe how Chaz was so they could tell me what to do when I took him home? But they wouldn't know what he was like unless they observed how he behaved.

When the doctor came by early that morning to do his rounds, he spoke with the nurse but not me. I thought that was strange and somewhat rude. After all, I was sitting right there. He could see me through the glass. But no, he didn't. I did overhear something about Benadryl, and he shook his head in agreement. Only I wasn't sure if they were talking about Chaz or not. For all I knew, it wasn't even a nod in the direction of the Benadryl.

I just knew that it was going to be a long day. Frank had to work till who knew when. I had to get used to another nurse in an hour or so. And I was taking care of a child that wasn't happy with anything I did.

* * *

Over the next few days, Chaz remained agitated. Nothing soothed him. Sadly, I looked forward to meal time so I could go downstairs and grab some food. That was the only time I didn't have to listen to Chaz scream and cry. Frank was working every day, so he didn't get to see Chaz but for a few hours each day. Chaz was crabby with him, too. He just didn't like anything about being in the hospital. I was starting to believe that Chaz just didn't like anything.

The next morning, I waited to catch the floor doctor as he did his morning rounds before I headed downstairs to get myself some breakfast. Well, he was a no-show. After a two-hour wait, I finally headed down for whatever was left of breakfast. Well, I got back up to the room quicker than the nurse expected me to, because as I turned the corner, I saw her enter Chaz's room with a syringe. I yelled, "No!" and set off running toward the room.

I must have scared the crap out of her because I saw her jump and whirl around quickly while dropping the syringe on the floor. The look on her face was one of surprise, fear, and a whole lot of panic.

My scream startled just about everyone on the floor because the next thing I knew the hallway was filled with curious onlookers. Chaz's nurse grabbed her paperwork, picked up the syringe that she had dropped from the floor, and rushed by me without even making eye contact. By the time her shift ended some twelve hours later, I didn't see her but one other time, even though I had to walk right past her to get ice chips and diapers. I felt confident that this incident was passed along, and that's why I never caught anyone else trying it.

I could see why the obsessive crying would bother the nurses. They were used to working twelve-hour shifts overseeing babies in incubators. They were not used to the normal sounds that babies made. If I were in their shoes, I'd probably give medication to quiet them at night myself.

During my time there, I noticed that I was the only mom that stayed with her child. Days would go by without me seeing any of the other parents of the preemies in Chaz's unit. And at first, that surprised me. Until one evening when it hit me: they were long-stay preemies. Some had been there for almost a year. They had parents that had to get back to their lives. Their work. Their families. Their homes. And more importantly, their other children. It took talking to Chaplain Daisy for me to understand this. I was fortunate to be able to take the time necessary to stay with Chaz during his hospital stay. Only I'm not so sure Chaz felt fortunate about that. He still wasn't happy with me. Nothing I was did made him happy.

THE REAL WORK BEGINS, NEW DOCTORS, SOME RESULTS

Finally! Chaz was going to be discharged from the hospital. No one was more grateful about that than me. Chaz's two weeks in the hospital felt more like two months.

On the drive home, I had mixed emotions about his discharge. I was glad he was out of the hospital, relieved that he had survived, yet totally terrified. What if I did something wrong? He'd only been out of his coma for a week. He'd only been off the respirator for a week. His EEG showed that he was still having seizures, so I was instructed to give him liquid phenobarbital three times a day.

I knew that once I was home, that would be when the real work would begin. For me, at least. Frank went back to work last week. And they had him working all kinds of weird hours, for not much more than minimum wage, to help make up for the time he missed. And because of the way scheduling was done at his store, employees didn't know from one week to the next when they'd be working and when they'd be off. So the responsibility of Chaz's care was left solely to little old me.

The first few days, I worried about everything, including feeding Chaz. Which, by the way, was so much easier with baby formula because you could physically see how much your baby was getting. And the hospital had provided me with written instructions on how much he needed and when. But on occasion, he would eat less, and I would worry. But he usually made up for it on the next feeding.

It was when I had to give him his seizure medication that I worried the most. It was liquid, and I would give it to him in a syringe. And occasionally he'd spit it out. Or sometimes he would just throw it up a few minutes later. So I was never sure if he was getting enough of it. This turned out to be trial and error. The first few times it happened, I would call Dr. White and ask, "What do I do?" I knew how important it was that he take the medicine, but sometimes I wasn't sure if it even had a chance to get into his system. Dr. White always got back to me quickly. It was obvious that he cared for Chaz and was concerned about him.

The pediatrician, on the other hand, not so much. The first two times Chaz threw up his seizure medication, I called her office and asked, "What do I do?" I always asked for the pediatrician, since I had no desire to talk to any of their nurses, seeing they demonstrated ultimate failure when it came to Chaz's needs the first time around. And the damn pediatrician didn't call me back once. That was it in my book. They were fired!

I tried. I gave them another chance. Two, to be exact. But again my phone calls were ignored. That was not the kind of doctors or nurses that I wanted in charge of Chaz's care.

I called Dr. White and asked if he knew any other pediatricians in the area that he could recommend. He suggested that I contact our caseworker at children's hospital. They would have a list. I did just that, and since Chaz was now on a Medicaid HMO, we had to choose one of the HMO's doctors. I chose Dr. Collins.

I then sat down and wrote a letter to the pediatrician's office telling them that we were leaving them and why. Then I wrote one to Dr. Collins giving him an update on Chaz and scheduled our first appointment to meet him.

When Frank got home from work, I told him about the change in doctors, and he drove me to the pediatrician's office to deliver the *you're fired* letter. It wasn't even so much of a *you're fired* letter as it was a *you've failed* letter. My letter mentioned all of the phone calls and all of the responses and all of the phone calls that were never returned. I wanted them to know that they were not putting my child's needs first, that they were ignoring my concerns over Chaz. It was bad enough that they had failed the first time, landing my son in the hospital. But even after all of that, they failed me by not returning my calls regarding the throwing up of his seizure meds. I had just had it!

So my letter requested that Chaz's record, what little there was, be sent over to Dr. Collins's office as soon as possible. I honestly think they were as glad to get rid of me as I was them.

When Dr. Collins took over as Chaz's pediatrician, he was thrown into the deep end of the pool with no float, just as Frank and I had been. He was not used to a patient with such complicated needs. And Chaz being on an HMO meant that we needed referrals for everything.

We continued to see Dr. White on a regular basis. Chaz was continuing to have routine tests such as MRIs, CAT scans, and EEGs, as well as routine blood work to see how much of the seizure medication was in his system. These blood levels were usually done at Dr. Collins's office. I hated these. I hated seeing Chaz being stuck by a needle and having blood drawn, even though I knew that it was for the best.

Of course, every time we saw Dr. White or Chaz had to have a test, Dr. Collins had to write a referral. If Chaz blinked, there needed to be a referral. And I had to remind myself that we needed a referral in hand every time we went for a test or went to see a doctor. It was slightly aggravating. Okay, it was monumentally aggravating. I started to feel like a bookkeeper. I learned quickly to take extensive, detailed notes about everything that referred to Chaz.

At first, I used a regular spiralbound notebook, then I quickly switched over to datebooks. I kept track of who I called, when I called them, why I called them, and what the outcome was. I did this for doctor visits and tests, too. It felt like I was constantly writing.

We loved Dr. Collins. He was a short, elderly man that was extremely patient and kind. He didn't treat me like some psycho mom that freaked out over everything. Even though I was and kind of did. He treated me like a concerned, extremely cautious mother that was rightfully so. That was what I loved about him.

Then there was Dr. White, the one person I didn't like in the beginning that I now depended on. Not only did I depend on him, I took what he said as scripture. Besides, he knew all of the details about what had happened on my end of this terrible journey, and he didn't judge me for overreacting. He told me, "If you're concerned, then I'm concerned."

This got me thinking. Chaz was now home, but he was still somewhat miserable. He hated taking seizure medication. And I got angry thinking about all that had happened to him. What happened to him was preventable and never should have happened. This actually kept me up at nights, even though I was up nights anyway, thanks to Chaz. He would often go three to four days without sleep. That meant I went three to four days without sleep. I decided to do something about it.

I did the only thing that I knew to do: I called our local newspaper, *The Virginian Pilot*, and told the person on the other end that people needed to know about this. They said that they would relay my message to one of their news writers.

It didn't take long for someone to call me back. It was health writer Elizabeth Simpson. She had written a heartfelt story a few days earlier about another child with a separate health issue. She was definitely the right one to address my cause.

My cause is that other moms need to know that not all women can breastfeed. And they need to know what can happen when you can't and you keep trying anyway. Bad things like this happens. And most importantly, moms need to know that they should trust their own maternal instincts. If mom is concerned, then the doctor should be concerned. The letters PhD and MD do not make you a genius. And it doesn't come close to the knowledge that a mom has about her own child. Yes, women have breasts. Yes, we can have babies. Or, at least, some of us can. But not all of us can breastfeed. We don't all produce breast milk. And not all of us can produce enough colostrum to keep a child healthy.

Elizabeth was interested in what I had to say and agreed to come out to my house the next day to meet Chaz and me and to hear more about our story. She was going to do an article on Chaz and would have one of the newspaper's photographers take some pictures.

When she arrived, Chaz was in his swing. Swinging was one of the few things that calmed him. She commented on how big he was, considering his age. I had been with Chaz so long that to me all newborns should be over ten pounds. So I never quite understood the surprise that people felt when they saw him.

The downside to having Elizabeth interview me was that I had to tell that dreaded story all over again. I kept reminding myself that Chaz's story needed to be told. Other moms needed to know what happened to Chaz, so it didn't happen to other newborns. I knew that Chaz's story wasn't the only one. That meant that others didn't have the courage to come forward. Chaz and I had been failed by multiple healthcare providers. And I was treated as someone that didn't know what she was talking about. Or, as one of the nurses had so kindly pointed out, "You don't have a medical degree." So it was high time that all of this changed.

Moms have a voice. We have our maternal instincts. And we deserve to be heard. We need to be heard. Even if a nurse or doctor disagrees, they should take our concerns seriously.

So I told Elizabeth the story from beginning to end. Then she asked me a few questions. She observed Chaz, and the photographer took some pictures. A few days later, I received a call from her saying that the article was going to be in the paper the next day. Even though we had daily newspaper delivery, I asked Frank to pick up a couple of extra copies for the relatives.

The next day, Elizabeth's article, "Mother Knows Best," came out. It highlighted exactly what I was upset about. One, mothers should trust their own instincts. Two, there is very little information out there about the possibility of some mothers not being able to breastfeed because they don't produce milk. Three, if a mother tries and tries, despite the challenges of breastfeeding, dehydration can happen. And it can cause strokes, seizures, even death.

The article was short but informative. The title summed up my mission statement. Even though I didn't realize that I had a mission statement until I saw it in black and white. Mother Knows Best.

EARLY INTERVENTION

Shortly after Chaz returned home from the hospital, I received a letter in the mail about early intervention. It said that Chaz had been referred to them by children's hospital. I ignored the first letter, though not intentionally. I was just overwhelmed with everything going on. I read it and then placed it aside to address later, then totally forgot where I placed it or that I even had it.

Not only was I a first-time mom of a newborn, but I was also the mom of a fragile child with special healthcare needs. And hanging with Chaz had become a full-time job. He was staying up three and four days at a stretch. I had continued my record keeping of everything that went into Chaz and everything that came out.

The day the second letter came, our caseworker from children's hospital called and asked me to please call the phone number on the letter. And after some phone tag, an evaluation was scheduled. I had no idea who these people were or what they did or what they were going to do. But if the caseworker at children's hospital recommended it, then it was necessary for Chaz's well-being.

On the day of the evaluation, I had no idea what would happen. I just knew that they said it would take a couple of hours. So I packed a bag with everything that I could think of. I had Chaz's tiny little plastic Enfamil bear, his blanket, his stuffed mouse, diapers, wipes, a set of plastic keys in various colors, a bunch of bibs, a couple of bottles of formula, his medication and a syringe, and an extra shirt since Chaz liked to spit up his medication and his formula.

Then I put Chaz in his carrier and carried him out to the car with a diaper bag, my handbag, and another bag filled with everything I'd need for a hospital stay. We looked like we were running away from home.

When I showed up at the infant program, I saw all of these little babies and stressed-out moms. I immediately knew that Chaz and I would fit right in. Though, to be honest, none of the moms looked as stressed as me. I was looking like someone that had escaped an insane asylum and was seeing daylight for the first time in a long time. Okay, maybe that's a slight exaggeration. I was at least showering every day. Sadly, all of my pants, including my jeans, had elastic in them. They were extra soft and extra big. Since Chaz was going days without sleeping, that meant that I was too. So I deserved to be comfortable.

I set Chaz's carrier down softly then dropped everything else in one big thump. The other moms looked at me as if to say, "Been there done that." A few gave me a "it does get easier" nod.

An occupational therapist, Dee, and a physical therapist, Karen, greeted us immediately. They took us to what they called a therapy room, where they would spend the next couple of hours evaluating Chaz. Even though the evaluation centered on their interaction with Chaz, I was asked questions throughout the evaluation, one of those questions being what happened. So I had to tell them the same story that I had already told half of children's hospital. One of them would take evaluation notes while the other one wrote down pretty much everything I said.

By the time the evaluation was over, I was sick of talking about everything. To be honest, I was sick of talking about myself. I was sick of telling the same damn story over and over again. Especially when I looked into someone's eyes and could tell if they were a breastfeeding advocate or not. Yes, surprise, surprise, some people doubted my inability to breastfeed. I don't like those people. I don't hate them. I'm just not fond of them. I feel that they are too close-minded. Not all women have the ability to conceive, so why should all of us be able to breastfeed? Or maybe, just maybe, some babies are not meant to breastfeed. Which was kind of how I thought about Chaz. He hated it. I hated it. It failed us. So we both have the right to hate it. Other people have the right to doubt us. And I have the right to not give a damn what they think. And there we were.

Thank God the two therapists doing Chaz's evaluation were not what I call judgers. At least I didn't get that vibe from them.

Once the evaluation was over, the therapists went over their findings with me. They told me that they would be adding some additional notations to Chaz's file—for example, everything that we talked about—and that they would be requesting his hospital and doctors' records for consideration, too. With my permission, of course. Did I have a choice?

Chaz's evaluation showed that he was significantly delayed in many areas. Areas such as cognitive development, physical development, communication, social-emotional development, and adaptive development. He would need to have every kind of therapy imaginable, and I would bring him here each week until he transferred out of the program at age two. Then he would enter another program that was not much different from this one. Honestly, I was even more confused now than I was before all of this ever happened. Maybe I'd catch up before he hit age two when he transferred to the next program.

SETTLING IN FOR A TIME
OF GROWTH, GUILT,
AND GOD

Fall had arrived. Or at least September had. It'd been a few months since Chaz's ordeal, and we were finally beginning to settle into a routine. We had our weekly appointments with the infant program. We were seeing Dr. White every three to four weeks. And we were seeing Dr. Collins every week or so. After what happened to Chaz and my being ignored by the medical professionals, I no longer relied on telephone messages with nurses or even doctors for that matter. So if Chaz blinked in a way that didn't seem right to me, we'd go see Dr. Collins just to make sure things were okay.

This had become routine for Chaz and me. Frank was working all kinds of weird hours. And he was working overtime since I wasn't working and bringing in any money. I had applied for disability for Chaz since Dr. White and the therapists said that Chaz would be permanently disabled, but that process was going at a snail's pace. And every time I turned around, they were asking for more and more information. But mostly they kept asking for the same records over and over again.

I'd gotten to the point where I literally called them and asked if anyone was actually reading the information that the doctors, the hospital, and the therapists were sending in. And then I'd send them letters asking the same thing. It'd taken a few months, but I'd finally come to realize that the people reviewing Chaz's records didn't have a clue as to what they were reading. It was as if the people in charge of his case were people like me before all of this happened. Because there was a time when I didn't know what all of that gibberish meant, either. I wished there was a database somewhere where you could look up all of this terminology. That's not to say that they would even take the time to do it.

I just didn't understand what the holdup was because not only did we have birth records but we had records from children's hospital, Dr. White, Dr. Collins, and the infant program. What more did these people need?

The letters that I received from them really made me question their abilities. They would ask for things like when did the incident take place. Did the incident cause permanent damage? What was the primary diagnosis? These were things that had already been answered in letters from doctors and the hospital. They were part of his medical records.

I was starting to feel bad about calling the same people over and over again asking them to please resubmit what they'd already submitted three times. Their offices were being as diplomatic as I had become. Upon receiving the second denial letter, I did the only thing that I knew to do. I gathered up all of my documents, took them to a copy shop, and copied them. Then the next morning, I got up early and went down to the social security office with Chaz in tow. I waited in line with everyone else just to hand over the same damn documents that they already had. At least this time I might get to speak to someone. Chaz was cranky. I was cranky. I really didn't have the time, energy, or patience for these people. My diplomacy was not at its best. But I was doing the best I could under the circumstances.

The shocker was after all of that, someone at a window collected my envelope of documents and said that they'd have someone review it. They couldn't tell me who. They couldn't tell me when. All they could say was that they had *x* number of business days, not including holidays, to review everything and that even then they might ask for additional information. And then they asked if all of my contact information was up to date. A part of me wondered if it really mattered.

I really wanted to strangle someone. I hated the social security office and the people in it. I understood that they had a job to do, but damn it, why were they making things harder for people like Chaz and me? I had report after report showing that he had irreversible brain damage. Irreversible being the key word. That meant that it wasn't going to get better. That meant that no miracle was going to happen. Unless, of course, Jesus himself came down to earth and touched Chaz on the head and healed him.

Speaking of Jesus, he and I were in the midst of making up. Sometimes. We still had our squabbles. Some days I loved him to death and thanked him for saving my son and for making him the happy little camper that he was. And other days, I cussed him to heaven and back for allowing him to have seizures and being miserable. And on the days he had a test at the hospital, Jesus and I went round and round. *Please give him comfort and keep him safe. Why the hell are you putting him through this? Please be there with him since I can't be. Just wait till I get my hands on you. I am going to kill you.* Yes, Jesus and I had a very complicated relationship. One that I hoped would one day work itself out. Until then, he and I were destined to go on this merry-go-round together.

To be honest, at times Jesus scared me. Growing up in a southern Baptist home, my mom would "put the fear of God in you," as they said. She was constantly telling me that God was going to punish me for this, that, and the other thing. You're listening to Elvis Presley, you're going to hell. You got your hair cut like Marie Osmond, you're going to hell. You cussed, you're going to hell. You disrespected me. You talked back. You're dressing provocatively. You're flirting with boys. You're wearing makeup. You looked left instead of right. You walked instead of running. You wore the color purple. It didn't matter what I did or didn't do, I was going to hell in my mother's eyes. By the time I was thirteen, I knew beyond a shadow of a doubt that I was going to hell. So at times, I wondered if all the rest really mattered.

Now that Chaz was going through all of this, I couldn't help but remember those words from my mom: "God punishes," so you're going to hell. She had even said as much during one of our many phone calls after Chaz had his stroke. She said that God was punishing me for being such a bad teenager. At times I couldn't help but wonder if she was right.

But the God that I grew up learning about didn't punish children for the sins of the parent. Okay, maybe he does in some parts of the bible. Hell, to be honest, God does punish a lot of people in the bible. Some deserve it. But not all. And why did God go from punishing in the Old Testament to forgiving in the New Testament? Did God have an epiphany?

Whatever it was, what my mom learned in church she drilled into me so bad that I would feel ashamed of even getting naked to take a shower because God would see me. I even felt uncomfortable having sex with my husband because of all her statements about sex sending me to hell. Let me tell you, growing up with a Southern Baptist mother that was all fire and brimstone fucks you up for life. And I am living proof. I'm not sure that I'll ever be normal when it comes to scripture and God. Maybe that's why we have such a volatile relationship. Maybe he is punishing me. Who the hell knows? Maybe one day I'll get to ask him.

One thing I do know is that Frank said he can't wait to see God because he wants to ask him why the hell he put Chaz through all of this. And he adds that he'd like to beat the shit out of God for what he did to Chaz. Though I understand, I also cringe. I don't need God coming down on our family any more than he already has. Whenever he looks up and starts shaking his fist at God, I want to run and hide. I just wait for the lightning bolts that will take him and us out. But if you go by what my mom says, then that lightning bolt would hit Chaz as punishment to us.

Like I said, God and I have a very complicated relationship. And it does become volatile at times. And even though I may cuss him out sometimes, I turn right around and beg forgiveness. I don't want any more strikes against my record. Or Chaz's. We've each had enough.

And I guess God was on my side that day I visited the social security office, because a little over a week later, I received a letter that said Chaz had been approved for Supplemental Security Income. Now I wondered if it was due to the fact that I actually took the time to carry the documents down there myself. Or was it that talk that I had with God? Or was it a game all along and he wanted to see how far I'd go? See, I told you. It's a very complicated relationship that we have. But we have one, and that's all that matters.

WHO GOT SHOT?

It was nice when Frank was able to tag along to Chaz's medical appointments. I really needed the assistance with the carrier and the diaper bag. Especially after I got shot. Okay, not exactly shot-shot. But it sure as hell felt like it.

One day, I pulled up in the driveway of our cute little beach house. Okay, it was more like a cottage. But it was home. I got out and unhooked Chaz's car seat. I bent down to pick him up and then *boom*! I heard shots. I felt shots. I winced in pain, and I hit the ground with tears in my eyes. All I could think of was, *I'm so glad I hadn't picked Chaz up yet*.

And I looked longingly at my little beach cottage and saw my trusty pals, Shaggy and Wolf, looking back at me through the patio door. They were so far away. I had no idea how I could crawl to them so I could call 911 and carry Chaz at the same time. After all, I couldn't leave him.

I felt my back, since that's where the pain radiated. And it was dry. No blood. I looked at my hand to make sure. Yep, no blood. What the hell?!

So I decided to stand up. But the pain radiated again, and I hugged the floorboard of the car. Chaz was starting to fuss, so I didn't have a choice. I had to stand up. This time, I managed to make it to a hunched-over position, and even that hurt like hell. So I grabbed Chaz and began hobbling my way to the front door. With every step, I cried. Only they weren't really steps. I was kind of dragging my legs and tossing my torso forward. I had to stop every two steps just to catch my breath because the pain was unlike anything I'd ever experienced, including childbirth. And that's saying something since I gave birth with no pain medication. Then my wrist started to give. Then I started praying. *Lord, just help me get us both into the house. Safely.* It felt like someone had a voodoo doll of me and was taking turns sticking me in the back and the wrist.

After a good five minutes or so, I made it to the front door, opened it, slid the carrier inside, and then collapsed on the floor, closing the door with my feet. Then I reached up and bolted it. Shaggy and Wolf were looking at me as if I'd lost it. They had their ears up, and their heads were tilted as they looked at me. They were sniffing the air around me. I think they sensed no injury, so they were confused. And so was I.

After lying on my back for a few minutes, I finally tried to move. The pain had subsided somewhat, and I was able to stand. I picked up the carrier, my wrist throbbing, and I placed it on the sofa. It was time to feed Chaz and give him his seizure medication.

I walked to the kitchen, feeling my back as I went. I just knew that I had been shot. So what the hell just happened? I didn't imagine that pain. And then it hit me again. I grabbed the countertop to stable myself. Through the pain, I managed to mix the Depakote sprinkles with the applesauce and walk to the couch before collapsing into a heap.

Feeding Chaz the applesauce hurt my wrist as it rotated. And the pain in my back was bringing tears to my eyes. I was confused as hell. What just happened to me?

I wasn't fully understanding what was going on, so I called the doctor and set up an appointment to see him about my wrist and my back. When Frank got home, I told him what happened, as Chaz and I were still on the couch. I had changed him and fed him and given him his medicine.

But I did it with as little movement as possible. He looked at my back and said that there was nothing there. He said that it was probably a back spasm, so suck it up. Suck it up. Talk about wanting to smack the shit out of someone.

The next day my, doctor kind of said the same thing. Back spasm and "new mother's wrist." Try not to do too much for the next few days. Amusing. Did he not see the child with special needs in the carrier next to me? We were forever tied at the hip. We were like conjoined twins. Wherever I went, he went and vice versa. So how did he expect me to rest? Dumbest advice I'd ever heard. Maybe that advice worked in the real world where people had normal children, siblings, nannies, relatives, neighbors, family, babysitters, and gorillas that could raise their children in the jungle. But not in my world. Nope. No way.

So I followed some other advice, and I sucked it up.

ANOTHER SEIZURE THREATENS CHAZ: ACTH, PART 1

Near the end of the year, I think God must have gotten lonely. He decided that Chaz having seizures and going to occupational, speech, and physical therapy several times a week wasn't enough; he needed more. Yes, God bestowed on little Chaz another problem: infantile spasms.

I begin to notice Chaz doing what I called "the muscle man." He looked like one of those bodybuilders doing a curl up using his right fist. He would do this movement while straightening his legs at the same time. And he would turn slightly to his left side.

At first, I just thought that it was something that he wanted to do. He wasn't doing it enough for me to call anyone. It took almost a week before he did it where Frank witnessed it. He was doing it daily, and I thought it was cute. That's why I called it the muscle man.

But then he gradually started doing it more often. And then more. Finally, I sat down one day and began counting them. He was doing them an average of fifty to sixty times a day.

I would talk to him during these and hope that he would turn his head toward me, but he didn't. He couldn't. It was part of the muscle man ritual.

So right after the holidays, I finally made a concerned call to Dr. White. He agreed to see us immediately. He was good like that.

I liked that he took my phone calls seriously even when they turned out to be nothing. I had spent the past few months reading books that I checked out from my local library, and I would ask him about different things I found in them. *Do you think it's this? Well, how about this? And this?* He didn't treat me as a moron. He would listen to my theories and kindly discuss them with me. He never once came out and said, "Mrs. Floyd, you're crazy." Or, "Mrs. Floyd, leave the medical stuff to those of us that have gone to medical school." This was why he was still Chaz's doctor six months later. He was the only one that treated me as a mom and as part of the team. We were team Chaz.

When we arrived at Dr. White's office, we were called back immediately. Frank set the carrier on the examination bed, and Dr. White was astonished at how many muscle men Chaz was doing. I told him that each day they had become more frequent. Now they were hitting as many as sixty times a day.

He knew what they were right away. Infantile spasms. He said that they could happen sometimes and that we were not to worry. They would not continue forever. However, he had three recommendations of treatment that we could try. So he began writing out the various treatments on the bedsheet that was on the examination bed. He provided the pros and cons of each. Then he left the room so we could discuss which one we wanted to pursue.

You had to love a doctor that actually gave you choices. It was refreshing. And since he was part of a teaching hospital, I prayed that other budding neurologists would turn out like him. We already had enough of the God-like ones. It was about time that doctors started taking patients and their mothers seriously.

So Frank and I went straight to option three. It was the only one that made sense. It took us less than five minutes to decide on ACTH. Unfortunately, that meant a hospital stay. Good thing we had brought along things for Chaz and me to spend the night. Since Frank had to work the next day, I was the lucky one that got to stay at the hospital. That also meant that I would be the one giving Chaz the injections.

The whole purpose of the two-day hospital stay was to make sure that I could give Chaz an injection and not freak out. Earlier I had explained to Dr. White that I used to give my dog insulin shots daily, so I could do this. He politely told me that even doctors and nurses had a hard time giving injections to their own children and that many of them couldn't bring themselves to do it. I said that as long as it made him better, I could do it. I knew that the injections would hurt him and that he would cry, but if they stopped the muscle men, then it would be worth it. Besides, it would only be one shot a day for thirty days. The goal was to stop the spasms within thirty days. But even ACTH can be dangerous.

It seemed like everything we did for Chaz was dangerous. In the past six months, I'd had my fill of danger. I had crammed twenty years of danger into six months. Chaz should be able to jump out of a plane without a parachute after this and survive. His first, middle, and last name had become danger. He could do anything that Evil Knievel did and survive.

"I was hoping you'd choose that option," Dr. White said as he let out a sigh of relief. "That's the option I would have chosen."

So Dr. White told us that he would call over to children's hospital and have them get Chaz ready to be admitted. He said that we should be able to get in there in about an hour. So we left and grabbed some food. Who knew when I would get to eat again? Frank was going to stay until visiting hours were up, which was around eight or nine o'clock. Then he'd go home, let the dogs out, and sleep for a while. He had to be up at four for work. He was a perishable clerk, and they started work in the early morning hours.

I tried to take comfort in the fact that I had packed everything that I felt Chaz and I needed for a hospital stay. I just hoped that it wouldn't be for more than two days. I didn't think I could take another long stay.

After we checked Chaz into the hospital, I stopped by the chaplain's office and left word for Chaplain Daisy that Chaz was here again and that we hoped that it'd only be for a couple of days.

We then went upstairs to Chaz's room and introduced him to his nurse. He was going to be staying in a large open room with four hospital cribs in it. And the entire outside wall was nothing but windows, making it very sunny in there. I hoped that it would be beautiful at night. As I looked around, I could see a couple of folded-up cots that were filled with clothes and blankets. That meant that a few moms were staying here so I wouldn't be alone. But honestly, I preferred to be alone. I've never been much of a talker. And when I'm stressed, I retreat within myself. And nothing stresses you out more than being in a hospital with your child.

The nurse was busy with another patient and his doctor, so she told us to go ahead and make ourselves at home. That was code for, "Grab your own bedsheets, pillows, and blankets, and set up over in your little corner of the world." Even though Chaz's bed already had a sheet on it, Frank and I changed it with our own. We knew from last time that Chaz would end up with a rash if he used the hospital's linens. I also brought his little blanket and his stuffed mouse, which had been given the nickname Chickems. It was because he had these short, thick little legs and feet. And since that was about all of Chaz that wasn't hidden behind tape or tubing the last time we were here, we felt that they'd make a great pair.

So by the time Frank and I got settled and, more importantly, got Chaz settled, here came one of the doctors from Dr. White's practice. He was there to make sure the nurse understood why we were there. Chaz was to receive a single ACTH injection, once a day, for the next two days. And that injection was to be given by me, his mom, to make sure that I could do it. Because if for some reason I chickened out, then Chaz would have to stay in the hospital for the next thirty days. The hell with that. Hand me that damn needle. Well, what happened next shocked the crap out of me. The nurse gave Chaz the injection, without including me. She didn't say, "Hey, come here and let me show you what to do." If I hadn't seen her do it, then I wouldn't have known that it happened. I was livid.

I raised my voice and became rather forceful as I said, "Excuse me! We are here so I can give the injections to Chaz and you're supposed to supervise."

Dr. Lawrence was sitting outside the room and hurriedly rushed in and interjected, "Well, since it's the first one, I asked that she give it. There will be time for you to do so later."

"How much later?" I asked. "We're only supposed to be here for two days."

"Well, we'll see. It might be longer," Dr. Lawrence said.

This time I screamed and didn't mean to. Okay, yes, I did mean to. I screamed, "Longer?"

Startled by my yelling, Dr. Lawrence stepped back a little. "Yes. We'll have to see how it goes."

"Okay, someone seriously needs to get Dr. White on the phone because that was not our agreement a couple of hours ago," I said.

And wouldn't you know it, Dr. White had left the office right after us and was officially on vacation. I didn't care. I told Dr. Lawrence that he had better get him on the phone or there was going to be a problem. But to be honest, I had no idea what I was going to do. What I did know was that after two nights here, we were going home. This time I knew what an AMA was, and I was ready to use it.

So Dr. Lawrence relented, telling the nurse to make sure that I gave Chaz the shot tomorrow. And she was to watch me give it and make a note about how I did.

I turned to Frank and said, "I have a bad feeling about this."

He mirrored my response. Then he wished me good luck. After all, he would be going home in a few hours. And I was the one left to deal with this.

I called down to the chaplain's office and begged them to let Chaplain Daisy know that we were there and that I needed her prayers more than anything right now. I left out the fact that without her prayers I might go postal on this whole situation. I was confident that I wasn't the only parent to ever do that. The hospital staff had to be used to parents going off on them. Only us parents didn't actually consider it "going off." We were, after all, "advocating" for our children. And in my case, I could only get burned so many times before I learned and fought back.

And I guess I must have scared somebody because Dr. Lawrence came back and parroted what Dr. White had previously said. Then an hour later, the nurse came in and reiterated what Dr. Lawrence said. Now, I just hoped that everyone complied.

Like clockwork, once the witching hour came upon us, Frank went home. Home to let the dogs out. And home to sleep in his own bed. With no beeping machines, no lights, no crying babies, and no yelling mamas. He would have a peaceful night's sleep. I would be lucky if I got to close my eyes at all.

ACTH, PART 2

The night went as I expected it to. Moms tried to quiet crying children. Some were in pain. Others didn't want to be there. Mine cried when he woke up and realized that he had an IV in him. IVs constitute continuous pain in the eyes of children. Especially babies.

Machines beeped throughout the night. TVs turned on and off. Nurses came and went. Mothers got up to use the bathroom. Some tried to read. Others stared out into the night sky. No need to close the curtains, seeing the night sky gave us a false sense of security that we needed. It was a way to feel as if we were still part of the outside world even though we were in this vortex that was sucking up our souls and that of our children.

Don't get me wrong, I'm grateful that this hospital exists. And its employees are some very special people. But if we were to be honest with one another, it is one place in the world that we would never want to be in if we could help it. It's a place that you just didn't want to visit, much less spend the night in. Because if you did, that meant that something was wrong with someone you loved. In this case, it was my seven-month-old son.

Chaz and I didn't have a lot of interaction with the nurse that night. Since I was the one changing his diapers and feeding him, all she had to do was bring me his seizure meds and weigh his dirty diapers. That was until injection time.

The next day, Chaz and I hung out with the other children and mommies. We watched TV and roamed the halls some. It was the weekend, and the hospital was nowhere near as crowded as it was during the weekdays, so we got to visit areas of the hospital that we normally wouldn't. Frank called to check on Chaz. He said that he'd be by after work. We had no idea when that would be because he typically had to stay until all of his shelves were filled and cleaned.

By the time late afternoon hit, it was time to give Chaz his injection. The nurse came in with it, and I jumped up anxiously. I was ready for this. I had no doubt in my mind that I could do it. I was like a dog begging for a treat. If she told me to jump up ten times and spin around four times and then do twelve jumping jacks, I would have.

So imagine my surprise when she showed me the injection and explained to me what it was and how to give it. Okay. The only thing the bitch did was pick a spot on his body, poke, and push. That's it. It was over in two seconds. Chaz wasn't getting some massive amount of medication. It was such a small amount that if you blinked you'd miss it.

So after she injected Chaz, I stood there with my mouth open. I didn't know if I wanted to yell at her or smack her. So I took another approach. Seething, yet quietly, I said, "I thought I was supposed to give that."

"Oh yes, you will," she said. "I have to make sure that you know how to do it."

"I believe I watched you do that yesterday," I said. "I didn't see you do anything different today. So what are you hoping to teach me?"

"Let's see how things go tomorrow," she said and walked away.

You. Have. To. Be. Fucking. Kidding. Me. What kind of statement is that? "Let's see how things go tomorrow"? Did she plan on doing that again tomorrow?

My niceness would be absent tomorrow. There was no way in hell that I was going to let her give Chaz another shot tomorrow. Then I thought about it, and I figured why wait for tomorrow? So I popped my head out of the room and asked her to please call Dr. Lawrence and tell him that we needed to talk.

Later that afternoon, Frank showed up as I was talking to Dr. Lawrence. I tried my best to act poised, but there was only so much I could do. He said that he understood my concerns and he informed the nurse that I was to give Chaz his injection tomorrow no matter what. And I added, "And then we can go home." To which he replied, "No. We have to witness you giving the shot twice before you can go home." Between gritted teeth, I said, "Then we'll go home the day after, right after I give him his second shot. Please have the discharge papers ready." Reluctantly, he agreed. Frank smiled. Yes, this was the new me. I didn't care where you went to medical school. I didn't care how long you went to medical school. I didn't care that you went to medical school. You were on mom turf now.

I was finally listening to myself and my motherly instincts, and I was advocating for my son. And I was doing it no matter what it looked like to other people. You want to call me a bitch? Then please do. If that was what it took to become a good advocate for my son, then so be it.

I missed dinner because of all of this arguing back and forth, so Frank and I took Chaz down to the cafeteria with us so we could grab something to eat. Again, the hospital social worker had been wonderful in setting us up with free parking passes and a meal card.

Frank hoped to get off early tomorrow since he had worked so many hours earlier in the week. So he offered to spend the night. I said that I would stay since it was a room for mommies and I didn't want him to feel weird or anything. But I told him that tomorrow we could explore the hospital some more and I could show him some of the things Chaz and I saw today. We had found a huge fish tank on this one floor. It was some doctor's waiting room, for what or who, I didn't know. I just knew that Chaz loved the fish tank. And since it was the weekend, it was quiet as hell. And I liked that. I didn't like the constant barrage of noise and activity that ran rampant in the hospital during the week. I, however, enjoyed being able to hear a pin drop.

The next day when four p.m. hit, I was standing by Chaz's bedside, ready and waiting. I knew that at any moment the nurse would walk in with his ACTH injection in her hand. And sure enough, she did at 4:02. She took one look at me, and I could see her wrestling with what to do when she finally relented. I knew it! She was actually going to try and do this herself. Again! But, by looking into my eyes, she stopped herself, and she allowed me to give him the injection. I did allow her to tell me what to do. I followed her guidance. After all, without her actually witnessing my doing a good job, we wouldn't get out of here tomorrow, either.

Boom! Done! Score one for Mom. One down and one more to go.

I wanted so bad to hug her and say, "I knew we could be friends." But I didn't. Now was not the time to gloat. I had to walk a fine line between being proud of myself and being intimidated by the whole process. I could be proud that I gave him the injection, but not overly satisfied, even though I wanted to say, "Wow, that was so medical in nature, I'm surprised that I could do it." At least without a medical degree or special training.

Here we were, spending another night here, even though Chaz had already had three ACTH shots. We should have been discharged today if it hadn't been for the nurse and Dr. Lawrence. But I laid my head on my cot that night knowing that tomorrow I was going home if it killed me.

Frank had to work the next day, so I knew we wouldn't see him until we called him. He knew that I was pushing for discharge after the second ACTH injection, so he promised to let his supervisor know that he may have to leave early. He knew that I would not be happy sitting for hours waiting for him to get off.

Since tomorrow was Monday, I knew the hospital would be bombarded with visitors. So that meant that Chaz and I would spend most of our time in his hospital room. I just wasn't one of those people that liked to walk down the corridors greeting everyone I saw. I grew up smiling and nodding at everyone I passed, and I had not outgrown that way of acting.

Come morning, a couple of Chaz's roommates got to go home. One had been in there for almost three weeks. My heart felt for his mom. Another boy had recently had surgery and was finally somewhat pain-free, so he was going home. That just left Chaz and a baby younger than him. The other baby had been there for two weeks. My heart went out to his parents, too.

I had finally gotten Chaz's disability approved so he had begun to receive supplemental security income. He was receiving the maximum amount of $434, which didn't even cover our rent. No, it wasn't a lot, but if I worked full time and had to pay for daycare for Chaz, then it would end up being about the same. Besides, none of the daycares that I spoke with had the ability to take care of a baby with a seizure disorder. And none of them wanted to be responsible for giving him his seizure medication. And trying to hire a sitter was out of the question because they would have to take Chaz to the infant program as well as to children's hospital for his various therapies. So it was sealed. Chaz and I would be no more than three feet apart from one another until the end of time.

Around three, I started packing up our things. The nurse would just roll her eyes at me when she entered the room. But I did see those discharge papers on her desk when I walked through once. So I was excited. When four hit, I was anxiously standing by Chaz's bedside again. This time, Dr. Lawrence and the nurse watched me give Chaz his shot. Satisfied, Dr. Lawrence agreed to let us go home, even though he looked more defeated than satisfied. But hey, Chaz got his walking papers, and we were out of there!

ACTH, NO MORE
SEIZURES, PART 3

Part of the agreement of letting Chaz go home was that children's home health would come by and visit each day. They were going to ensure that I was giving him his injection and that there were no complications. I had no problem with that. After his first hospitalization, we had home health visit regularly, just to make sure that Chaz was gaining weight and that all was well with him.

Of course, there was eventually a problem with that because they sent Betty out to our house on one of those nurse's visits. And when I saw her standing in my doorway, I had a post-traumatic moment. I couldn't breathe. I couldn't speak. I started shaking. I stood there with this shocked look on my face. What the hell?!

I let her in. She did her exam. I answered her questions. But I was so uncomfortable. To me, it felt like that moment when you have to choose your attacker out of a lineup. It was traumatic for me. After she left, I sat on the floor by the front door. She was gone, but I knew that I couldn't handle her coming back. So I called them and said that I was terminating their services. I explained to them why in detail, I might add. They tried to talk me out of it, but my nerves just couldn't take go through that torment again.

I never in a million years thought that they would send her to my house after all that had taken place.

So they informed Dr. Collins and Dr. White that I had "refused" further services. I called and spoke with Dr. Collins and Dr. White and explained what happened. They appeared to understand. Besides, as they both said, everything was going well, so there really wasn't a dire need to continue the service, and if I needed either one of them, they were there for me.

One of the other reasons I terminated their services was that Betty had failed Chaz once before. And now they wanted me to trust her again. I think not. But it was the post-traumatic emotions that I was having a hard time dealing with.

Dr. Lawrence explained to me that this time home health would come from a different agency. This time they would part of children's hospital home health. So I wouldn't have to worry about seeing Betty.

Since children's home health was to come in the mornings, Chaz's injection would now be given in the mornings. And for the first three weeks, we would lower the dose every seven days. And in that last week, we would lower the dose daily until all the medication was gone.

Now I had a plan. It was rather genius of me, if I say so myself. And I say so. I was so proud of my plan that I would tell it to anyone that would listen. When I would lay Chaz on his changing table, I would lay him with his head where my left hand was. This made it easier for me to change him. But it also provided me with something else. Since Chaz's stroke, he only turned to the left when you laid him down. This meant that he would be facing the wall. So I would give him his injection. He would cry. And I would pick him up and talk about the mean old lady that was giving him a shot. See, I could give him the shot, and he'd never know it was me because he would never turn his head, in my direction. It was genius, I tell you. Pure, evil genius. But hey, it worked. And that's all that mattered.

Like everything in life, though, things came up that weren't expected.

And so sometimes the nurse would be running late, and I'd have to give Chaz his shot without supervision. But it didn't matter to me. I was doing it, and I wasn't even flinching. All I could think was, *This is going to help him.* So I did it.

About two weeks in, I started to notice that the number of times that he did the muscle man each day was decreasing. I called Dr. White and told him. He asked me to keep a record, so I did. By time week three ended, he was no longer doing any muscle men. Of course, Dr. White kind of, sort of, doubted me. And the home health nurses made notes of my observations. Even Frank noticed. Of course, not until I pointed it out to him. But he wasn't the one with Chaz around the clock. And I mean around the clock.

I was just glad that we were able to be home during all of this ACTH injection mess. And better yet, we were in our own beds. Plus, I loved my doggies, and I missed them when we were away. Chaz got a kick out of our doggies. Especially Wolf. Wolf was such a beautiful Keeshond that sometimes acted like she had a few screws loose. She might have, who knows. But she made Chaz laugh. When she'd jump around Chaz would just giggle. As for Shaggy, about all he did was lay beside Chaz and Chaz would reach his hand over and grab his fur. I think this was his way of petting him. Especially because his right hand always remained in a fist. That is until the infant program got him this purple neoprene thumb splint. That kept his little hand open. Even with that on, he would still end up fisting Shaggy's fur.

Even though the number of muscle men that Chaz did daily had decreased significantly, he was getting more irritable each day. So for week four, Dr. White said that we would decrease the amount of ACTH each day for seven days and then we'd be done with it. So that was what we did.

By the end of January, we were through with the ACTH injections. And even though I was elated that I no longer had to give Chaz a shot each day, I was also extremely happy that his muscle men had gone away. And like everything else in life, that was short lived. Something else came in then and took its place. I began to wonder, out loud, if my son was ever going to be given a break. Wasn't it about time that God gave Chaz a break and picked on someone else for a while? My son hadn't done anything to anybody, so it mystified me how God could allow all of this to happen. Then the haunting words of my mother would waltz back in my head: "God punishes the child for the parents' sins." Well, God must have thought that I intentionally killed an entire village of people because he was laying the punishment on really strong when it came to Chaz.

With Chaz coming off of ACTH, Dr. White decided to add another seizure medication to his daily plan. This was in part because he had begun to have a different type of seizures, which appeared to be myoclonic jerks as well as some other seizures that began with some right face twitching that seemed to involve the rest of the body. Dr. White was unsure if these were secondary generalized seizures or if he was having some tonic seizures in addition to the infantile spams. Now Chaz had to see Dr. White weekly until he could stabilize his seizures.

You know what they say about when one door closes, another opens? Well, sometimes you just want all the damn doors to stay closed. You want them to stay closed and have everyone go away and leave you the hell alone and just let there be quiet. Unfortunately, life with Chaz was not working out that way. I felt like someone would forever be opening and closing doors in our lives. I began to feel like I was on the hamster wheel and couldn't get off. I couldn't even begin to fathom how Chaz felt. Nor did I dare. Since he was still a baby, I hoped and prayed that he would not remember any of the bad. I prayed that he wouldn't remember the coma or the seizures. I prayed that he wouldn't remember me giving him those thirty injections. And every time I fed him, I prayed that he would not remember, or notice, that Mama was putting Depakote sprinkles in his baby food.

Each day my list of things that I "hoped" Chaz wouldn't remember appeared to grow larger. I felt that it was only the beginning. My gut said there was much more to come. And I hoped that maybe I would not remember it all, either. I was beginning to push things aside and only remember them when necessary. At times I really wished that I could push them aside forever because I was losing sleep every time Chaz's health changed. I worried. I prayed. I cussed. Then I worried again.

I kept remembering what Dr. White and Dr. Lawrence said about some of the health professionals not being able to give their own children shots. It made me think I might be a monster. But since the ACTH injections were for the sole purpose of stopping Chaz's seizures, I had to do it. I had no choice. And if I hadn't been able to do it, then he would have spent thirty days in the hospital, and I didn't want that. So I did what any strong mother would do, and I did what was necessary. That's how I felt. I felt empowered. Because I was doing what was necessary for Chaz.

But to be honest, if Chaz didn't continually keep his gaze to the left, then honestly I probably wouldn't have been able to do it, either. But the fact that he would continually turn to the left, by my positioning him the correct way, I could get away with it. As they say, he didn't see it coming. But I would always remember.

CHAZ THE CELEBRITY

Nineteen ninety-four had definitely been a very stressful year. Let me fill you in. Since I didn't listen to my gut instincts, which I now call "mom instincts," I took Chaz to see Dr. Collins every time I suspected something was wrong. If he even blinked the wrong way, we went to see Dr. Collins. Which is a bad example, considering his rapid eye movement was a sign that things had gone south. So we basically saw Dr. Collins weekly. And Chaz had to have his phenobarbital levels checked regularly so his medication could be adjusted accordingly.

Chaz not only had therapies at the infant program, but he had weekly sessions at children's hospital as well. Since he received WIC, we had to see them regularly, and poor Chaz had to have bloodwork there. It took forever for them to allow me to bring them a copy of his bloodwork from Dr. Collins's office so he didn't have to get poked at the WIC office. Plus, to be honest with you, I didn't find the WIC office to be very sterile. I didn't feel comfortable with the office or the people, yet we really needed the baby formula that they were providing us. Actually, we really needed everything that they provided for us. Because we were always broke. And even though Frank and I went with no food or reduced food regularly, at least Chaz had his formula and baby foods. And another reason I hated going to my local WIC office was that they only took the first twelve people. So you had to get there an hour or more before the office opened to ensure that you and your child would get in. And I hated taking Chaz out because sometimes I had to go in the rain and the snow. And I felt like Chaz didn't deserve to be out in the weather. But since the appointments were for us both, there really wasn't any option on this. At least when I went to the food stamp office, I didn't have to bring Chaz. And that was another thing that I really hated. I hated going to social services. Those lines were long, and once you got in, you still had to wait forever to see someone. Then there was the social security office, which we had to see regularly as well.

That year was nothing but meetings and problems. That year was when most of my mental health issues started. I started having anxiety, panic attacks, problems with agoraphobia, and depression. Only I didn't have time to dwell on it, so I never saw anyone for it. It's also when a lot of my woman issues came to the surface. My periods had always been out of control, but after I had Chaz, they got worse.

We also began seeing Dr. Stephens every few months because she was the one that recommended therapies and equipment. She was the one that set us up with wheelchair clinic appointments, as well as splint clinic appointments. Then there were the follow-ups, not just with the appointments but with the insurance companies. I say companies because we had two. We thankfully had primary health insurance through Frank's work at the local grocery store, and Chaz had Medicaid as his backup since he received SSI (Supplemental Security Income). One thing I can say is that our primary health insurance was absolutely wonderful. Exceptional. When they received paperwork for Chaz's equipment, it was processed in like two weeks. And they approved 99.9 percent of the items that were medically necessary for Chaz. They were one of the few things that I never had to worry about. Now making sure that the paperwork got to them, that was where I went crazy. I would call and call and call people to ask them to please send in the necessary paperwork.

And 1994 was also when that article came out. I say that because when you make the cover of *The Wall Street Journal*, people listen. And here I always thought that they primarily reported business news.

At the beginning of July, Kevin Helliker called me to say that he had remembered reading the 1993 article "Mother Knows Best," which appeared in our local paper, *The Virginian Pilot*, and was written by the wonderful Elizabeth Simpson, while he was stationed in England. It had resonated with him, so he decided to do an article on a woman's inability to produce breast milk. Apparently, he had found a bunch of moms with the same problem as me, and their children had suffered as Chaz had. Many of them suffered worse than Chaz. And as bad as I felt about this, I couldn't help but take comfort in the fact that it wasn't just me, that it was an actual problem. A problem that had been going on since the beginning of time but a problem that women didn't talk about. No one talked about it.

But I wanted to talk about it. I had done my research without trying. I had read all of those baby books so I wouldn't screw up, and not one of them mentioned dehydration. Not one of them mentioned that not all women could breastfeed. I was mad. I was mad in 1993, and there I was a little over a year later, and I was still mad. So when Kevin called, I sang like a canary. I was an open book. I was reminiscent of a person visiting a priest. I told him everything that I could possibly think of. My goal was awareness.

It was time that the world woke up and realized that not all women could breastfeed. Society seemed to accept that not all women could get pregnant. So they should accept that not all women could breastfeed. Right?

I ended up speaking with a bunch of the people that Kevin had spoken with, and it was heartbreaking. And when he asked me to send him a picture of Chaz and me together, I freaked. I didn't do pictures. I didn't do family pictures or any kind of pictures. Not even publicly. But apparently, they had this guy that drew pictures of the people that appeared in its publication. I told myself that *The Wall Street Journal* was a huge newspaper, so we'd be buried in the back somewhere.

So when I got up early on the morning of July 22, Frank and I headed to the only newsstand that we knew of and bought a bunch of copies. I freaked out when I saw my very own face smiling back at me. I panicked. I couldn't believe it. I was positive that we would be buried in the back somewhere. But the cover? *Oh God. Breathe. Take a deep breath and just breathe.*

We went back home, and Frank called everyone we were related to and told them about the cover. I sat down and read the article. My wound was still fresh, so reading it was like reliving it all over again. Again, I panicked. It was not even seven a.m. and I was experiencing my first huge, full-blown panic attack ever. I took care of Chaz then laid down on the couch. I needed time to myself. Time to breathe. I was shaking inside. Honestly, I was a nervous wreck.

I had wanted to get my message out, and there it was. Those poor children. And the more I read, the angrier I got. Why in the hell didn't all of these so-called medical professionals listen to these moms? There were so many people that had failed all of us moms. My heart bled. It was beyond aching. My heart was bleeding. Just thinking about all of the unnecessary suffering that these babies and mothers went through was sad.

And thinking of all of the medical professionals that had failed them was even more astounding. Something needed to be done. We needed to get our message out. Things needed to change. Mothers needed to know about this. I wanted mothers to trust their own instincts. I wanted them to give a bottle if they felt that it was necessary. I didn't want them to be bullied into breastfeeding. I didn't want them to feel like failures if they didn't or couldn't breastfeed.

Frank headed off to work while I was lying on the couch trying to steady my breathing because all I really wanted to do was scream. My heart was racing, I started sweating, and I felt like I might black out. I'd never had a panic attack before and was still unsure if that was what was going on. So I just laid there until my heart stopped racing.

When nine a.m. hit, my phone started ringing. *Primetime Live. Dateline NBC. America Tonight.* The BBC. There was request from radio stations from all over the United States and even England, and California, for interviews.

And all I kept thinking was, *Why didn't Kevin tell me this was going to happen?* At least I could have been prepared.

But when I took the phone off the hook at lunch time so we could eat in peace, I knew that even if I was warned, I would still feel like screaming. I plugged the phone back in after I ate lunch, and it continued to ring up until evening. When Frank came home from work, I was sitting on the steps out front, and he walked up and asked, "What's wrong?" Then he heard the phone ringing and said, "Aren't you going to get that?" And he walked past me to answer the phone.

Though I could easily hear him from where I sat, I wanted nothing to do with whoever was on the phone. I had spoken to people all day today. Took notes about what they wanted and when they wanted it. I was done. Mentally, I couldn't take anymore. My panic attack this morning was nothing compared to what I was going through now. My insides were shaking, and from the outside, I looked like someone going through DTs. I was like hyper-vigilant. And I was doing everything I possibly could to block out everything around me. I had to retreat to within myself. I had to shut down.

Frank came outside and told me a reporter called. Then he asked if that's what had been going on all day. I nodded and showed him my writing pad. He was surprised by some of the names that he read.

We went inside, and he reheated his dinner while I filled him in on my day. At this point, I had a migraine coming on, and I was scared. I had this fear of all of these people coming to my house and demanding I answer questions.

When I went to bed, I prayed that tomorrow would be better. But that was only the beginning of my emotional and mental problems. I had a hard time sleeping because I kept hearing a phone ring. So the next day, I was tired as hell.

Not only had my migraine gotten worse, but I was very sleepy. My neck was aching and my body was tense. I felt like I'd been hit by a truck. And then ten a.m. hit, and the phone started ringing again.

Frank didn't want me to do *Primetime Live* since they had aired a special report on a scandal with Food Lion.

I had a couple of calls from impromptu radio shows asking me about how I felt about breastfeeding and what I had hoped to have accomplished by allowing *The Wall Street Journal* to interview me. At the time, I said that I had nothing against breastfeeding per se. If you can do it, great. But if you're one of the ones that can't, then don't. I wanted moms to trust their instincts. If they felt like breastfeeding wasn't working, then stop. Stop immediately. Don't allow yourself to be bullied into it. And if you didn't want to even try to breastfeed, then don't. My goal was to tell moms that it's not the end of the world if you don't breastfeed. But it is when you can't and try anyway. Thank God Chaz didn't die. By all accounts, he should have. The fact that he was living was an absolute miracle. And miracles should be passed along.

Have my thoughts on breastfeeding changed? Yes and no. The word alone causes my face to grimace. But I'm not against it. I am against those that push and push moms that aren't comfortable with it or those moms that feel that they can't. Now if you're a breastfeeding advocate that doesn't bully, then we might just get along. But if you are pushing breastfeeding down my throat like some people do religion, then we have a problem.

I want women to know that even though moms are touted as superheroes, we do have our limits. Not everything on our bodies works. Just like your thyroid might not work properly, neither do your breasts sometimes. And just like the heart stops working, so can the breasts. We are not bionic people. We are not perfect. And like I've always said, "If we can't all get pregnant and have babies, then it's just common sense that not all of us can breastfeed."

After what happened to Chaz, I just wanted to get the word out. I wanted people to know that this can and does happen. And it's not as rare as some would like for you to think. I wanted all baby books to be updated to show that this can and does happen. I wanted baby books to show the signs of dehydration. But it went a little beyond that. Yes, a child may need six to eight wet diapers a day. But he needs six to eight *wringing* wet diapers a day. That is the key word. Wringing. Chaz's diapers were damp.

Just damp. Not wringing wet.

One of the other problems was that I had reached out to all of these medical professionals and none of them listened to me. They did not take my accounts serious enough. Even if I had only called each of them just one time, that should have been enough for them to be concerned. But since I called them multiple times, that alone should have been a red flag. And unfortunately, I was always taught to listen to the ones in charge. Listen to the ones with the degrees. So I didn't question their advice. I never once thought for myself and stopped trying and broke open the case of formula that was sitting in Chaz's bathroom on a shelf. Besides, it didn't help that Frank was in my ear reminding me that they were the experts and I should listen to them. It felt almost like everyone was against me. But when so many people tell you that what you're feeling is wrong, you start to believe it. And that's where I fucked up.

AFTERMATH OF
HOLLYWOOD EXPOSURE:
THE PRESS DOESN'T
GET IT

So for the next few days, the phone rang and rang. Day by day, the number of calls lessened. And the following week, there were only one or two calls a day. I did so many interviews that I stopped counting. I couldn't even tell you who all I did talk to.

But I can tell you this. Frank called me from work one day to ask me if I knew that I was in a certain tabloid, and I said no. I didn't remember doing an interview with them. He said that one of the men that was responsible for putting the magazines on the racks had come across an article about us, and he showed it to Frank. All I could say was, "Well, is it a good one?" I had to know if they wrote on my behalf or called me crazy for speaking out against breastfeeding. He said that it was a good one. So I was like, "Buy me a copy so I can read it."

Around that same time, my mom called and told me that I was in another tabloid. I was like, "What?" She said that one of her friends down the street had read it when she was in the grocery store line. So I called Frank and told him to pick me up a copy. It too was good.

Then a week later, *Star* magazine came out with an article about us, and I considered it one of the better ones. It was short and sweet, and it said exactly what I wanted to say. It was almost as if I had written the article myself. This is not to say that I didn't like *The Wall Street Journal* article. I did. It was very investigative. The moms that were interviewed were treated fairly. They respected the tragedies that each of our children had faced. For that, I could not ask for more.

But now, when all of the breastfeeding advocates came out with their own articles and interviews saying that each of us had not been shown how to breastfeed properly, I didn't like that. I didn't like that they were belittling, insulting, shaming, bullying, and criticizing us moms. They were basically saying that the maternity wards that we were in were not considered "Baby-Friendly hospitals." I believe the wording was they were not considered breastfeeding hospitals. And I can tell you right now, mine definitely was. I had a nurse on top of me in my bed, holding Chaz, while teaching me various techniques. If that wasn't trying, I'm not sure what is. To me, their comebacks were so disrespectful. One woman's child died, for heaven's sake. And you're going to condemn her breastfeeding techniques when you weren't even there? Little did I know that I was going to become one of the advocate victims soon enough.

I had agreed to do a couple of talk news shows, and one of them made me so angry that I'm surprised I didn't have to be carried off the set. At that moment, I believe that I deserved a Nobel Peace Prize, because I did not go off on people. At that moment, I knew that I must have been raised right because any other person would have gone off at the mouth. A part of me regrets the fact that I didn't. A part of me feels like I failed Chaz and all the other moms by not taking a more verbal stand. I was told by this doctor, on television, that I was lying. He actually called me a liar on TV. He said that he didn't believe my accounts of what happened. Because—wait for it—because every woman can breastfeed. At that moment, I saw red. It took everything in me not to jump up off that couch and rip his tongue out. More so, I wanted to yell at the host, who had brought me there under false pretenses because that bitch had recently had a child and was breastfeeding successfully. And she had her doctor on her show because he was promoting the release of his new baby book. That's when I knew that I could trust no one from Los Angeles.

When we got back to our dressing room to wait for our escort down to the limo that had brought us there, Frank said he looked at me when the doctor called me a liar and knew I was ready to pounce the guy. I was so mad that a part of me was shaking. Not only inside but out. He knew that I wanted to. But I couldn't speak. Not yet. I was not going to let these bastards know that they had pushed me over the edge. Once in the limo, I let it rage. Thank God Chaz didn't scream along with me. I was mad as hell. When I got home, I wrote to him telling him that I thought that he was full of shit. Then I didn't mail it because I wasn't going to give him the satisfaction. To this day I hate, yes hate, them both. Hate. Hate. Hate.

That interview got me thinking about all of those radio show interviews I had done, from all over the world. What exactly were they saying about me because I couldn't hear them since I wasn't in the area of their broadcast? This made me shudder inside. I was probably branded a laughing stock and didn't even know it. Now I felt even more insecure. And I pulled back into myself. All I wanted to do was go home. At home, I was safe. I could trust the people within my four walls. And I had some illusion of control at home. In Hollywood, I was nothing but bait, and I didn't like it. And what bothered me the most was at the heart of all of this drama was my son. There was an innocent child that people were making assumptions about his life and spreading lies about it, and that really bothered me. That made me cry tears of heartbreak.

It sure as hell had been an interesting year so far. I never stopped to wonder what would happen next. I just knew that all of the media hype had died down and my fifteen minutes of fame had died down. I had helped a few people. I knew because I had heard from them. I had received letters and phone calls thanking me for sharing my story. I knew that Chaz's story had saved their child's life or the life of a friend's or relative's child. Chaz's story had made a difference, and that confirmed that he had not suffered for no reason. To some degree, that comforted me. But it has never fully helped me to recover from what happened to Chaz. I was still mad at all of the ones that didn't listen to me, and it made me quite angry that their children were not suffering as mine was. Their child was not taking seizure medications. They were not on the path to having multiple surgeries. They were not going to have to have thousands of hours of therapy or wear weird-looking devices. I hated them for that. Don't get me wrong, I never wanted anything bad to happen to their children, but I sure as hell wish they knew how Chaz and I felt. But I knew that they never would, and that angered me.

That anger I took and balled it up and put it into advocating. Not just for Chaz but for others like him that were going through challenges. These kids needed a voice, and I was just hopping mad enough to be the one to do it. Someone asked me once—okay, more than once—why I was doing what I do. My response was, "Someone has to." And I was that someone. And I was taking my role seriously. Honestly, if I hadn't have begun advocating, I probably would have gone mad. Or at least madder than I was.

Even though I had always been kind of a depressed individual, after what happened to Chaz, I became even more depressed. So I started taking medication for depression. And with that came highs and lows. Not just for me but for Chaz as well. Because his mom would be happy one day, sad one day, and then angry the next.

A week after that disastrous television show aired, we made preparations for our *20/20* interview. Actually, I prepared. They were going to be with us for two days to film us doing what we did regularly. So I spoke with Karen and asked if we could film Chaz doing physical therapy. She was a dear about it. And the fact that she was like eight months pregnant at the time showed how much she loved Chaz. No woman wants to be on television while pregnant. Unless you're a supermodel or something. But it wasn't just Karen that was going to be camera shy. So was I. We had to add another activity to our agenda: I agreed to let them film Chaz doing aquatic therapy. And guess who Chaz's swimming pool partner was for this activity? Me. Because we had been doing it for several weeks now, I remained the chosen one. At least Karen got to wear a shirt and pants.

I only wore a bathing suit. It was a one piece, but still, I was nowhere near bathing body friendly. But I did it for Chaz. Since we were trying to raise funds for a conductive education trip to London, they wanted to film me passing out fliers. I chose the area, and *20/20's* producer, Gail, sought approval from the businesses that I would visit.

And last but not least, we ate lunch at Doumar's. Now in case you don't know what Doumar's is, then you really need to find out. It's been featured on numerous travel shows about historic places to eat.

Then there was the actual interview with Lynn Sherr. I had seen her on television many times and was excited to meet her. When I finally did, she turned out to be a doll. And her questions did not exploit the situation nor did they discount the truth. It was final editing that I had some trouble with. There appeared to be more for the opposing side. Needless to say, I reached out to Gail afterward to tell her my concerns. And thankfully she apologized for how I took the episode. In her creative vision, it was a fair airing; in mine, it wasn't. But what's done was done. Another failure. And last interview. No more. I had been used enough.

I came to the conclusion that if you want something done right, then you need to do it yourself. But I had no idea how to reach people. Better yet, I was afraid of reaching people. I had been praised for my bravery in speaking out on the subject. But there was plenty of times that I had been attacked for doing so. I had received nasty, threatening phone calls and mail. Even one breastfeeding nut sent me a videotape of her talking. But she made sure that you could not see her face. I felt like if she was so adamant about what she wanted to say, then she should have had the guts to show her face. After all, I had put my face with my words. So all of the bad attention had also caused me to be a little afraid of going out. For a while there, I would look out for people following me. And I started taking different routes to children's hospital, the infant program, and home. I was scared. Really scared.

I had endured some negativity when *The Wall Street Journal* article came out, and now with the *20/20* thing, there was even more. I was so glad that I was officially done with this part of things. I didn't like feeling scared and unsafe. And let's be honest, there are some breastfeeding nuts out there. I had people wishing me dead, for heaven's sake. I mean, really. Who does that? I'm a mother of a child with special needs and you're wishing me dead? There is no reason for that extremeness. But breastfeeding is one of those topics that tend to have obsessive fans.

So I promised myself that I would only do local stuff from now on. No more national. National reached out to the homes and arms of the crazies. And I couldn't deal with that. At least not right now.

PICTURES

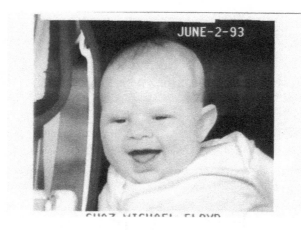

Figure 1: Chaz's baby picture – he even smiled when he was born.

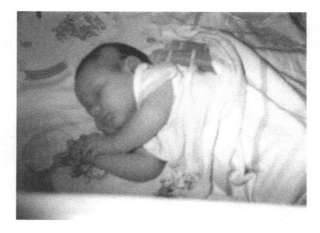

Figure 2: Chaz back home from children's hospital with a patch of hair missing

Figure 3: Chaz with Wolfgang (the gray dog) and Shaggy (the black and white dog)

Figure 4: This was the turning of Chaz's leg.

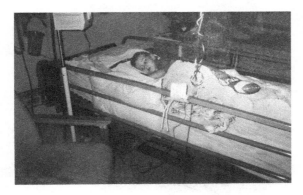

Figure 5: One of Chaz's many visits in the hospital

Figure 6: Lynn Sherr and the Floyd family

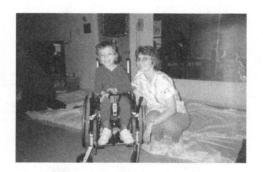

Figure 7: Karen C. PT & Chaz

Figure 8: Karen M. PT & Chaz

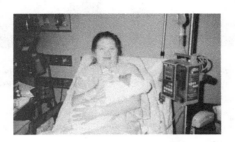

Figure 9: Me feeding Dustin

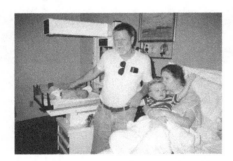

Figure 10: The Floyds with Pam's dad Robert

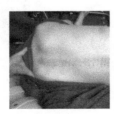

Figure 11: After surgery stitching (from neck to tail bone)

Figure 12: Dustin and
his great-grandmother
Florence

Figure 13: Chaz and his
grandmother Dot during
another surgery

Figure 14: Another
hospital stay

Figure 15: Dustin & a
high school soccer game

Figure 16: Dustin &
a high school soccer
game

Figure 17: Chaz &
Jackie at camp

Figure 18:Chaz wall climbing at camp

Figure 19: Chaz seeing how high he can go.

Figure 20: Chaz painted Marilyn for his mom

Figure 21: Chaz's Pink Floyd, Dark Side of the Moon

Figure 22: Chaz painted Prince
for me for mother's day

Figure 23: Chaz's graduation pic

Figure 24: President George
Bush with Dustin and Chaz &
the mascot that made Chaz cry

Figure 25 Chaz and
Denise at the NATO
parade

Figure 26: Chaz and Dr.
White at Elle King/Joan Jett/
Heart (Summer 2019)

Figure 27: Dr. White
and Chaz at one of
his birthday parties

Figure 28: The Floyd Family today

Figure 29: Chaz sees Dr. White for the last time when he's 21.

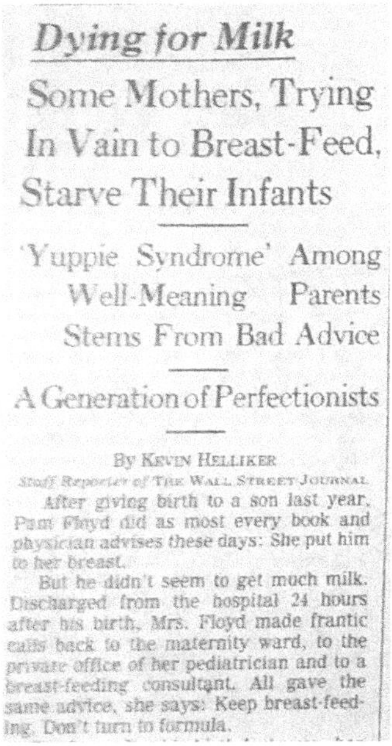

Dying for Milk

Some Mothers, Trying In Vain to Breast-Feed, Starve Their Infants

'Yuppie Syndrome' Among Well-Meaning Parents Stems From Bad Advice

A Generation of Perfectionists

By KEVIN HELLIKER
Staff Reporter of THE WALL STREET JOURNAL

After giving birth to a son last year, Pam Floyd did as most every book and physician advises these days: She put him to her breast.

But he didn't seem to get much milk. Discharged from the hospital 24 hours after his birth, Mrs. Floyd made frantic calls back to the maternity ward, to the private office of her pediatrician and to a breast-feeding consultant. All gave the same advice, she says: Keep breast-feeding. Don't turn to formula.

Figure 30: Article Title from The Wall Street Journal

Figure 32: Chaz and Roman

Figure 34: Chaz and Danny doing Karaoke

Figure 35:Chaz and Dustin (2015)

Figure 36: The Floyds going to a wedding

Figure 38: Tanner, Danny, and Chaz

Figure 39: Chaz and Danny out to eat

Figure 40: Wall Street Journal drawing

PART 3

CONSEQUENCES AND FIXING BROKEN

BRACES, SPLINTS,
AND HATRED

On the recommendation of his physical therapist, Karen, we had Chaz fitted for AFOs (ankle-foot orthoses) in their splint clinic. AFOs came in all sorts of shapes, sizes, and colors. And each child had some say in what color they would receive. The process was kind of harrowing. I had to sit there and hold Chaz as Karen made a cast-like mold of his foot and ankle, in proper alignment, mind you, and wait for it to dry. It took hours. I hated the process, and I hated the AFOs. And when I shopped for shoes for Chaz, if I didn't have him with me, I would carry one of his AFOs with me to see how easy it fit into the shoe. Easy fit determined the winning shoe.

I know that Karen and all of the physical therapists in children's hospital's therapy department were super excited that they were now able to provide their patients with Cascade DAFOs. Apparently, they had been pursuing Cascade for a while and were finally able to provide them to their patients.

Chaz hated it. He hated the casting process. First, she would put the sock-like material on him, up to his knee. Then she'd twist his ankle and foot into proper alignment. Then she would cast it, the same way you would do a plaster cast of something. Only this time it was Chaz's ankle and foot. Then I'd try to entertain him while she held his ankle and foot until the plaster dried. And I want to remind you that she did this twice. Once for each foot. Then we'd go home and wait. Because then she had to ship the molds to Cascade.

And when they came back, it was just as much fun. Only this time she would put his foot in the proper position and then place the AFO on him and hope it would fit right. But nope. She would heat the molded AFO until it held his tiny little foot into proper alignment. This meant more patience for me as he wiggled and cried. I think that was the moment that I was finally able to detach myself from a situation. This had become my coping mechanism. I just don't think I realized until that moment.

It's actually kind of weird when you think about it. I was there, in the moment. I could hear Chaz and KC and understand anything I was told. Yet I had placed myself in another—I don't like this word but humor me—dimension, and the crying wouldn't bother me. By having part of my mind off somewhere else, I was able to hold a wiggling baby that was crying and screaming the whole time this person was wrangling with his foot.

Sadly, Karen informed me that Chaz would need a new pair of these about every six months, orthopedic surgeries not included. Oh, joy. I would have to seriously begin practicing my detachment skills. I would need to master them before the next fitting.

Karen answered to Dr. Stephens, the rehabilitative specialist in charge of children's hospital's outpatient therapy program. So Dr. Stephens was always behind the scene of Chaz's care. When we finally met her, I felt as if I had just been run over by a moving subway. I say that because we would sit in a patient room while various people came in and out asking questions. One lady in particular, Elaine, came in and asked a jarring amount of questions. And she was accompanied by a medical student, who looked like she was lost in a tornado. I told you it was jarring. Then Dr. Stephens would come in. She was a pleasant woman, just a little older than me. In other words, she wasn't my parents' age, but she wasn't mine, either. She had short brown hair and round eyeglasses. She was pleasant. And she looked Chaz over as she related everything that she knew. Which was a lot since she had access to most of his medical records. So remind me again why we had to answer Elaine's jarring questions. And I know damn well that we scared off that medical student. But Elaine scared me, too. She was like a rocket ship. You had ten seconds to detonation.

So besides the obvious things, she mentioned that he had suffered intraventricular bleeding at six days old. She was glad that he had begun to spoon feed himself. She applauded him for self-feeding himself finger foods. He had a Cheerios container that he hoarded most of the time.

Dr. Stephens was excited that Chaz had been seen for bilateral AFOs. She touched his tiny right thumb splint and told him that she loved its purple color. Elaine wrote down that we had a bath chair at home, and she asked if it was working out all right, and we said yes. Chaz had begun to sleep through the night, which was a plus.

Then she noted that his truncal tone and lower extremity tone was hypertonic. She saw some evidence of his initiating trunk control. Even though Chaz was now eleven months old, he still didn't have the best head control, so we still supported him by the neck.

We were thrilled that he had begun to say "Mama" and "Dada" (just here and there, but hey, he said it). And Dr. Stephens gave us hope when she said that she anticipated Chaz being an ambulator. But he would probably not be functional for distances more than around the house. Her goal was that he would eventually be able to walk, even if it was for short distances and with some type of crutch or walker. She just didn't see him doing it all day long. That meant he'd always need a wheelchair. But we left that visit filled with hope. Hope that one day he'd be an ambulator. Just another fancy word that I added to my list of shit that did happen and shit that could happen. Anyway, she said that the adaptive seating clinic would order Chaz a prone stander since he was showing progress in his therapies. And we were definitely on board with that idea. Anything that could give Chaz the advantage.

As far as everything else went, also by July of 1994, Dr. White, with the help of Dr. Stephens, had collectively given Chaz all sorts of diagnoses. We went from simple things like seizures, cerebral palsy, and developmental delay to:

Chaz has several medical problems related to hypernatremic dehydration and subsequent venous sinus thrombosis and intracranial hemorrhage as a young baby. Seizures—initially controlled with phenobarbital, his seizures worsened with the development of infantile spasms, which responded initially to ACTH and later to valproic acid. Axial hypotonia—requiring special bracing and devices to maximize sitting and functional movement. Pseudobulbar palsy—which made eating and vocalizations more challenging. Spastic diparesis, which is asymmetric, involving the right more than the left, making the left upper extremity his most functional extremity. Developmental delays due to all of the above.

And hopefully, with the various therapies that he currently receives at the infant program and at children's hospital and all of the other interventions that he's receiving, he will hopefully learn valuable skills which will increase his chance for maximal independence as he grows up.

That was what Chaz now looked like on paper. But in real life, he was a happy, playful child. Yes, he was dependent upon his dad and me for everything. But he was happy and laughed a lot. He was extremely social. He loved the girls, and he wasn't even a year old yet. He smiled and flirted with all of the therapists and nurses. He even smiled at women when we were out and about. And these women loved to joke that one day he was going to be a ladies' man. I was starting to think that he already was. In his own way.

But that was Chaz. He was paving his own way through life. Dr. White always joked that when it came to Chaz, you had to throw everything that you'd learned in your medical textbooks out the window because Chaz was developing his own. Dr. White also loved to show the medical students that he was mentoring Chaz's initial MRI and early medical records then ask them questions. He would always ask if they thought he had a shunt. They would always say yes, and he would say no. Most thought that the child that they would see come through the door at any moment would be so spaced out that he wouldn't even know if he was there or not. So not accurate. Chaz had managed to beat all of the odds and overcome so many obstacles. And that made me happy. But...

It still didn't take away the pain and anger that I felt to all those that failed us in the beginning. All of this happened because I was seeking medical advice based on what Chaz was doing and how he was acting. And I embarrassingly admit that I would sometimes think how unfair it was that all of their children were fine. Normal. Without special needs that required constant attention. I would never in a million years wish something bad on a child, but I couldn't help but think of how unfair it was.

Some days I would sit there and think about how their children would grow up to play sports, date, attend college, drive. They would spend the night at friends' houses. They could run on the beach and jump in the ocean. These images came when I was having my dark days. Those days when my anger would hit the roof and I'd wish that they could feel just a tenth of what Chaz and I were going through. I wanted them to feel Chaz's pain. I wanted them to feel my heartbreak. Because it was all their fault! Their fault for not listening to me and for not taking me seriously!

Yes, I was going to have to live with the fact that I was dumb enough to listen to them. I also still needed to address the anger that I felt toward Frank when I would think back to his words, "They're the medical professionals, so they know what they're talking about."

I had to find a way to get over the guilt and grief of not following my own motherly instincts. Which, by the way, is the most important thing that a woman can do.

I was also trying to find a way to live with the breastfeeding junkies. You know, the ones that see you buying formula in the grocery store and tell you how bad of a person you are. Yes, that happened to me. The ones that see you give a bottle and make a rude comment about you being a bad mother for formula feeding your child. Yes, that too happened to me. And then there are the ones that see you giving your child a bottle and ask you what is in it. Yes, that, too, happened more times than I can count. These types of people have their own breastfeeding mafia going on.

While in the waiting room at children's hospital, while waiting for Chaz to begin his various therapies each week, I would talk to mothers who would tell me about their sore nipples, the fact that their children were "hooked up" to them around the clock, and how they wished that they'd never tried to breastfeed. Many had given up because "something just didn't feel right." These were the ones that I envied. They too had had a feeling that their breastfeeding wasn't working. But they were smart enough to do something about it. They didn't confer with other medical professionals. They followed that motherly instinct and stopped trying. They saved their children. I envied them because I couldn't save mine. I didn't save mine.

I was too busy following everyone else's advice. The books. The videos. All of those wrong voices. Dead wrong. I was angry at them all. But who wouldn't be?

It was because of them that Chaz was now the survivor of a brain hemorrhage and stroke. He was going to spend the rest of his life with a seizure problem. His hypotonia and cerebral palsy would always require special braces and devices for sitting, eating, mobility, and sleeping. He would always have trouble saying what came to mind. And his spasticity would always give him problems, even when he slept. Chaz was in for more than I could ever imagine. And I was imagining much.

I knew that he'd never ride a bike. That he'd not be able to hang with the "regular" kids. That he'd always need my help. He was my firstborn. And he was supposed to be my golden child. The one that would grow up to be a popular, handsome young man. He'd play sports and excel in not only those but in school as well. He'd eventually go on to a wonderful college and get a degree. Over the holiday break, he would bring home the girl that he was going to marry. And we'd love her as much as she loved our son. He'd graduate from college. Marry. Have kids. Live in a big house that he could afford with a job that made him happy. This was my dream for him. And now I was beginning to understand that none of this would ever happen. Never.

And you wondered why I hated God sometimes. That is why.

What sometimes made things worse was when people would come up to us and tell me that they were praying for my son. As much as I appreciated their kindness, what I really wanted to do was say, "But he allowed this to happen to him." He was responsible for allowing the medical professionals and the books and the videos to give me bad advice. He allowed horrible things to continually happen to my son. So why pray for him? He wasn't helping Chaz. He was allowing it. It felt as if God was actually making it all happen. This too was why I hated him at times. But he was also the one that I prayed to whenever I needed someone to listen and do something about it. I prayed to him daily to protect him and keep him safe. I prayed in part because he was already damaged and I didn't want anything else to happen to him. We had had enough. Chaz had had enough.

A BROTHER FOR CHAZ

When I got pregnant with my second son Dustin, I was excited. I always wanted two boys, two years apart. I wanted them close in age so they would get along. My sister and I are almost seven years apart, and we were never in the same place in our lives when we were growing up. That put a strain on the relationship, and it's never been the same since. Honestly, it's pretty much nonexistent.

Once Frank and I decided that it was time to have another child, I went off the pill, which was right before the holidays. So when January rolled around and I missed my period, I was a little surprised. It was kind of quick.

With my erratic periods and heavy bleeds, I wasn't jumping for joy just yet. Yes, I would miss periods. And then the following month I'd bleed like a walking crime scene. I can't tell you how often I had accidents. I had no idea when my periods would start and what they would be like. So missing one wasn't that exciting.

I never wanted to have girls because with girls came periods, makeup, clothes, and pregnancy scares. Plus, I was a girl, and I knew firsthand how much trouble we were. And I wanted nothing to do with that.

Of course, you don't get a say-so in what the sex of your baby is, but I really, really, really didn't want a girl. Can you imagine having a girl on top of having Chaz and all of his medical needs? Lord, my life would be over. I wouldn't have time to pee, let alone sleep.

But I was tired. Tired all the time and more than usual. I just didn't feel like myself. But I waited. I waited six weeks before I mentioned it to Frank. I scheduled an appointment with my doctor. And I told the therapist during one of Chaz's visits to the infant program. And I was right. I was pregnant with baby Floyd number two.

And as before, I was nauseated as hell, requiring home IV therapy a few times throughout the pregnancy. And it was a little challenging taking care of a heavy baby with very little head and trunk support when you had a needle sticking out of your arm and a long tube attached. But such is life.

That summer was a bitch. We literally had sixty days of one hundred–degree weather. Fortunately, we had an above-ground pool in the backyard. So Chaz and I spent a lot of time in the water.

Because of everything that happened during Chaz's birth, my OB/GYN team decided that this time they would not assist in getting the baby out. I would have to push him out, all by myself. And they would take him two weeks early to ensure that he wouldn't be huge. So during one of my OB/GYN visits, Frank and I sat down with Dr. Watson and picked a date. We chose September 12. The plan was for me to show up at the hospital that morning and they would induce me, and then I would deliver my baby while the doctor held his hands out as if waiting for the ball to be hiked in football.

When I got home that day, I called my dad and told him what was going on. Then I asked him if he and Grandma could come down for a few days so they could watch Chaz while I was in the hospital. Since Frank wanted to room-in with me, as he had done with Chaz, it would be great if they could come and stay for a few days.

Thank God they said yes. So now I would have someone to take care of Chaz. Besides, the infant program ended their services at age two, and starting in September, Chaz would be attending a special needs preschool. And he would ride the bus. So now I was expected to put my two-year-old on a school bus, in a wheelchair, and send him away to a strange place for part of the day. And this wasn't supposed to stress me out. Ha!

But when the bus driver showed up the day after Labor Day, Chaz just smiled at her and was super excited to get on the bus with the other kids. The bus driver was nice as could be, but I followed her the first two days anyway. I had to make sure that she was driving properly. Can you tell that I was a first-time mom?

Well, I typed up Chaz's daily routine and did my best to add everything that I possibly could to it so my dad and Grandma wouldn't have to worry about anything. Of course, they turned out to be old pros. And Chaz loved having them there.

On the morning of September 12, I kissed everyone goodbye, and they wished me good luck. It was strange knowing that I was definitely going to have a baby that day. All I kept thinking was, *I'm leaving pregnant, and I'm coming back with a little fella*. Only I didn't know if I had a little fella or not. Again, I didn't want to know the sex. I felt like that would be my surprise at the end of this long journey.

I had asked Chaz's physical therapist, Karen, if the pain was any different when you're induced. Because she had shared with me that she had gone through the same thing once. I also asked if she needed an epidural. "Yes! Of course," she said. "I'm not that much of a superwoman." I needed to know because I didn't have an epidural the first time around.

So into the hospital I went. I was giving Pitocin. And let me tell you, that shit hurts. With regular labor—and I know why they call it labor—the pains starts off small and several minutes apart. Then it works its way up to lasting longer for shorter periods. But with Pitocin, you go from zero to sixty immediately. That drug does not play around. You don't get those little ten minute apart contractions. No, you get sixty-second contractions a minute apart. Two, if you're lucky.

Oh God, did it hurt! At first, I had said no epidural. But it didn't take long for me to ask for one. I tried being a brave woman. I really did.

I walked around the maternity floor, but only a few times. Then I laid in my bed and cried. The question of an epidural was up in the air because I would have to remain completely still while the doctor inserted it into my spine. And with all of the fuss that I was making, the nurses were unsure if I could do it. I grabbed one of them by the arm and said, "Get me the doctor now!" And as I did this, I couldn't help but wonder who I was. It was like something out of a movie. I knew it was me, but it was uncharacteristic of me. I told you, Pitocin does not play around.

It didn't take too long for the doctor to come in. He asked me a few dumb-ass questions, then he proceeded to give me the epidural. And I guess I had an out-of-body experience because I was able to remain completely still, even though I was contracting like hell. I guess God was looking out for me.

The epidural didn't work right away. It took a few minutes. So I wasn't happy about that. But when it finally did work, I couldn't help but wonder why I hadn't gotten it the first time. I didn't feel the contractions to the extreme that I had before. Now I just felt pressure in my belly that felt like muscle spasms. And I couldn't really feel much from the waist down. Let me correct myself. I couldn't really feel anything from the vagina down. I was numb. I couldn't even will myself to move the lower part of my body.

And all I kept thinking was this didn't feel like all of those stories that I had heard from other moms about epidurals. The epidural was presented to me as some wonderful gift from God where you just magically felt nothing and went off into la-la land. I wasn't in la-la land. I was in what the fuck just happened land.

Soon after my epidural was inserted, Dr. Watson walked in. He was grinning and said, "Are we ready to have this baby?" *Sure. Why not? After all, I'm here. You're here. Frank's here. The baby is here. Let's get this pony show on the road.*

So two nurses came in and helped me move down the bed and into the stirrups. I wasn't able to move because of the epidural. I told you I was feeling nothing in the legs. Then Dr. Watson sat down onto his little roll-away stool and clasped his hands together and watched. Let me repeat that. Clasped his hands together. And watched. He had not been joking when he said that I would have to push this baby out on my own. But it was almost impossible to do since I couldn't feel the lower half of my body. Now I was tired. Exhausted. Mad. And numb. This was going to be a very long delivery. Only it was feeling more like a standoff.

It was like in those country western movies when the bad guy and the sheriff are standing in the center of town for a showdown. Well, that's what was going on with Dr. Watson and me. And unfortunately, he won. I pushed Dustin out all by myself.

And again the ultrasound at Watson's office was totally wrong. Two weeks ago, it predicted that Dustin would be around eight and a half pounds. No. He was nine pounds twelve ounces. Just like his birthday. But he was healthy. Nothing broken. And the best part was I was bottle feeding. After what had happened to Chaz, not one person asked me if I was breastfeeding. They all knew I was bottle feeding and had already stocked me up. The ones that didn't know me must have been informed about me because not one person asked, "Breast or bottle?" And I thoroughly appreciated that. Either way, I never once considered breastfeeding. I really liked the fact that they didn't ask me or try to persuade me differently. I was now the poster child for bottle feeding. Or at least I could have been. And ironically, this time, I did not get offered any free cases of formula as I had before. See, God has a sense of humor. Or at least that's how I felt.

BOTOX

Chaz's hamstrings were super tight. He couldn't straighten his legs out for nothing. He was always kind of bent at the knees, despite all of his physical therapy. He tended to scissor when held up in a standing position. And he was always in a frog-legged position when he laid down. But his hamstrings had gotten so tight that Dr. Stephens decided that we needed to "do something about it."

And since Botox had recently been approved for use in children, as a way to reduce tightness in the hamstrings, we followed her recommendation. They gave us some type of cream that was to be rubbed onto Chaz's legs and then plastic wrap placed over that to allow the cream to "sink in." The idea was to numb the area in which the injections were to be given.

So in February, Chaz went for his first set of injections. I watched as Dr. Stephens used very little medication to inject my son multiple times into his hamstrings and his adductor muscles. I bet she injected him at least ten times with what appeared to me to be the same amount of Botox as I had pumped breast milk in the hospital in 1993. It was probably even less than that. And he cried. His dad and I held his hand and talked to him the whole time, stroking his head. But let's be honest, that didn't take away the pain. I bet those injections felt like tiny little bee stings.

Dr. Stephens must have been used to children crying like that, but I wasn't. I was used to Chaz crying. God knows he'd done enough of it over the years. But it wasn't crying due to induced pain. Then there was the guilt of knowing that I had volunteered him to come in here and get those dang injections.

But Dr. Stephens promised us that this would loosen up his extremely tight hamstrings, mixed with his physical therapy sessions.

And since the Botox was to magically make his hamstrings looser, Dr. Stephens also set us up for a March appointment for him to have serial casts for the new bilateral ankle-foot orthosis, especially since his had been refabricated many times due to poor fit. Chaz's ankles were turning, and it was blamed on the hamstrings.

When May rolled around, it was time for Chaz to have his IEP reevaluated. I hated IEP meetings for several reasons. One, the school personnel seemed to suck the individual right out of the individual education plan. And two, these meetings were like walking into a courtroom with you as the accused. You had your jury, which consisted of his physical, occupational, and speech therapists. His school caseworker. A head special education personnel for the local school system. Though this person was there to make sure the I's were dotted and the T's were crossed, the truth was they acted as a gatekeeper. Their famous words were, "No. We can't do that." Or, "No. We can't allow that." Another favorite was, "We don't have the funding for that."

The therapists each gave their "up to the minute news" on Chaz. First was the occupational therapist. He could brush his teeth with minimal assistance. He bathed sitting up in a bath chair. He fed himself with his fingers, cup, and a spoon. He self-propelled his wheelchair. Then came the speech therapist. His speech was in the two-year seven-month range, producing four- to five-word sentences. His cognitive skills were in the thirty-two to thirty-six-month range, and his developmental level was twelve to twenty-four months. His physical therapist noted that he had a gait trainer and took steps to ten feet maximum. He sat with support, and he could also sit without support using his upper extremities for weight bearing in a tripod position.

With the Botox failing to work, Dr. Stephens recommended hamstring lengthenings, a fancy name for muscle-tendon releases. Her office sent us over to Dr. Owen, a pediatric orthopedic surgeon. It wasn't supposed to be a long procedure. Nor was it supposed to hurt terribly. And the only real inconvenience, we were told, was that Chaz would have to wear these leg splints for a couple of weeks, to keep his legs straight, in order to make the surgery a success.

And we were told that if that didn't work, then there was another option. But the doctor had only performed six of them so far, and they were tracking the progress of each child to see if it was viable for other children. Dr. Stephens said she'd let us know during our next visit.

We did inquire as to what the procedure was. It was called a Selective Dorsal Rhizotomy. And it would be performed by a neurosurgeon.

With Chaz being seizure-free since 1994 and drug-free since April 1996, I was kind of afraid of adding any additional surgeries or medications. But here we had Dr. Stephens, Dr. Owen, even Dr. Price, saying, "Yes, yes, Chaz needs this." Not just to improve his quality of life. That's where they get you. That quality of life statement gets you every time. But it would also assist him in his journey to one day walk.

So I did what I always did when it came down to making these kinds of life-changing decisions, and I contacted Dr. White and asked him what he thought. He was going to be my go-to guru as long as he was Chaz's neurologist. You would never know that at one time I hated the man. Dr. White knew all of the players in this particular game. He knew the six other children. He knew the doctor, and he was well aware of the surgery. And, of course, he knew everything there was to know about Chaz. Literally.

He told us that Dr. Northam, from his office, was also involved in those surgeries, as it was a two-person operation. Neurologist and neurosurgeon. So when he said that he felt like it was a good decision, we came onboard with the idea, too. But when the surgery was described to us, we couldn't help but have our doubts. Just one wrong move, one wrong decision, one wrong choice, and our son could be paralyzed for life. In our eyes, this was a thousand times worse than how he was now.

So while Dr. Northam sat at a machine looking at all of the nerves in Chaz's spine, Dr. Price would touch one of the nerves and they would see if it reacted correctly or not. If it didn't, then it would be cut. Severed forever. Never to be put back together. Forever severed. I cannot stress the forever part.

So if Dr. Price touched nerve L4 and biology said that it was supposed to make you move your toe and instead you move your right pinkie finger, then the nerve would be cut because it was considered damaged. Or say nothing happened when he touched that nerve. Then that too meant that it needed to be cut. And let me tell you, there are thousands of nerves in the spine because each nerve root has numerous rootlets connected to it.

Even though we had Dr. White's blessing, I was still skeptical. I didn't want my son to be paralyzed. He had gone through enough hell as it was. Yes, he couldn't do everything that kids his age could, but he was able to do enough to make himself happy. And that made us happy. So deep down, I was really on the fence about this one.

And of course Frank was with everyone else. The medical professionals. I wasn't so sure. I was waiting for my mommy instinct to kick in and give me its blessing. And so far that hadn't happened yet, even though Dr. White was on board. So I agreed to meet with Dr. Price and see where we go from there.

NEW AGE THERAPY:
SELECTIVE DORSAL
RHIZOTOMY

After recommendations from Chaz's therapists, Dr. Stephens informed Dr. Price that it would be a good idea to see Chaz as a possible candidate for a Selective Dorsal Rhizotomy. It took me lots of practice to be able to say "rhizotomy" where it came out sounding even remotely like a real word. So after reading all of the therapeutic and rehabilitation notes he received, Dr. Price decided to evaluate Chaz himself. Of course when I got that phone call to set up an appointment, that's when a little fear set in. So I called Dr. White, as I did with every major decision regarding Chaz, and asked what he knew about the procedure, the surgeon, and what about Chaz having the rhizotomy. He reminded me that one of the neurologists from their office was part of the surgical team that worked with Dr. Price on the rhizotomies. Of course, Dr. Price had only performed six of them so far. On children, that is. I never asked if he performed them on adults. I think a part of me didn't want to know. Even if I did, I wouldn't be able to get past the number six. This terrified me even more. Even though I had Dr. White's blessing.

So Frank and I spent many hours discussing the pros and cons of the surgery. But more so we discussed how comfortable we felt with putting Chaz through a surgery that technically wasn't necessary. In other words, he didn't have some life-threatening condition that required a rhizotomy. Even though the surgery would assist in the symptoms of his cerebral palsy, he would have that for the rest of his life. He had been through so much so far that it just didn't seem right to go through with something like this. Then again, it was supposed to increase his ability to sit, stand, and eventually walk. It would prevent the need for Botox and hamstring lengthenings. But it was still a big question of *what if.* The rhizotomy involved Dr. Price messing around, surgically, in Chaz's spine, which at this point in his life was just fine. Just one wrong slip and Chaz would be in worse shape than he was now. Again, like I said, it wasn't a life-threatening surgery. It was voluntary.

The road to the decision of whether to do the rhizotomy was long. It took months. I interviewed some of the other six families. I talked to adults that had had neurosurgery with Dr. Price. I talked to everyone I possibly could before I felt comfortable saying yes. Even though Frank was on board quicker than me, he felt more comfortable with his decision after all of my investigation.

I just couldn't blindly agree to something a doctor suggested. Not anymore. I'd been down that route before, and I wasn't about to go back. Again, I repeat, I don't care how many letters are behind your name. I need to know more. You need to earn my respect. And Dr. Price did by giving me his blessing when I said that I needed to talk to some people first. It also helped that he didn't have this godly air about him that a lot of doctors, especially surgeons, tend to get. That played a huge role in my decision.

So I finally called Dr. Price in late summer and said, "Okay, let's do this."

Since the procedure required a ton of therapy afterward, this included an agreement that Chaz would stay in the hospital for thirty days, where he would receive therapies, especially physical therapy, for six hours a day.

That's not including the need to wear Dynasplints on his legs at night to keep them stretched out. It would also mean schooling while he was in the hospital. Basically, for eight hours a day, Chaz would have people working with every part of his body to help loosen him up right after surgery. This was to get the most out of the surgery. And then he would need physical therapy three times a week as outpatient once he left the hospital.

So the procedure was scheduled for fall. Frank told work that he needed to work certain hours during those thirty days because he would have to take care of Dustin while I was in the hospital with Chaz. My grandmother agreed to come down for two weeks to take care of Dustin while all of this was going on. And for the other two weeks, Dustin would take Chaz's place in preschool. And Frank would stay with Chaz at the hospital during his two days off a week. Only he didn't ever have two days off in a row. But we had to do it this way since we couldn't afford for Frank to take off. And I needed to see Dustin so he wouldn't think that I'd abandoned him. And because this was supposed to be a miracle surgery for Chaz.

I contacted Chaplain Daisy and gave her the details of Chaz's next visit to children's hospital. We were going to need her support through this. She had become my on-land link to God. It was just so much more comforting to me when I heard her pray to God on Chaz's behalf. I couldn't help but feel that she had a little more power in that department than I did. It's not that God and I were on the outs at the moment, but our relationship had been a bit peculiar after Chaz's stroke. I was still in a love/hate relationship with him. But to be honest, I hadn't really bothered him much lately. We were okay, as far as I was concerned.

But a chaplain had a direct link to him. He took her words seriously. I'm not saying that he didn't take mine seriously, but I just feel that with her being a third party, she had a little more clout. Plus, that was her job as chaplain at a children's hospital. She was to pray for the children and their families. So she and God had an understanding. And I respected that. And I relied on that. I counted on that.

Again, children's hospital tried to help us out as much as possible with free parking and meal tickets during our stay. And they had various services for Chaz. He was visited by Santa Claus and by therapy dogs. I love therapy dogs. I think every hospital needs more of them. Nothing is greater than getting a visit from a therapy dog when you're lying in a hospital bed. At least not to me, there isn't.

The morning of Chaz's surgery, we were told that it would take six to eight hours. As we waited, we talked to other parents in the surgery waiting room. One poor mom and dad were waiting for their son to have heart surgery. He was twelve, and he had basically had one surgery a year since he was born. So they were old pros at this. They were looking at a twelve-hour wait. So as we came and went during the day, we watched as families came and went. When dinner time hit, around six o'clock, there was only a handful of us left. We had been there more than eight hours already. And of course, that meant that heart mom was still waiting, too. Chaz came out shy of ten hours.

By time Chaz was in recovery, the only person left in the surgery waiting room was heart mom. Since Chaz was going to the PICU after recovery, I couldn't stay with him. But I did stay with him until visiting hours were over. I stopped by to see heart mom. It had now been sixteen hours, and she was still waiting. But she assured me that the surgery nurse was assuring her that everything was fine. At that moment, I prayed for her and her son. It was no longer about us.

I took Frank home, and then I came back to the hospital. I couldn't sleep, so I figured I could sit with Chaz for a few hours. Frank thought I was nuts. He said that I would be better off sleeping at home. But I couldn't help it; I felt that I had to be there, just in case he woke up and I wasn't. I at least wanted to be in the vicinity where I could make it there in a matter of moments if he called out for me.

His PICU nurse took pity on me and gave me a reclining chair to sit in, and she brought me a TV/VCR combo on wheels. I remember her saying, "You're going to love this movie." She popped in *A Field of Dreams* starring Kevin Costner. I saw the opening title and credits, and that was about it. I slept through the entire film. I woke up when the ending credits were rolling. The nurse asked me how I liked the movie. I thought this was a strange question. Wasn't she standing there with my son the entire time? Even if she wasn't, wasn't there some other nurse standing there? I was confused by that, but I told her the truth, I missed it all. Then I thanked her and said that I thought I'd head on home now.

She did have someone show me to a cot room where she said that some of the interns slept when they needed a break. But I didn't feel very comfortable there. I didn't feel safe. There was no one there, and it was at the end of a very long, dark hall. And I was a woman on very little to no sleep. So I drove home.

The next day when we visited, Chaz was fussing a little. I asked the nurse if he could have some more pain medication. She put in the order. Then the head nurse came over and said, "That's Dr. Price's patient." They looked at each other, and then they both disappeared. I was more than curious as to what was going on. So I asked. I was told that they had to contact Dr. Price directly. He didn't like the PICU doctors making decisions on his patients when he wasn't there. And apparently, all of these people were terrified of him. I wasn't sure if that was a good thing or not.

I was on the fence about this because I had had the misfortune of interacting with god-like doctors. And I felt like, hey, it's Saturday, if you're not here, then the PICU doctors should be able to see that a child's in pain and give him medication. A few minutes later, they gave him some pain medication, and Dr. Price showed up a couple of hours later to evaluate Chaz, read his chart, and talk to us about him. I guess he wrote some different orders to assist with the addition of more pain medication when he was not present. I'm really not sure what happened. But we didn't have that problem again. Though I did overhear the words, "He's Dr. Price's patient," several times during the rest of the weekend.

Come Monday, Chaz was released from the PICU and sent to the rehabilitation floor. Dr. Price informed us that Dr. Stephens would now be checking on him daily but if we had questions about something to please contact him. And he added that Dr. Stephens would keep him informed as needed. I believe these two were sharing notes on everything to do with these seven rhizotomy kids. They had to keep track of how the surgery worked on these kids so they could make more informed decisions. But then again, one couldn't help but think of the bias in that particular sharing of information.

I'm not saying that they were not on the up and up. The problem was I pretty much doubted everyone in the medical field to some degree. All but Dr. White. Doesn't make sense, does it? The person I used to hate was the one person that I relied on for information and guidance.

I actually wished that everyone that had a child with special healthcare challenges had a Dr. White to rely on. And if I could have him there until Chaz turned twenty-one, then I'd be more than grateful.

Twenty-one appeared to be the cut off for everything. For school services, for being a patient in Dr. White's office. Even for most of children's hospital's services.

On Monday, Chaz was taken to a private room with a private bath and a window seat that doubled as a bed for parents. The hospital had completely redone their rehab floor, and now they had these little pods. There were five rooms to a pod, and there was a nurses' desk in the middle of them. So whenever we needed a nurse, all we had to do was open our door and there one would be.

We were set up for the day with towels, washrags, bedding, and extra bedding for Chaz and me, along with a small kit of shampoo, soap, toothpaste, and a toothbrush. Everything else I brought from home for my stay. There were dry erase boards on each child's door that consisted of their daily schedule. And there was another board with their name and any allergies that they had. The schedule was posted so not only would the nurses know where each patient was during the day but so the patient and his family members would know and schedule visitations accordingly. Chaz's day was jam-packed with therapies, as promised.

I figured that since we were getting settled into his room, which included signing papers to attend school at the hospital and for the use of various rehab equipment, that we'd get the day off. But nope, later that afternoon, there came his physical therapist. He was going to the playroom to see if he would sit up, roll over, and crawl.

My head was spinning. He just had surgery on Friday, and there we were on Monday asking him to move around. Were they crazy? But this was what we'd signed up for. And imagine my surprise when Chaz sat up, unsupported, for the very first time in his life. I got so excited that when I shrieked, he almost fell over. So the therapist ran and got an instant camera so I could have a photo to mark the occasion.

The rhizotomy appeared to have aided Chaz in sitting up straight. By being able to extend his upper torso fully, he was also starting to talk more. We were told that by his being able to extend his upper torso, he was able to get more breath into his lungs. This meant that he could speak more than two to four words at a time before taking in long breaths. It was remarkable, really. From that day on, he hasn't stopped talking. And talking. And talking.

I felt like I was beginning to understand what it meant to have a "normal child." Only I don't like that word, normal. Is anybody really normal? I don't think so. We all have something dark or weird in our past or abnormal or different going on in our lives and in our minds. We all have some sort of medical problem or mental issue, even if it's something like ADD, or ADHD, or depression and anxiety.

RHIZOTOMY, POST-OP,
AND THE FAMILY

And here my normal child was going to have a not-so-normal life for the next couple of weeks. Frank would drop him off at preschool, where he would spend six hours with special needs children, most of them older than him. But Dustin was a trooper, so I wasn't too worried about him.

He would get to do normal preschool stuff while he was there. The only difference would be that some of the kids there were in wheelchairs or walkers and some didn't speak. Other than that, he would play on the playground, go on field trips, eat lunch, have snacks, color, and make things while he learned. To this day, I don't know how to tell them thank you for that. There is one person in particular that I want to thank, and I hope she knows who she is. Then again, I thank everyone from the cafeteria staff to the therapists, and the administration, for helping us out with Chaz during that trying time.

While Chaz was busy getting his torso, arms, and legs stretched out several hours a day, Dustin would get to see what preschool was like. I was torn between the two. I'm not sure who I felt sorrier for. Chaz was a social butterfly, so I know that he didn't mind preschool, but Dustin I wasn't so sure about. Dustin was a homebody. An independent homebody. Plus, he thought he was part dog. He hung onto Shaggy and Wolf as if they were his playmates. I think that's because Chaz couldn't actually do a lot of wrestling and hugging and touching since he was always in his wheelchair or prone stander. Chaz always had a metal device attached to his person at all times unless he was rolling around on the floor. And even then Dustin didn't mess with him too much. Part of me wonders if he was afraid he'd hurt him.

Either way, they bonded. Just maybe not as much as Dustin and the dogs. And by now Shaggy was seven years old if the SPCA gave us the correct age when we adopted him in 1990. And Wolf was five years old. So they were still quite young enough to entertain a two-year-old. Though at times I felt sorry for them. Dustin could be rough. I nicknamed him the Dust Cloud and the Dust-a-Bust. He was always running around. That kid had energy, the kind of energy that I wasn't used to. You have to remember that I had spent the past four years with a child that wasn't able to run around. He could roll around once he got in his wheelchair, but that wasn't even close to what Dustin could do. Dustin could run laps around Chaz. So he kept me thin by always having to keep up with him. And this made Chaz laugh. So I guess it was all worth it. In a very tiring way, of course.

It's near impossible to have a toddler and not lose weight. They're like these toys that you wind up. Once they get going, they don't stop until whatever wound them up stops. Then it's a quick nap. And then they're up and back at it again.

And when Frank was at work on the weekends, I would put on some old albums, and me and the kids would dance together. We'd even get Shaggy and Wolf into the groove. Dustin and Chaz loved to see the dogs dance with us. And I was losing calories and didn't even know it. I was concentrating on having lasting fun memories with my kids.

So the first two weeks went by rather smoothly considering all of the changes each of us had experienced. Dustin liked preschool for the first few days. But then he started to miss us, his blue blankie, and the dogs. So he started taking his blue blankie with him after that. And this helped his anxiety a whole lot. But it still wasn't the same. He wasn't seeing me as much as he was used to. And he was not used to his dad being his primary caregiver. They would come over after school and hang out until visiting hours were over. And some evenings, Frank and I would switch out. Dustin did enjoy playing with all of the toys and devices that Chaz had in his room and in the hospital. One afternoon, this couple was going around visiting children on the rehab floor and handing out new toys. When they saw Dustin and heard his caregiver story for the month, they gave him a toy, too, and he beamed with excitement. But nothing could ever take the place of that little blue blankie.

Since Frank had arranged with his work to drop Dustin off and to pick him up each afternoon during the week, that meant that he had weekends off. So for those first two weekends, he stayed with Chaz, and I got to be home with Dustin. At first, Dustin was afraid to fall asleep, fearful that I would end up back at the hospital when he woke up, and that broke my heart. I felt like the worst mother in the world. So I had done a lot more praying than usual. I not only needed God's help to get each of us through this but I needed reassurance that what I was doing was the right thing. Only by now, there was no going back. What was done was done. Now we just had to ride this particular wave till the end. And it was exhausting, frightening, and heartbreaking.

Chaz was so worn out daily that by time dinner showed up, he was too tired to eat. And not eating in a hospital is a no-no, in case you didn't know. So Frank and I got where we would do one of three things. One, we would eat part of his food if it was edible, which wasn't often. Two, we would dump some of it in the bottom of the trashcan and cover it with some dirty diapers. Or three, we would move the food around so it looked like he ate something. Because every time Chaz was given something to eat or drink, we had to tell the nurse approximately how much he had eaten and drank. You may call this lying; we called this surviving. We even brought snacks from home for him to eat, things we knew he'd most likely eat. But there were no guarantees when it came to what Chaz would eat and when. Besides, Chaz had never been a very big eater. He would eat till he was full and that's all anyone could ask. Besides, doctors and nurses had these norms that they expected of all children. But as we have learned from children with special healthcare needs, each child is different. So whereas little Tommie might eat a whole hospital tray of dinner, little Scottie might only eat three-quarters of his. And then comes little Chaz, who would only eat half of his.

And whenever he didn't drink what the nurses considered was enough, the nurses would bring him various juices and ice cream. No matter what I said, no one believed me when I said that Chaz wasn't an ice cream eater. They would offer him popsicles and cups of ice cream in all sorts of flavors, and he would always say no. He just wasn't an ice cream eater. Of course, the nurses, even his doctor, found that unusual. Eventually, I got tired of them asking and him rejecting, and I told them to give it here, he would at least try it. And that's what he did. He took one wooden spoonful, and that was it. The nurse watched. She couldn't believe it. A kid that actually didn't like ice cream. I had two of them. Dustin wasn't a big fan, either. And the irony was their dad ate ice cream every night. He went through half a gallon in a few days. So it's not like my kids were not offered ice cream or told that they couldn't have it, it was readily available, and still, they didn't want it.

One thing I did like about the rehab floor was that the same nurses worked for the same pods regularly. So it was rare that you got someone that you hadn't already had. But if someone got sick, then you'd always get this one nurse that came in there as if she was an admiral and you were a recruit, and you'd have to set her straight. These would typically be the people that treated you as if you did not have experience in taking care of your own child. And most of the time, I could bite my lip and let things slide, especially if it was an evening shift nurse. Because you didn't really see those evening shift nurses much. But then again, you always got that one, that one that insisted on coming into the room in the middle of the night and waking your child up to ask how he was doing. I hated this, and Chaz did, too. When this happened, Chaz would give one of two responses: "I need you to leave me alone," or "Sleep. I need to sleep." One time it got to be so bad with this one nurse that I made a sign and put it on his hospital room door that said, "Do not disturb." When that got ignored, I told his rehab doctor. I wanted something in the chart that said that they would not wake him up. They could check on him, sure, but do not wake him up to ask him if he needs something. I found that to be asinine. That's why they have that little call button in the shape of a nurse's hat.

For someone that didn't have a lot of experience with hospitals or medical people, I was getting a full-blown crash course with Chaz. And with each hospital stay, I got more and more confident and assertive in his care. Yes, I could be a bitch. I'm sure if you pull his medical records, you will read that in several places. But when you're a mom, you do what you have to do. And if you're a mom that has already been failed by healthcare professionals, then it becomes part of your DNA. I would tell people that. My DNA had forever been altered. This shy, quiet, nonconversational girl became a woman that wasn't afraid of any doctor, nurse, therapist, or surgeon. I honestly didn't care about your experience in the field or the letters behind your name. You know that old saying, "Fool me once shame on you, fool me twice shame on me." Well, my slogan was, "Fool me once, shame on you, and you can mark my word that there will be no fooling me twice." Okay, so it's not the prettiest slogan, but I'm sure that moms and other caregivers out there understand what I'm saying.

RHIZOTOMY AND
THERAPY FROM HELL
AND THE FAMILY

After we survived the first two weeks, we were gearing up for a change in our remaining two weeks. For one, my dad would be coming down for a week. He was bringing my grandma, who would be staying for two weeks. My dad was going to do some work around the house while he was there. Frank and I owned a HUD home, so it was constantly under repair and in need of repair. No, it wasn't necessarily the prettiest house that you'd see on the street, but it was our home. And we had lived there since March of 1994. And best of all, Dustin had been born in that house. So it was no longer just a house, it was our home.

So my dad was going to do a few little things around the house while Grandma took care of Dustin and helped out while Frank was at work. The weather was great, sunny, but not too hot, so it was nice when she hung clothes out to dry. I loved the smell of clothes laundered outside. And she was doing some cooking as well. Only I didn't get to really benefit from this since I was the primary one holed up in the hospital.

It was during this time that Frank got his first case of vertigo. He missed work, couldn't get out of bed, and was throwing up. And because of this, he was unable to come to the hospital to relieve me. My dad felt bad for me, so he did come over and spend about five hours one afternoon so I could just leave. I had been at the hospital for ten days and nights, and I needed a change of scenery because I was going cuckoo. I had already complained to anyone that would listen and even a few that didn't. My dad let me borrow his Jeep, and I did fun things like go to the grocery store and walk around, dreaming of what I could buy if one, I had money, and two, if I was actually going to be home to enjoy any of it. Then I went into a Dollar Tree and bought a couple of books. I had already read everything that I owned, and I had managed to fill up two journals so far. Then I grabbed a burger and fries at Doumar's, with an ice cold Coke. I sat in the Jeep since Doumar's had a car hop. And then I tried to relax.

Dustin had managed to get sick around the same time that Frank did, so my poor grandma had her hands full. I stopped by the house to see Dustin, but he felt so miserable that he took one look at me and then rolled over in his bed and went back to sleep. So I hurried back to the hospital to relieve my dad, who was going back to my house to help my grandma out. Grandma was trying to get them healthy with soup and fluids.

So as I headed back to the hospital, I was stuck between a rock and a hard place. Again. I was sad that Dustin and Frank were sick. But I was also sad that I was going stir crazy. And I swear I think I did and just don't remember it. I remember taking Chaz for walks around the hospital. We even went outside. We hit the gift shop. We sat in the cafeteria. We watched the ambulances come and go from not only children's hospital but from the general hospital beside us. Chaz played video games and watched TV. Weekends were boring as hell. And the chaplains were on call for emergencies only. This felt like an emergency, but I knew better. I bothered them enough during the week.

By week three, I begged his doctor to let us go home, for a day if nothing else. She finally granted our wish, and Chaz was able to go home that Sunday for a few hours. Five hours, to be exact. Let me tell you, it went by very quickly. We had a turkey dinner to celebrate the occasion. The dogs were glad to see us. Even though I had been home a few times over the past three weeks, they hadn't seen Chaz at all. So here they were again wondering what happened to one of our family members while wondering why we had added guests. But they were being fed and watered, so it was all good. We had a dog door for them to go outside and potty whenever they felt like it. And you have no idea how wonderful that is. It is such a relief when you know that you don't have to get up at a certain time and go outside in the whatever weather and take your dog for a walk or to let him out. So Shaggy and Wolf were pretty much low maintenance.

When it came time for Chaz and me to return to the hospital, it wasn't too bad. After all, we'd had a nice break. And we knew that our time at the hospital was coming to an end soon.

So the next week at the hospital flew by. It was chaotic, though, so when evening hit, Chaz and I were exhausted, him physically and me mentally. His routine hadn't changed. It was still filled with hours of therapy. I was meeting new people and representatives every day. Sometimes more than one a day. I had to sign off on equipment that had been ordered for Chaz to use instead of using the hospital's. These would be things that he would take home, and I had to make sure that he had to use them regularly. I signed so many papers that week that I felt like I had signed away my house. His hospital schooling would turn over to homeschooling through the public school system. He would have physical therapy three times a week, occupational therapy twice a week, and speech therapy once a week. And guess who would be carting him to all of this? Yes, me. And Dustin, of course. He would have to tag along. This kid was going to need a medal for attending all of these appointments while remaining as still and quiet as possible. Again, we were all in for changes.

Chaz was allowed to go home one more time for a respite from the hospital. And we prayed that he'd be going home two to three days after that. Unfortunately, we couldn't leave until everything was in place. Thank God I had purchased that calendar from the Dollar Tree because there was a ton of appointments that I had to keep up with. And each day we were adding more and more appointments. And my folder of paperwork from this thirty-day hospital visit was mounting daily.

Our second respite was fun. We all ate in the living room while watching the Washington Redskins play. Frank was a huge fan, and he had already converted Chaz. Dustin wasn't quite on board yet. Me, I was more player loyal. I was fond of Jim Kelley and John Elway. But we were all together, and that's all that mattered.

When Chaz and I returned to the hospital, we said a prayer, begging God to please let us go home in a couple of days. And God answered us with a huge yes, two days later. Of course, it took us several trips. Chaz had so much equipment that we couldn't fit it all in one vehicle. And sadly, Chaz and I were the last things to leave the hospital that day. Frank took the equipment with him. He made two trips before coming back to get us.

Chaz and I were grateful to be home. Again. At home, he was happy and relaxed. And tomorrow it would all start all over again. By that, I meant that all of those outpatient therapies would begin. But at least we could sleep in our own beds. And Chaz wouldn't have his food and beverage intake monitored. And better yet, no one was going to wake him up in the middle of the night to ask if he needed anything. Home sweet home.

WHAT IF WITH DUSTIN
AND GRANDMA

I remember my grandmother coming down for the birth of my second son, Dustin, in 1995. I was formula feeding Dustin, and my grandmother was a great help in recognizing that his crying was for more food and not crying because he was fussy. Even though I was feeding him the recommended amount of formula, with him being a big baby, the recommended amount wasn't enough for him. My grandmother walked into the bedroom on our first night home and said, "Feed him until he doesn't cry anymore." That was advice that I used with Dustin from then on. And guess what? He rarely ever cried.

I can't help but wonder what would have happened to Chaz if she had been there. Do I wish that I had asked her to come and stay with me for a week or two after Chaz was born? That answer is simply hell yeah! I know that she would have been the one person that would have saved Chaz's life. Then again, I'm a firm believer, thanks to Chaz, that everything happens for a reason. And I truly believe that Chaz's stroke, brain hemorrhage, and seizures due to dehydration, because of my inability to produce breast milk, was meant to happen to save many more lives over the years to come.

I have a picture of my grandmother sitting in my hospital room holding Dustin. She is grinning ear to ear. This was the first time that she'd ever gotten to hold one of her great-grandchildren on the day that they were born. Now, my grandmother had two distinct bonds with both of my children. And Dustin is the only grandchild that my dad got to hold on the day that he was born. I hear that that is something that one doesn't forget.

TURNING OF THE LEG

Even though Chaz had endured physical therapy once a week since he was only three months old, had worn AFOs daily, and was seeing a rehabilitation doctor regularly, his orthopedic problems were far from over.

It was brought to our attention that while trying to stand, Chaz's hips were popping out of joint. I wondered if it was all that therapy and their twisting and pulling of his legs throughout the years that had ruined his hips. The only way to solve this problem was for him to have hip reconstruction surgery. An osteotomy. This osteotomy was supposed to help correct the malposition of his hip joints. Dr. Stephens was on board, and so we were off to see Dr. St. Plow.

I wasn't a huge fan of St. Plow. He looked at Chaz as if he was a bag of bones as opposed to a human being. When he walked into the room, he would ignore Chaz until it was time to examine him. And when he talked, he talked about the procedure as if he was going to perform it on someone that was in a coma or something. He didn't view Chaz a child, or as a child that had feelings, or as someone that deserved to be part of the conversation about his body.

Then again, he barely spoke to us when he entered the room. He also wasn't one to look you in your eyes when he spoke. And when he did, it was all medical terminology. I don't think he knew how to interact with people. He appeared to hide behind his profession. And when he spoke, it was the short version. So you always had to ask a bunch of follow-up questions. And when you questioned him, he tended to get upset. Not exactly in a *how dare you question me* way. It was more of a *why didn't you pay attention the first time* kind of way. He made you feel like you were bothering him. And if you couldn't keep up, that was your problem. Not his.

He had been referred to us by Dr. Stephens. And several parents that I spoke to spoke very highly of him. They were praising him for the work he had performed on their children. But each one did tell me that his bedside manner left something to be desired. So I weighed my options, and I chose to stay with him because of the good work I was told he did. Even though his bedside manner needed extensive help.

Even though Chaz was with us during the visit to St. Plow's office, he had questions for us. Hell, I had questions for us. But I did my best to answer them the best I could. He was scared, and I knew it. But like with every surgery before it, we prayed. We prayed that God would send us a sign. We needed to know that we were making the right decision and had the right people in place. That's not to say that I always agreed with God.

It had been eight years now, and God and I were still not on the best of terms. I still questioned him and his signs. But that didn't stop me from relying on him. I prayed to God almost every day. Sometimes more than once a day. Sometimes I just needed to know that he was still there and hadn't abandoned me. I was, after all, not the easiest person to get along with. One thing I knew for sure was that even if he didn't love me anymore, I knew he loved Chaz. And it was during these surgeries that I needed him to show me that. I needed the reassurance that he was going to take care of Chaz no matter what. And I couldn't help but wonder if God's love for Chaz was shaped in any way by my love for him. Did God punish the child for the sins of the parent? My mom thought so. And unfortunately, I honestly don't think that little tidbit will ever leave my memory.

But it was the parents that I had spoken to that was my sign in this case. And maybe that was wrong. I'm not sure. St. Plow had done hundreds of these surgeries, successfully. So there was nothing to worry about. Right?

A couple of days before the hip reconstruction osteotomy, Chaz had to see St. Plow to make sure that he was cleared for surgery. St. Plow was, as always, in a hurry. I had written down a few questions that I wanted to ask him. And I could tell that I was bothering him. Apparently, he had somewhere else he wanted or needed to be. But this was my son, and I wanted some answers.

That morning I pulled Chaz's hospital bedding out of the dryer. Since he was allergic to the hospital's strong detergent, we were given bedding ahead of time to take home and wash. I had my piece of paper reminding me to remind them that Chaz broke out to the plastic, durable tapes and that only paper tape would do and that he required a latex-free operating room. And let's not forget his allergies. Penicillin, sulfur, and latex. Even though I could quote most of this in my sleep, I always brought it with me because I never knew who may need a reminder. Besides, every doctor and nurse that interacted with Chaz would always ask what we'd already answered. I felt like they skimmed charts but not actually read them.

I may sound cynical, but do you blame me? After what Chaz went through from birth to now, you better believe that I am cynical. I honestly didn't know any other way to be. My son was already disabled from medical people that didn't pay attention, so now I demanded that everyone pay attention.

ORTHOPEDIC GURU
BECOMES A MAJOR
PLAYER

C haz first went to the University of Virginia, otherwise known as UVA, and the pediatric orthopedic clinic at the age of eight. He was sent there, as the referral read, because he had an attempted osteotomy for correcting the malposition of his hip joints, and this had failed and required revision surgery. In August of 2001, he underwent successful revision surgery on the left hip and had the hardware removed from the right hip. In December of 2001 or January of 2002, he sustained a right femur fracture when his leg was twisted. He does have weaker bones as a result of the fact that he does not ambulate. This femur fracture was treated with internal rods, which were ultimately removed.

After Dr. St. Plow decided to turn my son's leg around, I decided it was time to go elsewhere for care. We had watched Chaz go through hell this past year, and it was time that I stepped in and stepped in strong and did some advocating.

After hearing that Dr. St. Plow wanted to break Chaz's thigh bone and just turn the bottom half of his leg from the break down, I said enough was enough. So I did what I figured was the best course of action. I took to the internet and started searching for the best pediatric orthopedic surgeons in the United States. I cast a wide net, even though I preferred someone on the East Coast. And I looked at *USA Today*'s best doctors list to find out more about these men. And they were all men. It was sad that I didn't come across a woman. You would think that in this day and age that there would have been at least one woman on the list, not that I was looking for a woman. But as a woman, I noticed.

I decided on three doctors and emailed them a condensed version of events. I didn't want to overwhelm them with a three-page email, so I sent them what I considered to be the most important information, which in the back of my head was that I was in no way going to leave Chaz's femur turned to the side for the rest of his life. It had already been that way for six-plus months, and that was way too long.

It was December, so I knew that getting a reply might take a while. I just assumed that doctors took long Christmas vacations. So imagine my surprise when a doctor from the University of Virginia got back with me immediately. He wanted to meet Chaz. So I scheduled an appointment right away. But a new patient appointment took longer than I had hoped. And if he could fix Chaz's femur problem, then we'd only have to travel for two hours. I took it as a sign. Sadly, none of the other doctors got back with me. That did bother me quite a bit. I couldn't help but wonder how you could be a great healer but not have great communication skills. But I put aside my animosity and prayed that our UVA doctor would be the one.

As we all know, UVA is a teaching hospital, just like children's hospital, but on a much larger scale. They also have a larger hospital with state-of-the-art equipment. And their doctors are up on the latest technologies. They even have the Kluge Center. It appeared that this was going to work out. But I didn't want to get my hopes up too high. But I couldn't help it. After what Chaz had gone through that year, I couldn't help but feel better thinking that a change was going to happen. And soon.

When we arrived at the Kluge Center, they definitely had their ducks in a row. We walked in, signed in, and boom, boom, boom, we were taken to the back before we had a chance to enjoy the playroom. There was this colorful lady seated at a craft table. She was wearing just about every color imaginable, she was very vocal, and she reminded me of an older Cyndi Lauper. Dustin, loving art and crafts, decided he would stay and make things with her while we went to the "boring doctor's meeting," as he put it. She said that was fine, parents did it all the time. And there were therapy dogs to pet. Chaz wanted to stay there, too, but that wasn't an option for him. So we told him that he could make something after he saw the doctor.

They sent Chaz upstairs for x-rays. They preferred to do their own, right there in their center, even though we had brought ours with us. And I had signed a release allowing Dr. Abel to view anything that children's hospital had on Chaz. He was granted full access.

Once we were back downstairs, we were taken back to the room where we were going to meet the head of pediatric orthopedic surgery at UVA. Of course, the first person to enter the room was an intern. But he was shortly followed by Dr. Abel himself. He had already looked at the images that children's hospital provided, he had read the doctor's notes, and he had looked at the x-rays they took not twenty minutes before. He had an answer. The best part was, when he entered the room, he immediately held his hand out for Chaz first to shake and introduced himself to Chaz. And he asked him how he was doing. He would always greet us second. This gave him huge points in my book. Because I had always felt like Dr. St. Plow looked at my son as a skeleton and not a person.

Dr. Abel then told us that yes, sometimes they had to turn the femur around when a staph infection had set in that was causing the ball at the top of the femur that fit into the hip socket to be soft. And even though it was something that they sometimes did, they preferred not to unless they had to. In this case, it was probably a good idea.

The first thing he wanted to do was wait a couple of months for some more healing to take place. Then he would go in and remove the hip osteotomy plates and screws so he could get a good look at what he was in for. Then he would go in and turn the femur using a computer navigation system.

MAJOR JOINTS AND
BRITTLE BONES

So in June Dr. Abel took all of Chaz's hip hardware out. What he found was deep infections in both hips. He cleaned it up the best he could.

He gave Chaz the summer to heal from that surgery before he went in in August to turn the femur around properly. He didn't agree with the thigh-cutting idea, saying it would create a whole other issue. That was what Frank and I thought, too. So with all of us on the same page, I was able to talk to Chaz about it and have him not be afraid.

Every time Chaz was due to have a procedure, Frank and I would talk to him about it and answer any questions that he had. Yes, he might be young, but he deserved to know the truth about what we had allowed to happen to his body. I felt bad every time I had to sign paperwork allowing someone to operate on Chaz. I couldn't help but feel like most of these things were optional and not always necessary, even when I knew that they were necessary. It's hard to give someone permission to cut into your child, regardless of the proposed outcome.

And Chaz would always ask, "Is it going to hurt?" And I always responded honestly, "Yes." Since UVA was closer to our relatives than it was to us, Frank's sister Leslie and his mom, Dot, would come up to be with Chaz on his surgery days. He loved having them there. He loved it so much that he had Leslie go back with him and his dad as they prepped him for surgery and gave him a mild sedative to knock him out. I know what you're thinking: "Were you jealous?" And the answer would be no. When it came time for Chaz to have surgery, I didn't care who went back as long as he was happy with it. And she made him feel safe. They have always had a special bond, and for that I love her.

When Dr. Abel came by to see Chaz before the surgery, they joked around with each other, mostly about the anesthesia doctor that was going to be with Chaz. He was wearing a Cowboys surgical cap, and Chaz was a diehard Redskins fan, just like his dad. So Chaz told the anesthesia doctor that he would have to change that surgical cap before he could be in the room with him. Funny thing is he did. Dr. Abel had another man with him. Apparently, they had flown him in for the use of this new piece of equipment that the man had a part in developing. So Dr. Abel was getting more points as time went on.

A few hours later, Dr. Abel informed us that the operation was a success and that he had turned Chaz's leg fifty degrees. It was officially in proper alignment with his body. I cried. It was finally over. Chaz could now ride in his wheelchair without having his leg hanging off to the side of his wheelchair.

But like everything in Chaz's life, this celebration was short lived. One evening in February, after Frank and I had put Chaz to bed, Chaz fell out of his bed while trying to retrieve a stuffed animal. One of us had forgotten to put the gate up on the side of his bed. And Chaz was wailing. I had seen him cry before but not like this. He was screaming; he was in so much pain. When Frank or I would try to roll him over—after all, he was lying face down on the floor—he would scream, "NO!"

We looked at each other and knew what we had to do. We had to call an ambulance. They got there in under five minutes, and Chaz was wailing the entire time. Chaz didn't want them to touch him, either. Since his bedsheet was under him, they picked that up by its corners and placed him on the stretcher that way. The sounds that he made broke my heart. I was crying and blubbering so bad that Frank said that he would ride in the ambulance with them. They would call us once they knew something.

A few hours later, Frank called and said that children's hospital had taken some x-rays and that he had a small fracture, here's some pain pills, follow up with your orthopedic doctor. And when I picked them up, Frank was mad as hell. He knew that for Chaz to be complaining like he was, something was definitely wrong. Something more than a "small fracture."

So the next day, I called Dr. Abel's office and left a detailed voice message. Surprisingly, his nurse called me back a few hours later. It was Sunday, and she had come in to take care of a few things, and she listened to my message and scheduled an appointment for the next business day. In the meantime, Chaz was to take the pain meds the doctor gave him and hope for the best. We didn't sleep during those forty-eight hours. Chaz had had plenty of surgeries, so for him to be crying and complaining like he was, we knew that something had happened.

Now you want to talk about guilt. I had so much guilt about not ensuring that the gate was up on his bed that I couldn't sleep with Chaz in pain. And I was also upset that he tried to get his stuffed animal off the floor instead of letting his dad or me know. So guilt and anger tend to go hand in hand. But the guilt was bad. Really bad. Sleep deprived, I ended up with a migraine. And when I get a migraine, it's bad. I have to lie down because I get nauseated and dizzy. But this was one time that I couldn't let my migraine take me out of the game because the next day we headed to UVA.

Turned out Chaz had what was called a Joe Theismann break. He had actually broken his thigh in several places. Dr. Abel was mad as hell. Sorry to put it that way, but that doesn't even describe how he felt. Even though he had performed his own x-rays, Dr. Abel said that you could easily see in the children's hospital x-rays that Chaz had several breaks in his thigh. He told us that they never should have sent him home and that surgery was required to fix the problem.

While he was talking to us, his nurse was arranging for Chaz to have surgery at UVA, as soon as an operating room opened up. And the break was so bad that we weren't allowed to drive Chaz over to UVA; one of their transport teams was on the way to Dr. Abel's office to pick Chaz up. Our parental instincts were right about there being something wrong with Chaz. And I made a note to contact children's hospital as soon as I got home. Dr. Abel already had. Like I said, he was furious. And he was a usually happy, pleasant man. But today he was mad, and it showed in his face. There were no smiles nor were there any jokes. This was serious. And all of this commotion was scaring the hell out of Chaz. He had no idea that he'd be having surgery today. He felt relieved that something could be done to stop the pain.

Eerily, Frank and I predicted that we'd be staying in Charlottesville for a while. So we had packed some clothes and some things for Dustin to do. I contacted Dustin's school to let them know what was going on. And I called Chaz's. And then we called the parents. I was having a feeling of deja vu. Again, here it goes, I couldn't protect my child. Or at least that was how I felt.

Frank and I said goodbye to Chaz when the transport team showed up. We kissed him and told him that we'd be there when he woke up. Then we retrieved Dustin from the craft table and told him the bad news. Since it was going to be a few hours before we would be able to see Chaz, we decided to get something to eat. We ate, only because we weren't sure when we would be able to again. I wasn't really hungry. Neither was Frank. But like I said, we did anyway.

Frank and Dustin would be staying in a nearby hotel tonight, and I would stay with Chaz in the hospital. As we waited, Dustin colored, played games we had brought with us, and enjoyed the attention of the women that were complimenting him on his beautiful blue eyes and dimpled smile. I purchased a monkey string puppet and walked through the hospital with it. We had a tradition of giving Chaz a fun stuffed animal with every surgery. By fun, I mean stuffed animals that move and sing. So the monkey fit right in.

When Chaz came out of surgery, he had several flexible titanium rods in his thigh, sticking out of his leg. He had holes in his leg that you could see through. When I saw this, I just burst out crying. Dr. Abel said that they would send Chaz home in a day or two. He had the rehabilitation clinic technicians working on a stretcher for us to carry Chaz home in. He didn't want him handled unless necessary. Chaz would have to ride back home, two hours without traffic, on a stretcher they were making for him.

My mind started wandering. What if we got into an accident? What if traffic was bad? What if we broke down? Guilt. Guilt. Guilt.

When Chaz woke up later that evening, he was in some pain, but he said that it wasn't the kind of pain that he was in before surgery. I was grateful for that but still feeling bad that this happened. And now I had to show him the rods sticking out of both sides of his thigh. I knew he was going to freak out. I knew that he wasn't going to take the news well.

So when he asked what Dr. Abel did, I pulled the bedsheet back slowly, expecting him to start crying at the sight of two rods sticking out of his leg. But he didn't. He was just relieved that he didn't have the kind of pain that he had before. And his foot no longer bent toward his ear. That made me feel a little better. But the guilt was still there. And there it would remain forever.

Two days later, the handmade stretcher was ready, and it was time to go home. Chaz had a partial hard cast around his hip and thigh area. So Chaz had to be lifted carefully. And since he was incontinent and still in diapers, he would need to be moved to be changed. So for the next month and a half, Frank and I tag-teamed changing Chaz. One of us had to clean him up while the other one turned him onto his side, very carefully.

Chaz was scared to have the rods removed, but he also really wanted them removed. He was as conflicted as I was. And I was twenty-eight years older than him. Signing surgical papers for your child never gets any easier. And as they wheeled Chaz in the back for surgery, my guilt sank in again. This was hopefully going to be an outpatient surgery. But like everything else in our lives, we didn't count on it. Fortunately, this time God was on our side and Chaz was allowed to go home. No more rods sticking out of the leg. No more holes that we could see through.

And as much as I loved Dr. Abel, I really hoped that we wouldn't have to see him again. One could hope. Couldn't we?

CHAZ FLOYD AKA
JOHN WAYNE

ell, I had signed up to be a waiver mentor, and I had to attend this two-day training in Charlottesville, the same time that Chaz had his surgery. And looking back, I know that I should have said hell with it. But I didn't. I was so set on changing the world for each and every child with special needs that I was determined to attend the training. This meant that when Chaz was released from the hospital, Frank had to drive an hour back to his mom's to pick up Dustin and then another three-and-a-half-hour drive home from there. And here Chaz had all of this equipment in his back. I felt like crap the entire weekend. I wanted to abandon it so many times. Yes, that was selfish of me. Or was it? I really don't have the answer. Because it changes daily, depending upon which criteria I use to answer it.

Chaz never spent much time in the hospital after surgery with Dr. Abel. Mostly because he would forgo pain medication afterward. When the nurse would come in to ask him if he wanted some, he would always say no. I would say yes. And then he'd yell, "NO!" And sometimes he'd yell no with tears streaming down his face. And on several occasions, the nurses would ask him if he was sure, reminding him that they could see him hurting. And he'd still say no. I only got away with a nurse giving him pain meds one time, and that was because she was able to put it through his IV. But that was the only time I got away with it because when he woke from that, he told me not to do that again. So from then on, when the nurse would come in with a syringe in her hand, he would ask her what it was. See, the other thing about Chaz is that he does not like to be kept in the dark about things. He prefers to be in pain and aware of his surroundings than to be sleeping through whatever is going on.

I can say this with confidence: Chaz is stronger than I have ever been. That kid has gone through hell and back and manages to keep a smile on his face through it all. Even when he is in pain after surgery, you can't help but feel like you're in the presence of someone special. Someone confident. A fighter. John Wayne. That's what Dr. Abel and the UVA nurses call him. John Wayne.

And by now I was aware that I was the one feeling all gloom and doom about his life while he was enjoying his life. I'm not saying that he enjoyed the surgeries. What I'm saying is that he has never connected the dots on why all of these surgeries were necessary. He has looked at each one as a separate event. And I followed the dots all the way back to that stroke on June 8, 1993. And when I connect those dots, I tend to get angry and feel guilty. I've been trying hard not to go there, but sometimes I can't help it.

I always dreaded the day that Chaz would ask me what happened, why he was in a wheelchair. And even though I have told him and even though he has heard the story repeated umpteen times, the truth is I don't think he truly understands.

Chaz has this uncanny ability to believe that all people are good. I used to think that. Some days I wished that I was more like Chaz. I wished that I could see the world through his eyes. Then reality smacks me in the face, and I am glad I don't. Because if I did, then I would be unprotected from those that intend to do us harm or to take advantage of us. But it is just fine that Chaz sees the world through his rose-colored glasses.

GAME OVER

y now, Chaz was done. And I mean done. He came to me and his dad one day, and he said, "No more therapy." He had had therapies since he was three months old. He was finished. And we had to respect that.

At one time there was hope that Chaz would spend his daytime hours in a wheelchair but would be able to go out in the evenings as someone that walked. But he had endured so many strikes against him that we all knew that this was out of the question; we were just waiting for one of us to say it out loud. And when Chaz said no more therapy, Frank and I knew that it was game over.

We had pushed him all of these years, and now that he was older, we didn't feel right pushing him any longer. It was a sad day in the Floyd household.

So the next day, I contacted children's hospital and canceled all therapy appointments and mailed them a letter telling them why. I did the same with the school system. Of course, that one turned out to be a shit show.

With Chaz turning down therapies with the school system, that would cause the school system to lose money. So we had to have an IEP meeting, which I hated. I hated all the IEP meetings. They were like court trials. When you walked in there, there would be a bunch of people sitting at this huge conference table, some of which you didn't always know. And they would present their case, and you would present yours. And then you'd fight to the death or come to a compromise.

And like Chaz, I too was tired of fighting. So we came to a compromise. No more therapy. But they could be listed as a therapy evaluation. Meaning, they could check in on Chaz once a month to make sure that he had the proper equipment at home and school for being a successful student. I looked at it as a second pair of eyes for Chaz's needs.

Besides, they didn't really do actual physical therapy and occupational therapy in high school. Not like children's hospital did. So it was a waste of time to begin with. Or at least I felt that way. But some of these people had been in Chaz's life since elementary school, so they were sad to see him leave their services.

But by the time high school rolled around, Frank and I viewed it as glorified daycare for students with special needs. Like I said, they couldn't really do the kind of therapy that an outpatient rehab facility could because there wasn't time. And when you had a room full of people getting "individualized" service, there really was only so much "individualized" attention you could give them.

So I looked at it as a place that Chaz went to hang out with friends. And even though Chaz was in self-contained classes in high school (meaning no regular education students), we did make sure that he had at least one or two regular education classes. With Chaz being so sociable, he needed to be around regular kids. By regular I mean the ones that tend to talk in class, even when they're not supposed to. Kids that tend to play practical jokes on each other and the teacher. Kids that were well on their way to a diploma and not a sealed diploma.

Chaz liked these regular education classes himself because he was always the class clown. Whenever we had our annual or biannual meetings, we would find out from his regular education teachers some of the hijinks that he performed while in class, or sometimes out of class as the case would be. His brother was in one of his art classes one year, and the stories that he would come home and tell me literally shocked me. I had no idea that Chaz was that comical and outgoing. I knew he could be both of these things, but he was on a whole other level at school. This kid would tell the teacher these sob stories to get out of class or to get out of an assignment. And one time he locked the teacher into the photo development room. I swear he was egged into that, but either way he did it.

And I couldn't help but laugh at some of the stories told to me. I knew that he shouldn't be acting up in class, but I was always glad to hear that he could act up like a regular student. I hate that word, regular. I like it better than normal. Because, as far as I believe, none of us are normal. We might appear to fit into certain categories, but let's be honest, we all have our quirks and issues. Maybe one day someone will come up with an alternative way to say normal. For now, I refer to it as regular.

But things were not all that bad for Chaz and high school. He made friends in special education and regular education. He made friends of all the staff. He was a social butterfly.

And when his brother, Dustin, attended the same high school, he was a soccer player for his four years. And Chaz got to know all of the people on the boys' and girls' soccer teams. He preferred the girls' team for two years. The most beautiful girl in school played soccer, and she kind of took Chaz under her wing. And like high school, when one popular girl likes you, they all do. So Chaz would sit with the girls' soccer team during games while his dad and I were in the attendee section.

With two popular high school boys, things appeared to be going good for the Floyd household. But we all know that all good things must come to an end. Dustin was hit by a player during one of the games, and it caused him to mess up his knee. From then on, he had issues with his knee wanting to go one way and the muscle wanting to go another. So we got used to seeing Dustin on the sideline with ice on his knee. When he played, he was good. Damn good. But if he was hit just right, he would go down for the count. And during one game, I watched as the other team plotted to take him out.

One of the players was instructed to hit him in the knee because they knew that he had issues with his knee. I wanted to run down there and stop them. But I knew I couldn't. That was just the way sports were played. And sure enough, he was hit in the back of the knee and out he went. When those little bastards stood on the sidelines and snickered, I wanted to go down there and smack the shit out of them all. But I was learning to not get involved. I had a problem with that. I had been so used to "fixing" things for Chaz that I automatically wanted to "fix" them for Dustin. But Dustin didn't want me to fix anything. Parents tend to make matters worse. So I followed his advice and stayed out of his business. Especially where sports were concerned. I agreed to only "help" him if he asked me specifically. That was hard to do. Very hard. Because every instinct in me wanted to help. I wanted to fix the things that weren't right or fair. I wanted to make things better.

So while Dustin spent his high school years battling knee complications, which included some intense physical therapy, Chaz had a few orthopedic problems of his own. His bones were weak because he did not ambulate. And since he wasn't getting stretched out as he had been during physical therapy, he had to see Dr. Abel for additional surgeries to improve his knee extension and to overcome severe flexion deformities in his feet. The muscle tendon surgeries were required because Chaz developed contractures due to his relatively reduced mobility and his tighter muscles secondary to his cerebral palsy.

And on top of that, he started complaining of back pain again. So Dr. Abel suggested that it might be time to take the spinal hardware out. That it was possible that it was aggravating him. So in 2012, Dr. Abel removed the upper portion of the spinal hardware since it was causing inflammation. And again in 2013, the lower portion of the spinal rods and screws were removed. And Dr. Abel scraped away as much of the inflammatory tissue that he could. Fortunately, Chaz handled these two surgeries like a trooper. Not that we were surprised.

PART 4

THINGS YOU SHOULD KNOW

ALL MY ROWDY FRIENDS

s Chaz has grown older, he's mixed his love of people with a newly discovered twenty-one-year-old habit: beer drinking. Chaz enjoys a glass of beer with his dinner. Especially if he's out with friends. Especially when those friends are his attendants.

Over the years, he's had a few attendants. There was one, I'll call him Dylan. Dylan was originally one of Dustin's friends. But after Dustin discovered working for money, no one saw him much. And for about five years there, he worked two jobs. And we hardly ever saw him. Well, since Dylan, Dustin, Chaz, and all the other people that kept coming in and out of my house were all around the same age, they used to like to go to restaurants that had pool tables where they could eat, play pool, and drink beer. They did not overindulge. And they were never gone that long. And they did this a couple of times a week. That's when I knew that attendant care was paying for itself because Chaz preferred to do those things with people his age than with me. And he preferred to do it with guys that would flirt with girls instead of having Mom around. Though I did go with them once or twice.

One of his other attendants promised to take him to a go-go bar during her shift because she worked nights. Frank dropped them off with lots of dollar bills and went back later to pick them up. Oddly enough, one of Dustin's friends was now the bouncer there, so he kept an eye on them and texted Frank throughout the evening. Apparently, Chaz was a hit with the dancers and not just because he had a stack of ones. He just has that personality that draws people in.

We'll be at events and people will come up and just start talking to him or vice versa, and next thing I know they're Facebook friends, they're swapping numbers, and they're making plans to meet up at another event. And I'm left trying to organize it all.

One of his friends, John, is the lead singer in a band that he met through Dustin. He was the dad of a girl that Dustin dated. I liked to call her ShaNaNa. That's how I remembered her name, even though that wasn't her name. Chaz loved to attend places they played at. He not only loved John and the music, but he liked hanging out with the other band members, especially their wives. I believe almost every attendant got to see John in concert. I did a couple of times. See, the thing is, after what happened to Chaz happened and he was let down by so many so-called qualified people in his life, I have to spend the rest of my life making up for it. So I do whatever I can possibly do to make him happy. And does it get exhausting? Yeah, you bet it does. Are there days I want to take off? Yes. But I can't. So off to concerts we go.

For instance, I've had to sit through KISS. I am not a KISS fan. I'm more of a Def Leppard fan, which we did see. Keith Urban, Little Big Town, Aaron Carter, Heart (I grew to like), Hunter Hayes, Lady Antebellum, Little Big Town (which I did love), and a few others. I've also had to see Motley Crüe, Styx, Foreigner, Buckcherry, Chevelle, Kid Rock (okay, that one wasn't so bad), Reverend Run, Evanescence, and more. I go to these for love of my son. And his crazy ass drinks a beer that turns hot in the first fifteen minutes that you're at these outdoor concerts because he's a dedicated concertgoer. I sit there and smile at him as I sip my water. Most of the time I usually know a song or two or some words to a few songs because I hear the music blaring through the house. So I'm not totally out of my element. But I try.

When it comes to fist-pumping, Chaz can outdo pretty much anybody. I've never seen anyone that does it as much as he does. He can get his wheelchair rocking when he gets into a rock song. But it's not just rock. It's all genres of music. He listens to everything. I've even had to endure bluegrass music, folk music, and dub step. Don't let me forget the Blue Man Group. They turned out to be pretty cool.

ANGELS AMONG US

When I thought about the possible closing of Waterside in Norfolk, I wanted to stand up and scream, "No! You can't!" Waterside was special to my family and me because it is one of the first places that we as a family encountered an angel among us.

Back in 1999, we were going to Waterside every Friday to eat and watch the boats. It was a time for us to hang out and talk about our week. That same year, my son, Chaz, who was six at the time, had reconstruction surgery to prevent his hips from popping out of joint due to the contractures he had related to his cerebral palsy.

Chaz had to be in a full body cast with a bar that separated his legs. He was in that upside down V-shaped contraption for almost two months. Despite this, he was a very happy camper.

We made sure that we never missed going to Waterside weekly, so Chaz could get out of the house. After all, he had to spend a lot of time at home, since he couldn't go to school in a body cast. So, every Friday, he had a change of scenery and was able to be around people. We tried to keep his routine as normal as possible. He even continued playing tee-ball. We just had him propped up in a reclining manual wheelchair. He gave the term "laid back" a whole new meaning.

One afternoon when we were at Waterside, we heard a rather deep voice say, "Well, hello, Floyd family." We looked up from our food and were startled to find a tall man standing beside our table. He asked how Chaz was doing. This man continued to talk to us as if he knew us. We were positive that we had never met him before. He surprised us by knowing things that we knew that we didn't tell him. He knew about my mother-in-law's visit the previous week, and he asked how she was. He knew about Chaz's surgery. He even knew that we came there every Friday.

We were really surprised by how well this man knew us. Even though none of us remembered meeting him before, we treated him like an old friend. Each week that we were at Waterside, this man would just suddenly appear at our table. He would inquire about the family, but more importantly, he would talk to Chaz to see how he was doing. Of course, Chaz loved the attention that this man gave him, and he looked forward to seeing him each week. Each visit from the nice stranger was brief. Each one putting a smile on Chaz's face.

When Chaz finally got his cast off, the doctor saw that a staph infection had set in. This explained the discomfort that Chaz had started having a few days before.

Over the next few months, Chaz had to have several surgeries to scrape the staph infection away and a new body cast put on each time to protect what they could of the original hip surgery. We continued to go to Waterside each week throughout this whole ordeal. And as luck would have it, that nice man would stop and talk to Chaz.

Here's where it gets weird. We never actually saw him walking toward us. He would just suddenly appear. Each time he would tell Chaz that things were going to be okay.

Well, one week, with my curiosity getting the best of me, I asked the man where he worked. He pointed as he said, "Joe's Crab Shack." So, when he left our table, I followed him into Joe's. I was no more than ten feet behind him the entire time, and I unbelievably lost him. I asked the bartender where the man had gone. He had not seen anyone walk by. I described the man, and the bartender said that there was no one working there by that description. I was shocked. After all, I had clearly followed the man into Joe's. I knew it. My family knew it. But the man didn't exist, at least not at Joe's.

Each week, we had made our best attempts to look for the man in hopes of spotting him before he appeared at our table, but each time we failed.

At the end of those extra few months of surgeries and body casts, the man stopped by our table one last time. He took one look at Chaz, out of the final body cast, and he said, "I knew you were going to be just fine, my man. With your smiling face and winning personality, I knew you were going to make it through." Chaz shook the man's hand, and the man bid us farewell, and we watched him walk off into Joe's, where we watched him disappear. It was as if he faded out, like something in a movie.

Chaz was finally well, and we never saw the man again. To this day, my family still talks about the angel that watched over Chaz when he needed it most. It has also made us firm believers in angels among us.

CHAZ IS CHOSEN

Chaz had this friend, Tony, who was also in a power wheelchair. And each time Tony would see Chaz, he would tell Chaz he needed to go to these weekly church socials with him. They had them at high school, but it wasn't the same. He told us this for a year before I agreed to get off my lazy butt and take him.

So one Monday evening, I drove Chaz to one of the local churches and was surprised when I pulled up. For one, top forty rock was playing. I was thinking, *This is a step up from anything I had to endure as a kid.* I unloaded Chaz, and we walked inside. And there were like twenty other kids with special needs, dancing, eating potato chips and dip, and drinking soft drinks. Chaz left me at the door. I admit that I stood there for a while because I was not expecting this. I was super thrilled by it!

This girl with super-long hair and an image to match her name came over and introduced herself to me. "Hi, I'm Gypsy." I introduced myself and gave her Chaz's name and told her that he was Tony's friend. The music was loud, my voice was low, and Chaz is not a name you hear every day, so she asked me to repeat it. So on autopilot, I said a little louder, "It's Chaz. C-H-A-Z." She thought it was cool.

I gave her credit for not asking if it was short for Charles. So many people have done that over the years. And I always have to say, "No. It's just Chaz." To which they always think it's such a wild name, when it's been given entirely on its own. Then they usually ask how it came about. I tell them it came from a dream that I had when I was in my early twenties. And my lead character was a blond-haired, blue-eyed boy that was popular but sweet named Chaz. I did write that dream into a screenplay.

Gypsy went onto tell me that for the next hour and a half, they would socialize, eat, listen to music, hang out, listen to a Bible story, and pray. And they did this every Monday. I wanted to drop to my knees right there. That meant that I would have to bring him every Monday. Because the kid was already in there dancing and stuff, and I hadn't even left the building. And in case you haven't noticed, Chaz basically gets what he wants. And I don't mean that in a bad way. For instance, this church social. It was for people his age with disabilities. How could I not take him to that each week? He needed this type of socialization.

Anyway, when I went to pick him up, he had a tag on that said, "My name is Prince Charming." The two leaders that brought him out to my van said that with his long, wavy blond hair, he reminded them of Prince Charming from *Shrek*. It wasn't the first time I'd heard that or the last.

Over time, this group grew. They changed churches over the years. They expanded to different cities. They even started an annual summer camp, which by the way is the only thing that Chaz lives for. It's like the social event of the year. No other event matches their summer camp. I'm just saying.

One year Chaz decided that he wanted to get baptized at camp. They usually do this on one day of camp, and Chaz spoke up and said he wanted to do it. Fortunately, that day, his dad was at camp with him helping his attendant, Jackie, because some muscle and assistance would be needed in the pool. I was missing that day because I was in school. I was nearing the end of my degree and couldn't miss. Plenty of people took photos for me. But still, I missed it. But I am so proud of him for deciding on his own that he wanted to do it. His certificate hangs proudly on his wall.

Poor Jackie had attended camp for five years with Chaz. She was Chaz's attendant. She worked with him during the week to help us with his activities of daily living. Put quite simply, she helped us with bathing, changing, transfers, cleaning his room, giving him his food, pills, beverages, and going places with him. And she'd hung in there longer than anyone.

Last year was rather rough because both of them went swimming during lunch time, which was nothing unusual. But for some reason that day, no matter how much they reapplied their sunscreen, they both got burnt bad. By bad I mean I'm squirming in my seat as I write this. Chaz turned shades of purple and red that I didn't know existed. On top of that, he developed these blisters that were more like huge water bubbles. Those things were several inches long, and they were half an inch to three quarters of an inch in height. Oh Lord, they looked bad. And he was in pain. Jackie called out of work for a few days with the same complaint.

We took Chaz to the doctor. He prescribed some ointments for Chaz and an antibiotic just in case anything became infected. We were not to pop anything. We were to change the dressings on the ones that had. Chaz hated this. We hated it even more. His skin had a discoloration until Christmas. Chaz's doctor had instructed him not to go out in the sun for the rest of the summer. So he only did night swims.

Jackie was a good person, though. She really cared about Chaz. We hated to see her go. But when you work as an attendant, there is no stepladder to other positions. And she was ready to move up. So she went to CNA school, got her license, and went to work at one of the local hospitals.

But for five years, she attended Chosen camp with Chaz. She helped him rock climb, ride a horse, swim in the pool, shoot a bow and arrow, and run around in the heat dodging water balloons while Mom stayed home.

For the record, Chaz has been attending these weekly meetings for almost two decades now. Sadly, Chaz's friend, Tony, has passed, as well as some other friends that he's made over the years at Chosen.

He did accumulate a friend and a relative. Here's a funny story for you. A few months after Frank's mom died, Chaz told us about this lady that bowled with the therapeutic recreation center with him. And he said that she looked just like his nanny, which is what Chaz and Dustin called Mrs. Floyd. So I stopped by bowling one day, and I had Dustin and Frank with me, and we all agreed that yep, she looked like Mrs. Floyd.

So we started talking to her. Over the next few months, we got to know her a little more. Over the next year, she started showing up in some of Chaz's other therapeutic recreation events. So I asked Chaz if he'd like for Denise to go to church with him. Of course, he said yes. So I invited her, and she said yes. That's been quite a few years ago. Here's the thing that makes Denise special. She is twelve years older than me but has a developmental issue. She soon adopted our family. She started calling me "Ma" and Frank "Pa." And she called Dustin and Chaz her brothers. She would ask if this was okay. I would say yes. Then she started telling people that we were her relatives. And I was still okay with it. But I was afraid that maybe, just maybe, it would cause a problem with the people that oversaw her care.

Well, that too has been ages ago. I'm not sure how long ago Denise adopted us and we adopted her. But yes, she has become one of the family. We include her in all holidays and birthdays and whatever events. And I pick her up and take her to church each week with Chaz. But there's one more thing. They're both Starbucks fans. And there's a Starbucks by the church they now attend. Or have been attending for about four or five years now. So each Monday, you'll find us at Starbucks getting drinks to go so they can waltz up into church with Starbucks. Starbucks owes me some stock. I'm just saying.

CHAZ, THE ARTIST

Chaz is now an artist. One of the former leaders from the church socials he attends does art therapy. We thought it would be good to give Chaz something to do. So we began weekly lessons. I didn't hover around. I remained absent so that student and mentor could create whatever their hearts desired.

At first, she had to get Chaz to follow instructions. The thought of that made me cringe because I'd tried in the past and blew a gasket or two hundred. And there were times that I could hear struggling to get him to cooperate. But within a short time, he was cranking out some really cool work. Turns out she had to get him interested in doing things that made him happy. And he like things like band logos. Hello, Pink Floyd. And anything WWE. His first was of a match with Asuka. He loved the different colors that made up her world. This meant that she was happy. And with that, she brought happiness. At the request of Dr. White, he did a Dean Cain Superman.

For Mother's Day, I have a stunning piece of Prince's *Purple Rain*. I felt honored that he thought of this particular piece for me, because I love Prince and I love *Purple Rain*. I grew up on that album. And it is the best Prince picture you will ever see. And it hangs proudly in my office where I get to look at it every day.

One day as we made our way through the Chrysler Museum, he saw Andy Warhol's *Marilyn Monroe*, and he really liked it. Apparently it spoke to him as an artist, and he had me take several photos of it so he could show his art instructor. He was determined to make one himself. I wasn't going to talk him out of it. I've also wanted to own one. So I asked him if I could keep that one. And I was happy when he said yes. I know if I'd let him sell it, he would have made a small fortune. But it was the Chaz Floyd version of Andy Warhol's *Marilyn Monroe*. I couldn't let that go. That was beautiful in its own way. And I had already picked out a spot in my house where I wanted to display it. And I get to look at it every day.

When he recreated Pink Floyd's *Dark Side of the Moon*, he got a lot of praise. He put a picture of that one on Facebook, and the crowd went wild. So he ended up making a few replicas that he sold. They were of course a little smaller than the original. The original Frank and Chaz decided to keep.

He had an art show and silent auction with his instructor, and he sold almost everything. We have a few pieces left and are thinking of starting an Etsy store. I'd call it Chaz Floyd's Art Studio. I'd also love to find another art instructor for him since ours left. With COVID-19 going on, the Therapeutic Rec Center has been offering some four-week painting classes. So he's signed up for all of those. We're collecting more paintings than we have wall. That's another reason to sell them.

I thought for sure Chaz would be happy to take a break from weekly art lessons. Especially since he took a month off for the holidays. But it turns out that he couldn't wait to get back when the new year hit. He's the one that asked me when the instructor was coming back. And he was sad when he found out that she wasn't. I was, too. They were creating beautiful work together.

JESUS AND GRADUATION

Graduation is every parent's dream. For our family, it was a little bit more complicated than that. Even though Chaz could attend high school until he was twenty-one, he wanted out when he hit twelfth grade. He wanted to graduate his senior year just like everyone else. And we were fine with that. We had provided him with the choices and allowed him to make his own decision, and he did. He was leaving high school as a senior.

We couldn't wait to see him roll down that ramp with his Jesus hair and accept that reward. See, Chaz had dirty blond, wavy hair that was shoulder length. And even strangers would come up to him and say that he looked like Jesus.

Chaz decided he was going to let his hair grow. He wanted to look like a rock star. So for several years, he didn't cut it. And one would think that he would look as if he just walked out of the 1980s, but no, he looked like an old picture of Jesus.

First, it was people he knew saying it. Like people at school, at church, his other friends. Me. He looked like my grandmother's picture of Jesus that hung in her living room from when my dad was growing up. I think the shape of the face and the color of the eyes added to it. Plus, his natural ability to talk to people and make them feel comfortable, happy, and just want to be friends.

Well, a couple of years into this hair-growing thing, he ended up in children's hospital because of a sudden seizure. He hadn't had one in ten years, then all of a sudden he had one. The nurse that got him situated in his room couldn't believe how much he looked like Jesus. And of course that just made him smile, which made her smile. And then the two became best buds. And that's how things went in his life.

But a few minutes later, another nurse came in and was like, "Oh my. You do look like Jesus." Then she took her phone out of her pocket and asked, "Do you mind if I take your picture?" I said, "Please do." She said, "My mother is never going to believe this. You look just like the picture of Jesus my mother has in her living room." I completely understood.

Then over the next few hours, more and more people came in to see the boy who looked like Jesus. And I sat quietly in the corner reading my book. Frank and Dustin just smiled because it never got old. Because we saw it, too.

So it was about time for Jesus to take the stage and say goodbye to high school and special education forever. You have to remember Chaz had been in some form of special education since he was three months old. And he was getting ready to hit nineteen. Because his stupid parents decided to hold him back a year in elementary school when he lost so much time due to a surgery. And we'd regretted that every school year.

And as much as I was smiling that day in the back of my mind, I was grinning at the fact that I would never, ever, ever have to put up with the special education department ever again. That alone was worth celebrating. And I could not wait to celebrate.

I mean, me and the special education department were on speaking terms, but they hated me as much as I them. And the same could be said for the department of transportation. I'd been a thorn in their side since

Chaz was two years old because he started riding a school bus at age two when he started Easton preschool, which was just like early intervention but held as a school day.

I cried the first time I had to put him on that bus. I actually followed that bus the first week to make sure the driver knew what she was doing. Of course, Chaz did care that he was on the bus because he got to hang out with more women. He loved women. He was a Casanova and didn't even know it yet.

But back to what I was saying. In celebrating my goodbye from all things special education related, as much as I wanted to throw away those IEPs, I couldn't. I had to save them. They would be guiding lights to help other family members stuck in the same horrendous situations. And with IEPs, wording is everything. Once a parent gets something in an IEP, they need to leave it in there, and once you get it in there, share it with other parents so they, too, can get it in there.

So the day came for Chaz's graduation. He had my mom and dad, Frank's mom, sister, and her husband there to cheer him on. Dustin was there and a bunch of his friends because they knew a bunch of the people that were in Chaz's graduating class.

So when it was time, Chaz's his special ed teacher, Paula—I have to call her out; she was great, and still is, actually—went up with him. Chaz was smiling away. People cheered. He grinned. He almost pulled a wheelie, if Paula hadn't been there.

Instead, we went home and had a party.

HELLO, MR. PRESIDENT: IGNORE THE LADY BEHIND THE WHEELCHAIR

A t the time I was the representative for our local challenger league and the coach of one of our teams when I got word of our invitation to play tee-ball on the South Lawn of the White House. President George W. Bush had invited our challenger league to play ball, meet the president, and have lunch. All on the grounds of the White House. That's if we could pass our background checks. Little did I know it was the beginning of the end in so many ways.

Since we could only have two players from our team and two buddies from our team, I thought it only made sense to let the two coaches' kids go, along with their regular buddies. By regular buddies, I mean their brothers. Keep in mind these are players with special needs, some of which have autism and only relate and/or react a certain way with their brothers.

We decided to make a family vacation of it because we loved going to Washington, DC for fun. Chaz and Dustin loved the museums. I loved that they were free. And to be honest, I never stayed at a hotel or visited a restaurant where I met a rude person. It was always a pleasant experience.

So the day of the trip, we stood in line with countless others just to get into the White House. And wouldn't you know it, Frank got stopped outside the White House. Someone with dyslexia had transposed the numbers on his identification, and they had to run something all over again. On top of that, he had back surgery and some nuclear tests involving dye recently, and he lit up like a Christmas tree on the second part of entry. So here I went with two kids following a ton of adults that were not letting the kids go first. That I didn't like.

So when President Bush landed in his helicopter with his dogs, we missed it. The kids couldn't see past the adults. Hell, I couldn't see past the adults. Dustin got nauseated. I walked over to the table where the water was. I was told they were out. So Dustin walked over to some flowers, I believe they were rose bushes, and he threw up. While I was assisting him and trying to find someone to help me, Chaz disappeared. And still no Frank. And keep in mind that this was the home of the president. You were not allowed to just walk around and look for someone. You were not allowed to do anything. It's like you were cattle being herded. You always had that sheep dog baring its teeth threatening you over your next move. Only we had SWAT with all these devices attached to them.

So after Dustin threw up in the rose bushes, he looked horrible, the poor thing. We found a place to sit where no one was telling us to get out of the way and to hurry up. Besides, all of the adults were taking photos of the president, his helicopter, and his dogs. After a few minutes, I told Dustin we had to at least find Chaz. Frank was an adult; if they ever let him in, they would point him in our direction. So I slowly and very cautiously walked over to this one entrance where I saw a lot of SWAT and other armed men kind of smiling. I didn't know they were allowed to smile on duty. But they seemed happy, so I approached them. I was pushing Dustin to my side so that he was clinging to me. I asked if they'd seen a boy with blond hair in a power wheelchair.

About that time, here came Chaz doing a wheelie up the homemade wheelchair ramp. And one of the guys asked, "Is that him?" Another guy said, "He's been doing that for about ten minutes." That's when I told them what happened to Dustin.

So I watched Chaz fly up and down the twenty-something-foot ramp a few times as he smiled and grinned as if he was going around a NASCAR track, and then I patiently told him we had to go. Deep down, I was ready to leave. So he came along, and the guys smiled at him as he left. I felt like a single parent because Frank still wasn't inside the grounds yet. I wasn't even sure if he ever would be. And I was ready to go home. Dustin looked like he was ready to throw up and pass out. Chaz was just caught up in the excitement. He was displaying enough for all of us.

The Secret Service finally corralled us over to another area where they decided to take our children first. Parents were not happy. Frank showed up in time to see our two children being led away by the men and women in black. He asked what was going on, and I said, "Hell if I know." And some parents were still strongly voicing their concerns. I didn't blame them. You couldn't just take all children with special needs from their parents and expect that there wouldn't be tempter tantrums of some sort. And not just from the children, which were at least mostly disability related. And sadly, the kids kept looking back at us as they walked away, and I really wanted to leave now. I'd had enough. We'd have more fun at the hotel, the restaurant, the museum. Anywhere else in DC but here.

Finally, the parents were allowed to walk the route the children had. The children were in the field area. We were escorted to the bleachers. We didn't get a say in where we sat. We were forced to follow one another where we were escorted to. So Frank and I ended up at the top of the bleachers, which made me kind of height sick. But I wasn't up there long when one of the challenger reps came and told us that Chaz had not stopped crying and he needed a parent. Frank volunteered me. So I went down to where the kids were. The focus of Chaz's problem was the mascot. Chaz did not like characters in costumes. So I relayed that to one of the Secret Service people, and they did that cool little thing where they talked into mid-air and they told the other mid-air to keep the mascot away from the crying boy in the wheelchair.

As the mascot moved to the other side of the field, Chaz calmed down.

Dustin, though, looked like he was going to barf any minute. I tried to get Frank's attention. I did. I waved for him to come down. We needed to leave. The Secret Service wouldn't let him leave his seat in the bleachers. We were stuck. It was hell.

Finally, the game was getting ready to start. President Bush came out for the singing of the national anthem. When he came out, the White House photographers started to take pictures. I was stuck there with my two kids. So I got on my knees behind Chaz's wheelchair, so I wouldn't be seen. And what did the president do? He decided he'd comes over and stand beside Chaz for the national anthem. He even put his arm around him as he began crying again because the mascot wanted a photo with the president. So mid-air had a conversation, and the mascot moved back enough for Chaz to let up his crying. And the president looked back and down at me during the national anthem. I gave him an uneasy smile. A part of me wanted to talk to him about the state of special education in the United States, and the other part wanted to say, "You have no idea how bad this day has gone. Can I go home now? Please."

So as this game happened, I stood off to the side, hiding from cameras. Why? I've hated having my picture taking since I was a kid. I'm just not photogenic. And maybe it's because a picture adds ten or more pounds. And it's the window to the soul. All I know is I have yet to see a picture of me that I like. Thank God the game was quick. Now the kids lined up to get a signed baseball from the president and a picture with him. Don't worry, he didn't actually sign them. A machine did it.

Then we were released to go to another part of the White House grounds, where we were provided lunch. That was where we met some interesting people. Our table was the best, I'll gladly say. It was our family of four and three interns. We asked them all kinds of stupid, embarrassing, crazy questions about working at the White House and with the president. And we feel like they answered honestly because they came back with some wacky stories, stories I cannot and will not share with you. But let's say it was the best part of the day. After we ate, we were free to leave. I must admit that I was never so happy to leave somewhere in all of my life.

I LOVE ROCK 'N' ROLL

Chaz loves music. When he was a baby, I would play the radio for him when we were in the car. At home, I would play albums on the record player. I would play music when I cleaned (this was to give me energy). I would dance with the dogs. Shaggy loved to dance with me. Wolfgang would but only because she had to. As he and Dustin got a little older, we would dance in the living room. This was something we did at least once a week. And the kids had their devices so they could play their own music. And might I add that Dustin and Chaz had always had the same but different taste in music. By that, I mean, yes they both may listen to the same genre of music but from artists on opposite ends of that genre. See, same but different.

Chaz has always like various genres of music, whereas Dustin tends to go through spurts of favorite genres. Well, when the kids were tweens, Frank and I owned a medical equipment company, and we made a fair wage. So we took the kids to quite a few concerts. Some of our most memorable are Aaron Carter. I picked confetti out of Chaz's wheelchair for a year. No joke. Remember, it's a power wheelchair. It has numerous small areas where that stuff can get caught, and it did. And all I could say was, "Oh, Aaron."

When Def Leppard came around, I dragged the whole family to see them. I didn't actually drag them; the kids knew their songs. I mean, doesn't everybody? And Chaz does this fist-pumping move when he really gets into a song. But it's not your normal fist pumping. No, he really gets into it. He pumps at supersonic speed. He can make a power wheelchair shake. And if he's in his manual wheelchair, you have to make sure he doesn't tip it over. To this day, Dustin says no one fist pumps like Chaz does. For Def Leppard, let's just say that he was singing and fist pumping the entire time.

But our most memorable will always be Joan Jett & the Blackhearts. I remember the year before Chaz had said something to me about us not attending any concerts that year, and well, he was right. I was pushing myself through a master's degree in journalism and barely had time to breathe. So I made him a promise that as soon as I found a concert worth spending my money and time on, we would go. So a couple of months later, I came across a little notice on Facebook. I had to double and triple check it before I opened my mouth. Then I went running into Chaz's room, and I said, "I just found what concert we're going to." His eyes got huge.

I started singing, "I saw him dancin' there by the record machine. I knew he must a been about seventeen." Before I could go on, he screamed, "I love rock 'n' roll." I added to that, "So put another dime in the jukebox, baby." And we both screamed, "Joan Jett!" I'd been dying to see her for three decades. And then I told him that Elle King and Heart were coming with her. Now, everyone has heard of Heart. I don't care how old you are; you've heard of Heart. Elle King didn't ring a bell, so we looked her up. As soon as we typed her name into Google, we knew who it was. I mean come on, "Ex's & Oh's." "America's Sweetheart."

So I ran back into the next room and ordered tickets. They had some special deal or gimmick where I had to order four tickets. So I did. I didn't care if I couldn't find a fourth person to go with us; we were going. So the concert was several months off, and I was recovering from foot surgery and finishing my master's, so I basically forgot about it and didn't invite anyone. No one.

So Dr. White came by one day for a visit. After all, he was an old friend of the family at this point. He'd been in Chaz's life since he was six days old. Chaz told him about Joan Jett, and I said, "You should come. We have an extra ticket." See, I knew I was saving that ticket for someone, I just didn't know who until that specific moment in time. Next thing you know, we were going to see Joan Jett with Dr. White. It's a good thing to have a neurologist with you when you're at a rock concert in hundred-degree weather, even though he wasn't Chaz's neurologist anymore. Dr. White retired when Chaz hit twenty-one. I'm glad his retirement coincided with Chaz turning twenty-one, because children's hospital was going to make us find a new one before he hit twenty-two.

The very first time we took Chaz to see the circus, knowing that the lights could have an effect on those with seizures, I got a little anxious. Right before the show began, who did I see a few rows down from us but Dr. White? See, again, a good time to have your neurologist with you. But Chaz was fine. He's never had a light-induced seizure.

Poor old Dr. White has been invited to some of Chaz's birthday parties. The ones where we have a pool party and cookout. There's usually lots of people, loud music, dogs running around, and people all over the place. Fortunately for him, he always has a reason to come in quick and get out early. I still feel the effects for several days. That's why we don't do them every year. But Chaz loves them. Plus, Chaz and Dr. White share a love of the Washington Redskins. So not only do they have something to talk about, but Chaz gets Redskins stuff as presents. Honestly, the kid has a ton of Redskins stuff. But every year, I realize that he really doesn't. They just keep coming up with more and more.

THANK GOD IT'S FRIDAY

When our downtown mall opened in 1999, I couldn't wait to go. I didn't have money to spend. But they had these awesome stores and restaurants that we'd never had before, and I wanted to see them. Of course, everyone in the Hampton Roads area did, too. So at first trying to visit there, especially in the evenings, was torture. You had to go during the day or fight hordes of people.

Dustin loved the Rainforest Café. He loved the elaborate rainforest décor. He even didn't mind the occasional simulated thunder, lightning, and rainstorms. Chaz could do without them. He liked the rain, just not the thunder and lightning. But at home he didn't mind it. So who knows? They did like the animals that moved occasionally. Of course we couldn't leave there without buying some animal from the gift shop. We only ate there when relatives came to visit. The lines were too long and the gift shop too expensive. But it was fun. At least we could say we did it.

Johnny Rockets was fun with their little jukeboxes but too crowded for someone in a wheelchair. But I must proudly say that my kids knew just about every song that was played while we ate. You can thank me for that. I grew up on 1950s, '60s, and beach music.

But the one that stole our hearts was Max & Erma's. And there were so many reasons why. For one, there was this table. Table number seven. It was set at an entrance on one side and the bar on the other. Other tables were not within earshot. There were a handful of two-people booths nearby. We'd go every Friday. We'd pick the kids up after school and head there. We'd always call ahead to let them know so they wouldn't seat anyone there. We basically eventually ordered the same thing each week after trying the entire menu.

And we did this for almost thirteen years. The kids liked the attention. We got to know the waiters and waitresses well. We became like family. Real family. They meant a lot to the kids and us as well.

They left the mall before the city started their First Friday's adventures. They would block off several blocks of the main street downtown and have a live band or two sometimes perform. There would be vendors. Alcohol. People with dogs. People with chairs. That was me. People would buy food and eat it as they watched the bands. There would be dancing in the street. Everybody would get to know everybody. It was just one giant party the first Friday of each month during the spring, summer, and early fall.

And Chaz made sure we never missed it. Dustin was usually working or out with friends, so he didn't join us that often. We would eat at the local pizza joint before the band started, and Chaz met some really cool people. Turned out he already knew some really cool people, too.

Chaz would be out there on the dance floor alone, then all of a sudden a lady would leave her husband or her friends and come dance with Chaz. If the lady had friends, they would usually join in, and then he had a few with him. He met some of Norfolk's local celebrities this way. One in particular was a *New York Times* bestselling author that I had been trying to get into her class for two years and had been unsuccessful. They danced and danced, and she gave him her cowboy hat. He danced every month with the richest man in the area's wife. The biggest attorney in the area's wife. There were other writers and newspeople as well as just plain ole' citizens having a good time on a Friday night. First Fridays was Chaz's thing. We'd show up. I'd put my chair somewhere in the back but where I could see, and there I would sit for two and a half hours. Because Chaz didn't need me. People would buy him beers. They'd dance with him. They'd take selfies. They'd joke. And all would have a good time.

Even though dancing in the street was fun for Chaz, he preferred to be up close and personal with the band. He would get up on the sidewalk so the only thing between him and the band was three steps. So he and the band members got to know each other.

Two bands he became good friends with were The Fuzz Band and Guava Jam. Let me tell you about The Fuzz Band. They have some huge hearts. They would interact with Chaz during the show, after the show, and even before the show. As for Guava Jam, they had no choice; like I said, there was only three steps separating them. But honestly, a couple of their singers and band members got to know Chaz and made him feel special among the other thousands of people there.

Speaking of bands making him feel special, John, the lead singer for As the World Burns, and his bandmates and their significant others have all been great to Chaz over the years. When John's around, to Chaz, he might as well be Jon Bon Jovi. And to John, Chaz might as well be the Dalai Lama due to his compassion, joy, and laughter that not only he has but that he brings to others.

One of Chaz's past attendants, Will, was into hard rock, so he didn't mind taking Chaz to concerts at the Norva. The Norva has hosted top bands and local bands. I like that it's small enough that I drop Chaz and an attendant off and not have to get in traffic. Will has taken Chaz to see a bunch of bands there, bands I can't even name because I'm not into hard rock. But yes, they did see As the World Burns. One I do know of is Fun House. That one sticks out because their drummer, Nathan, is one of Chaz's friends. They went to high school together. Nathan actually stood up for Chaz one day when someone tried to bully him. Chaz tells everyone that story. Even complete strangers. So I'm following suit and sharing it with you.

HAIL TO THE REDSKINS

One of Chaz's biggest loves is the Washington Redskins. I don't like the term "biggest fan." But let's just say that he's so close, he should be the team's owner. Yes, he has all the clothes, hats, shoes, blankets, footballs, cups, and other stuff that fans can buy. But Chaz goes beyond that. Chaz has stuff created just for him. For one, he uses Washington Redskins antenna balls as the controller topper for his power wheelchair. He's used other antenna balls in the past, but he prefers the Washington Redskins. His room is painted in Washington Redskins colors. His floor is made to look like the field of the stadium. He has a huge Washington Redskins bookbag on the back of his wheelchair that people notice ninety-five percent of the time and they strike up a conversation, even if they're on the opposing team. This would totally give me anxiety, having to talk to people or strike up a conversation with a dozen people everytime I went out the door. Though in a way I do. Because guess who is standing there with him, making sure he comes along? Yes, me. I turn fifty shades of red, move my head around slowly as if I'm listening to their conversation yet not listening to their conversation. Then I have to nervously tell Chaz to come on because it's time that either I, them, or him goes. And we do this a few times, every outing. E.V.E.R.Y. outing.

Anyway, I have to interrupt this story to tell you another one as it does have something to do with this one.

During one of my Chosen Ministry emails, I had read about a special needs airshow, and I thought, *Why not?* So I signed Chaz and us up. It sounded pretty cool. We were to get special parking, not only because we were handicapped but because we were with the Noblemen and had a parking permit. But we also were to be in a special tented area that would have chairs, tables, water, and pizza for lunch. All at no cost. And best of all, our very own port-a-potties so we didn't have to venture off somewhere. Well, it was the coolest thing ever. We had front row seats, literally. And Chaz rode around the tented area meeting all of the Noblemen. Well, that started a friendship that is sealed forever. Chaz loves, loves, loves those guys. And they (and some of their wives) love him, too. As Chaz has gotten older over the years, he graduated to the over-twenty-one part of the experience and now can drink from the keg with the guys. Did I mention that people working the event get to drink?

So one year, Frank was talking to Pete, one of the Noblemen, and mentioned that Chaz had never been to a game because we could never get tickets to a game. Well, Pete knew a guy that was helping out families like ours. He said he would give him a call. This man was getting kids like Chaz and their families into a game with a free hotel stay the night before and dinner. It sounded too good to be true, so Frank and I didn't get our hopes up, but of course, Chaz was telling everyone, "I'm going to a Washington Redskins game." And then I'd have to go behind him and explain. Well, within a week, we were provided several dates to choose from of games we were interested in. So we picked one, and it was set in stone. We were shocked. We were grateful. Oh Lord, were we grateful. Chaz was ecstatic. But then again, so were we.

About two weeks before the game, my fibromyalgia had taken a turn for the worse. It was so bad that I even had to cancel going to class.

Thankfully, my professors understood and allowed me to turn assignments in from home, though being at home was not a walk in the park, either. I was home because I couldn't walk. I could barely bear weight to go to the bathroom. Even lying in bed hurt. I was constantly changing positions, which also hurt. And this was before binge watching was a thing. We were going into week three of my fibromyalgia attack when it was time to go to the game. Me walking out to the van caused tears. Me getting into the Jeep caused tears. We decided to take the Jeep instead of the van because it was more compact and we were taking Chaz's manual wheelchair with us. Frank had painted it Washington Redskins colors and placed a few Redskins stickers on it but not too many. And he took an old jersey to cover the seat backing. We just had to drive to Arlington, Virginia. It was the weekend, so it took us less than three hours to get there. For me, it might as well been twenty-four. I complained all the way there. I felt like I was in a sardine can. And not being able to stretch or move my legs or adjust the pressure from my hips and thighs when the pain hit made me cry at times. I had the feeling that no one had any empathy for me at all.

After we checked into the hotel, we met our guy and his grandson for dinner at Cracker Barrel because it was within walking distance of the hotel. I lagged behind terribly. Each step made me want to jump in front of a car, if only I had the ability to jump. I honestly don't think I exerted myself that much, ever. Not even during childbirth. And the pain was monumental. But I did it for Chaz and for the family to see the Washington Redskins.

The next day, we drove to the stadium. We parked what felt like a mile away from the entrance to me. But it really wasn't for everyone else. Chaz got to tailgate with the Hogettes and Chief Zee. The camaraderie between fans was unbelievable, and Chaz was right in the middle of it. And so was Dustin and Frank. I believe I was standing on the side in a pain-induced coma because I didn't see me being any fun at all. And I'm sure I didn't smile unless it was my "I'm in pain but I'll be polite" smile.

Well, we went into the stadium, and I do recall the heavens opened up. You know how the holy gates make this magical sound when they open?

Well, that's what happened when Chaz and Frank walked into the stadium. Dustin and I aren't that big on football. The plan was Frank was going to sit with Chaz and I with Dustin. Then Frank saw that Dustin and I were sitting on the sixth row and Chaz was in the handicapped section, which might as well have been the nosebleed section compared to row six. But okay. Whatever. Well, first Frank and Dustin got to go down on the field. Then Chaz got to go down on the field. I could have gone but I couldn't walk. I was in my seat. I wasn't moving till it was time to leave. And I also made it. But I eventually had to pee. Remember, we were on football time.

After the game, we were to head to the entrance of the locker room where Chaz would have his football signed and Dustin would have Chaz's wooden Redskins photo signed. And the man's grandson also had a football to sign. The cheerleaders came out first. Chaz grinned from ear to ear. He looked like he'd just won the lottery. He didn't need to see the players. He saw the cheerleaders. Then Kirk Cousins walked out. And so began the signing of the memorabilia. I stood by and took photos and video.

It was a day that would go down in history for the Floyd family. And it was a day that Chaz would always remember.

ALL INSURANCE SUCKS!

In the beginning when Chaz was a baby, I thought Medicaid was a wonderful thing. It covered his special formula and all of the tests and exams and doctors' visits that he had to endure in the first few years.

Then when it came time for equipment like wheelchairs and bath chairs, I didn't worry that much because we had Frank's insurance through Food Lion, and they were great. They paid for everything. We actually got spoiled for a few years with his Food Lion insurance.

Then when we lost that, I became a different person. I became a research assistant into various health insurances, including Medicaid and Medicare. I also became a bit of a bitch, AKA advocate.

I learned the hard way that they're worse than IEPs, and they're worse than the IRS. What you say and how you say it matters. Before Chaz started talking, his speech therapist ordered a Cheaptalk 4 device for him so he could communicate his wants and needs. The insurance considered it "educational." I eventually got fed up with fighting it and found a place that gave Chaz a grant and got it that way.

Then there was the time that our state decided that everyone that had Medicaid, whether it was primary or secondary, would be put on an HMO. Those of us with primary insurance knew how ludicrous this sounded. Someone, won't say who, asked if I would speak to Congress about this. I said sure, no problem.

So I contacted a bunch of parents that were in the same programs as Chaz and asked what their complaints were. They told me, and I sat down and wrote up what I was going to say. I was only supposed to talk for something like five minutes. My written response was a little more than that, so I made a bunch of copies and put a photo of Chaz on the front of it so when it came time to give my speech, I handed them out to all of the congresspeople.

I had sat there for about an hour listening to people talk and Congress listen with not much interaction. I got up there, and they asked me questions, so many questions that I went way over my time and still didn't finish. But I did walk away from there with the head of Medicaid saying that they would not require people with primary insurance to have Medicaid as primary also.

I did find out over the next month that just about every problem I had mentioned in my written speech had been addressed by Congress and fixed by Medicaid. I tell people that it pays to let those in charge know what's going on. And most of the time, it doesn't pay to go to the person in charge of the program you have a problem with. You need to go over their heads. I also learned that with special education. I'm all for due process and for filing Department of Justice complaints. If we don't stick up for our kids, who will? And Chaz will be my kid no matter how old he is. And I'm fighting to the death.

When I first started advocating for Chaz, I had met a mom that told me I needed to start writing my own letters of medical necessity. I looked at her in awe. I told her that I could never do that. That was on the upper echelon of education. She asked me, "Who knows your child better than you?" Well, okay, she had me there. So I started looking into it, trying it out. And surprisingly, it started working. It was time consuming. But all it took was keeping up with my son's medical information and putting it with what the insurance was asking for.

Now when it came to getting wheelchair ramps installed in our vans, I left that to Frank. If he needed my assistance, I'd give it to him, but I preferred to stay out of the automobile arena.

One thing I can tell you that is a bitch to get approved is a power wheelchair. Even if you already have one. Even if you've already had several. The insurance companies treat you as if you're trying to steal something from them. They do. They make you feel dirty and cheap.

But it's not just the insurance companies. It's also the DME companies. It takes them f.o.r.e.v.e.r to obtain an item for you. I know from experience that it does not take six months or more to get a piece of equipment. What usually takes the most time is getting the DME company to do the paperwork and send it to the doctor for a signature and then actually follow-up with the doctor. Like call him weekly and say, "Okay, I faxed over Chaz Floyd's wheelchair certificate of medical necessity to you last Tuesday. Can you tell me when I can expect it back?" And most likely he's going to say he hasn't seen it if you have gotten it back in a week. So then you ask who you should address it to and what number you should send it to. And then he knows it's coming. Again. And you'll usually get it back in a day or so. But the key is to keep tabs on what you fax your doctors. And it doesn't hurt to keep tabs on when you fax things to the insurance companies. The key is to make sure that everyone is doing their job in the proper amount of time. But no one holds anyone accountable, so it takes you six months to a year to get a wheelchair. And I can say that because I used to own a medical equipment company.

It's one giant pain, and it's never going to be perfect. But parents, you've got to keep a call sheet of everyone you talk to, what they say, and when they say it. Because if you don't, you will never be able to keep people in check.

Now I'm going to be honest and say that there have been times, meaning several spans of months to a year or so, where I have my fuck-it attitude and

I honestly don't care when something happens. I'm not going to follow up on anything. I'm not going to fight for anything. I'm just going to let it all slide because my Xanax has kicked in and I need a break. Sometimes you just need a break. And I take a mental health break. And I just let things slide for some time. You have to. You just do. If you don't, you'll go nuts. And that's all right. Even Wonder Woman and Superwoman had their down time. And I'll take it right after I write the letter of medical necessity for that power wheelchair. Can you say Bible?

THE SPECIAL NEEDS
CLUB

Not only was Chaz attending physical and occupational therapy with the early intervention program, upon their recommendation, but he was also taking it at children's hospital each week. I had officially become an infant chauffer. I would sit in the waiting room and eavesdrop on parents' conversations. But to be honest, they didn't mind sharing whatever information they had come across.

Turns out, we parents learn more from each other than we do from the medical professionals surrounding us. Then again, we had a huge network. I got where each week I would take such copious notes that I had a bright idea. Or at least to me, it was bright.

Each week, or sometimes two if it was a slow week, I would go home and type up whatever information I came across on a newsletter that I developed entitled *The Special Needs Club*. It seemed a fitting title because it's kind of what we were. We didn't ask to be in this club. But here we were.

And I would make a hundred or so copies and leave them in the waiting room each week. As more information came to me, the more copies I would make. Before you knew it, I was making close to five hundred copies. I realized that I didn't have that kind of money. Especially since the newsletter had started to turn into more than one or two pages, front and back.

So I decided to start a nonprofit to help me with the cost. That's when Snap4kids was born. It stood for the Special Needs Assistance Program for Kids. Over the past twenty-plus years, Snap4kids has done several things. We've shared our newsletter. We've given grants for things like special needs car seats and special needs bikes and other equipment not covered by health insurance for the physically challenged. When our funding grew low, so did our ability to provide grants. We've provided workshops on special education and waivers. We did develop our very own care notebook, which we called our Snappy Finder. But our biggest area is advocating. We have spent most of our time assisting parents when they are having problems with their IEPs. Now I'm lucky if I tweet. My blog is an abandoned step-child. But I do keep the resources up-to-date as much as possible.

Now when the tee-ball league Chaz initially played with for quite a few years ended in a parental political defunct fiasco, I decided to start my own tee-ball league with the help of Snap4kids. I named it SNAIL. It stood for the Special Needs Assistance Independent League. And if you're wondering, I did have a snail as our symbol. But our teams were named after things like the Blue Jays and the Cardinals. And I reached out to a very nice man to do our logos and another one to do our photos if people wanted to buy them. And for the end of the season, we always had our trophies and cake and ice cream. My trophy guy was a little bit of a drive away, but he was the only one that had male and female wheelchair tee-ball toppers. And it was important to me that the trophy represent the person. But the most special thing I did for the kids was strike up a relationship with Heather, who handled the media for the Tides. They were our local baseball team. They were constantly losing players because they were being drafted for higher-ranked teams. Players would come to play tee-ball with our kids, take photos, and autograph Tides baseballs. One year we got lucky, and some managers and coaches came instead of players. Even though the tee-ball season only lasted about ten to twelve weeks, it took a lot of planning to make it happen. So I only kept it up for as long as Chaz was interested in it, then SNAIL ceased to exist.

So you see what having Chaz did to me. It turned me into one of those women that sees a problem and goes after it. And when I don't get my way, I'm like a dog with a bone. It's like everything I did after giving birth, I did for my kids.

Because I did stuff for Dustin, too. Who do you think drove to all of those soccer practices? And let's not forget the Boy Scouts. And the BMXing. And if there was an injustice to Dustin in school, I took care of it as if it happened to Chaz. The schools didn't like me. At times, the feeling was mutual.

During all of those years of hours of physical, occupational, and speech therapy at children's hospital, poor old Dustin had to tag along. And to my amazement and everyone that's ever met him, he has always been remarkably quiet. I would give him art supplies, and he'd be fine. He is an artist at heart.

MY, HOW MOM HAS CHANGED

I've gone from being a shy young woman into someone you didn't want to cross. And I don't mean that in a bad way. I was shyly pleasant. But once I was crossed when it came to Chaz, it was near impossible for you to get my trust back. Oh, who am I kidding? It's been twenty-seven years, and the only person that has survived that is Dr. White.

I became the woman that carried a personal organizer around with me. The bigger, the better for me because I needed room to take copious notes. I needed a place to keep track of appointments; to write down who I called, why I called them, what they said, or what time I left a message; to record when I mailed something and when I was promised something. I wrote everything down. And then I wrote reminders to check back on a promised day or in a week. This was the only way that I could keep track of everything.

And it was nice to have at therapy and doctor appointments. You could jot down those little things that you knew you'd forget once you left the office. I still have mine after all these years. And you should see them. They have different colors of ink and even writing on them. (My mood reflects my handwriting. Always has.) I have things written sideways and in between stuff. But I can look at it today and still make sense of it all.

I highly recommend one even today. I know most people put everything in their phones, and that's great and all. But some of us are visualizers, and we like to be able to see our world on pages that we can flip. Besides, by this point, I had also added a few more things to my plate at different times. I had become PTA president. I had sat on a local and regional special education advisory committee. I was giving speeches about where insurance, mostly Medicaid, was missing the mark, especially as it involved primary insurance as well.

I was working on *The Special Needs Club* newsletter while having multiple, how shall I say it, female surgeries along the way. I was arguing about doctors and vendors about products. I had to argue with Chaz's rehab doctor to get a pronestander. I didn't think we argued as much as we disagreed. But the notation in Chaz's chart says differently. Chaz did well with the pronestander, by the way.

I had to argue with his orthopedic doctor to take a body cast off because I knew that he was having muscle spasms in it. And the doctor wanted to just keep giving him medication for pain. So I gave him an ultimatum: remove the cast or I'd do it myself or having someone else do it. Red-faced and all, he removed it bright and early the next morning. That's how we found out he had a staph infection. And yes, he was having muscle spasms in a body cast. And that one still makes me cry today.

The medical equipment vendor that provided Chaz's diapers would every so often send us these horrible ones that would crystalize when Chaz peed in them. And then there would just be a huge mess. I even had the school call me one day and send me a note, too, and say, "Please do not send these brand of diapers ever again." So I told the diaper company that, and they miraculously got Chaz a new brand of diaper. It wasn't great, but at least it didn't crystalize. We went through this for years and years.

Every quarter, or so it felt, I had to go argue with the WIC office. I had to bring my script showing that Chaz needed a certain type of formula and that he got his bloodwork from his pediatrician. I had to go to the health department, with paystubs in tow, to prove that he still qualified for Medicaid. (As his secondary, since his dad's insurance was primary.) And I had to go to social services to make sure he kept his social security income. I hated going to all three. I would come down with a migraine while visiting all three. It would slowly start the day of, and by time I arrived home, I was into a full-blown attack.

And as much as my migraines kept me from doing anything, I remember this one time I had to keep my appointment with the lady from the city. I needed handicapped parking signs put in front of my house. I needed them for several reasons. One, my neighbors parked there, and then I had nowhere to park. Two, Chaz's school bus had nowhere to park but the middle of the street to pick him up and drop him off, and this was dangerous because idiots would try—and most would succeed—going around the bus while he was getting off the lift. And then there's three: I had a van with a lift, and I, too, needed the extra space to put my lift up and down when taking Chaz back and forth with his therapies and appointments. All I had to do was get a doctor to write a letter saying why I needed the signs and that the need was permanent. Dr. White came to the rescue. So I spoke to her, and she said they'd be out tomorrow to put our signs in. To today, I love and appreciate those signs. Because I have no idea what I would do without them. Can you imagine living in the city and have to use a wheelchair lift on a daily basis and not have the room necessary to move the lift up and down? I know I would be very bitchy.

Someone else I had to contact each year, and each IEP meeting, was the head transportation guy. See, our school system was famous for putting special education students on buses for an hour and fifteen minutes. Well, the first few times Chaz came home, he was completely bent over. And I didn't like the way that looked. So I asked his doctor about it. And yes, this was not the way for a child to ride; it could cause breathing problems. And I noticed the ride getting longer. After thirty minutes, I was calling the school and transportation, wondering where they were at. After all, they were only fifteen minutes away.

So I discussed it with his doctors, and we got a note written for a fifteen-minute bus drive with the complications of why longer was not acceptable. Then I called an IEP meeting. And I had one of the area's top advocates go with me, and guess what? Our IEP was written for a fifteen-minute bus ride. Now I didn't care if they were five minutes late. But I did get concerned after that. And here's where I give you some of the best advice I could ever give you. Once you get something in an IEP, keep it there. It's a lot easier to have something removed than it is to try and add it, even if it's been in there before. So just leave it. I left everything that I had to fight for in Chaz's. I wasn't about to fight for those things again. Of course, they would ask each time if it was needed or if it could be changed. And I would always reply, "No."

Let me tell you something else you need to do when you're a mom. You need to go in there with several attitudes. Yes, I said several. The first one is you're the boss, and you won't be messed with. Two, they will not see you upset. Three, you're not a hostage, so you're not going to sign something just so you can get out of the room.

Come prepared. I never walked into an IEP meeting without my trusty sidekicks, which were:

- *The Complete IEP Guide: How to Advocate For Your Special Ed Child* by Attorney Lawrence M. Siegel, purchased from www.nolo.com
- *From Emotions to Advocacy: The Special Education Survival Guide* by Pam and Peter Wright, founders of The Wrights Law website, purchased from www.wrightslaw.com
- *Special Education Law* by Peter and Pamela Wright, purchased from www.wrightslaw.com

I used the IEP one to help craft my IEPs. I used the advocacy one to help me write letters without expletives. And the special education law one I carried with me everywhere. That way, when someone told me that they couldn't do such and such, I asked them where it said that in the special education law. Show me where it says it, and I'll believe you. I'll be honest with you, I got my son through all twelve years of school, and not once did someone show me where something was in the IDEA (Individuals with Disabilities Education Act). And if you haven't visited the Wrights Law website (www.wrightslaw.com), you must. It will help you on the road to becoming your own advocate.

And remember whenever the school system says we can't do that or we don't offer that, ask for proof. And as for the "we don't offer that." If you have documentation that shows your child does need it, then they have to find a way to offer it. Most likely, "we don't offer that" is code for "we don't want to pay for that." And that is not your problem. They have to find a way to make it work. Remember to learn to stand your ground. You will not be liked, and you will be talked about. But your child will get what he or she needs.

DR. DOOLITTLE

Chaz has always been a huge animal lover. He'd pet anything from a slimy snake to a furry dog. He's always loved going to the zoo and the aquarium and anywhere else he can see or pet an animal.

During one of our visits to Lynchburg to see the relatives, we decided to look in the newspaper for puppies. We figured there would be a better selection in the country than there was in the city. And sure enough, there was a man that had golden retriever puppies mixed with flat-coated retriever. We figured we couldn't go wrong with that kind of mixed breed. And he only wanted $50. So we decided to get the kids a puppy. You read that right. I said a puppy.

So I called the guy up and asked for directions. We drove out to his house, and he told us how his prized golden retriever got mixed up with his neighbor's flat-coated retriever one day, and well, he held his arms out to show us these gorgeous puppies. The puppies looked like either Mom, a golden, or Dad, a flat-coated. Dustin walked over and picked him up a golden that was walking around. Chaz asked his dad to pick him up a dog and set him in his lap. He picked up a black flat-coated. Frank and I played with the other puppies as we looked at them. They were all so adorable that it was hard to decide.

We asked the kids which one they wanted. Well, Dustin started walking to the van with his and Chaz refused to let his go. So Frank and I looked at each other and did the only thing good parents who were out of their fucking minds would do and asked the guy if he would do a two-for-one deal. And he did.

Frank's mom wasn't too happy about us coming back to her house with two puppies, especially since it was close to bedtime and we still had a few days in our stay. Of course the puppies whined and did all of the things that puppies do. But Casey, our flat-coated, who was named by Chaz before we even pulled out of the man's driveway, lived for thirteen years. She was a wonderful dog that spent each night on Chaz's bed and floated in the swimming pool with him every time he got in there. She did like to walk around the pool at times and play lifeguard. Casey had some attitude, though. Sometimes after Chaz went to bed, Casey would want to come in the living room with me and Frank and hang out and see what's what. And I didn't care that she did that. But from the other room, all you could hear was Chaz going, "Casey, Casey, Casey." So I'd tell her to go back in there. That didn't always work. So as she grew older, all I had to do was point. I'd point to Chaz's room. She'd start walking that way, stop in the hall, and look at me as if to give me a second chance. I'd keep pointing. I swore I could hear her cussing me out. Then she'd walk super slow back to his room.

Snappy, our golden, was Dustin's buddy and lived to be fifteen. She's the only dog that I'd ever owned that I'd never had to walk on a leash. They were sisters, or litter mates as the vet called them. And they spent the first part of their years in the same bedroom as the boys. And Snappy was one of the most beautiful puppies I ever saw. She too floated in the pool and played lifeguard. She liked to get in the pool even on days when we didn't. Sometimes we would grill out or hang out on the deck. And Snappy would get warm and go for a swim to cool off then join back up with us.

Snappy did scare us to death one day. When the kids shared a bedroom, Frank had made a top-only bunk bed. The bottom part was Chaz and his hospital bed. It faced one way and the top part faced another way, and that's where Dustin slept. But to make it so Snappy would be able to get up there with no problem, Frank built an actual staircase to the top so Snappy could come and go as she pleased. When she was about five years old, she kind of fish flopped down those stairs one morning as the kids were getting ready for school. I panicked. I freaked. That made the kids freak. She laid on the floor for a few minutes afterward and then got up. But she was weak. So we got the kids to school, and we headed to the vet. Turns out she had a seizure. She would have one every few years. And when she hit fourteen, they became more frequent. And when fifteen came along, we had to tell her goodbye.

When Chaz was in elementary school, he owned a Moluccan cockatoo named Jake. Chaz named him, too. He saw him in a pet store one day, and well, the bird was cool. He loved to dance to music and Chaz loved to play music, so they were meant for each other. Jake was cool. I would sometimes take him, on his leash, to the boys' soccer practice so the other kids could see him. He was the chillish bird. I miss him. I think we all do.

After he died, we went out and got another one, and Chaz named him Prince. Prince had his moments of being chill. But Prince got a little too stressed for us, so we had to sell him. We hated to do that because we've never gotten rid of something we've owned. Even the ferrets that Dustin got, Queen Elizabeth and King James, lived their lives out with us. They too liked to swim in the pool. They also liked to walk around the house and pick at the dogs.

We had a community dog, a Dalmatian; we called him Pongo. He was a nutcase. And he absolutely loved Snappy. There was no hanky panky. He just constantly had to make sure that she was nearby, that he could brush up against her, be beside her. He just loved her.

HE'S MY BEST FRIEND

Each year the place that handles Chaz's case management services and service facilitation has a Christmas party. And Chaz doesn't miss it. The best part is that it's during the day so his attendant, whoever that is at the time, gets to go with him. There's food, dancing, socializing, lots of picture taking, some gift raffles, and lots of holiday enjoyment.

Well, this one year, without any warning, Chaz meets this other guy in a wheelchair. They are both decked out in Washington Redskins stuff. So of course they gravitate to each other like moths to a flame. They start talking and realize that they have even more in common. They love playing video games, and they love WWE. That was it. They were now officially friends. They kept talking and getting to know each other. And of course their attendants talked with each other to ensure it was a good fit. And you would have thought that the red-haired boy that was three months older than Chaz came from the same mother. This is something Danny's mother did later say to me. And I too later said it after I saw the two of them in conversation. They were like twins. They had so much in common that it was unbelievable.

So they started talking to each other every day through FaceTime. By that I mean they stayed on there all day and into the night. So every time you went into Chaz's room, Danny was basically there also. That's kind of how I got to know what little I did know of his parents.

Arrangements were made for mall meet-ups and lunches. They saw each other when their case management place held meet-ups at their place. And there were things like football games, a cookout at our house, and the air show. We did what we could to get them together in person. But they logged some hours on FaceTime. And it did feel like Danny was in the room all the time. And we would have conversations with his mom and dad because they were there on video and loudspeaker. I thought of it as a new way of communicating. It was a new way of communication for people who have special needs and can't always get out and about and for those who are homebound for whatever reason. For example, a quarantine during a pandemic.

Chaz has another friend that he FaceTimes with a lot, and that's Tanner. Now he's known Tanner a little longer than Danny. But they met over the love of video games and because of their disabilities and the disability community that they come from. You can find them on there for hours. The thing is they are usually never alone. They usually always have other people with them. That's what drives me nuts. I'll go in the room to ask him something or to give him something, and he'll want me to say hello to four, six, or eight people.

Oh yeah, that reminds me. Chaz has this weird belief that if he's on FaceTime with someone and I walk in the room that I, too, should be on FaceTime with them. And he'll turn the phone rather quickly at me and go, "Mom, meet Tanner." Or, "Mom, meet Jeff." And then I'm standing there going, "Okay, hello." Then what? So I have to ask them a few questions. You know, how are they doing. General stuff. Nothing personal. And then I bail out really quick. It's best to say that I have something on the stove or in the oven. And then I give Chaz a mean look.

But he keeps doing it. He's immune to mean looks. I think that's why I don't even bother anymore. I just roll my eyes and go with it.

Oh, and then he has his PlayStation friends. He gets online with PlayStation sometimes just to talk to people. He doesn't even play a game. He just talks to "his friends." In a way, it's adorable. In a way, it breaks my heart because he has been bullied before and quite often at that. He's even had a pedophile come after him online. It's just sad that you'd want friendship so much that you would talk to people you don't know just to have someone to talk to. We have finally gotten his PlayStation list down to people that we do know who their screennames really are. So we currently know the actual people that he talks to online. But it's still scary because someone will always bring someone new in and then someone else and that's how it goes. But you can't constantly stay on top of all of that. Now we do ask the attendants to try and help out. But it's hard and time consuming, though we do our best.

One thing is for sure: I can die happy knowing that Chaz does have great friends that will be with him for years to come. And they are Danny and Tanner. Thanks, boys.

I AM LION HEAR
ME ROAR

When I decided to go back to school, Chaz was getting ready to graduate and Dustin had one year left. I figured that they were at a point in their lives where they didn't need me full-time anymore. So one day, I sat in front of my computer and signed up. Then it took me a couple of months to do all of the necessary paperwork. But I did it. And I chose the home of Big Blue. For those of you that don't know, Big Blue is a lion. And a very cute and fuzzy one at that.

Since I was a student, I got in free to basketball games, so I started buying tickets to the girls' games and drag the family along. But it was Chaz who went most of the time. So for four years, we sat up in the corner of the 200 section of the sports arena, ate popcorn, drank huge sodas, and cheered the girls along. And just about every time we showed up for a game, Big Blue would be at the entrance greeting people. And Chaz had to have a picture every time. It took about a decade, but he finally got over that fear of mascots.

Chaz loved attending the girls' games. He had a couple of favorites over the years. But his favorite was the girls coach, Karen Barefoot. I attended a fundraiser on campus once where a silent auction was held and one of the items was an autographed basketball by Karen Barefoot. There were other items, like baskets of bath products, reading materials, tea drinking, and other baskets that a mom like me would have loved. But I saw that ball, and I had to have it. So I circled that table up until time was called, and I made sure that I made it home the lucky winner. That's been quite a few years ago. That ball is still displayed proudly on his shelf.

But let me tell you something funny about Big Blue. He has some super fans. One in particular is Danny P. Danny has a labradoodle named Charles that he shaves to look like a lion. Funny thing is Charles got loose way back when and people actually thought there was an actually lion running loose. Since then, Charles's popularity has grown. There's even a book, *Charles the Lion Dog*.

But things get odder, as they often do in Chaz's world. We were in one of the pizza joints by the college one day, and Chaz, who has to stare at people when he's out—I swear he's a sociologist at heart—was staring at the people at the bar while we were eating. They were eating and laughing, whereas our family was just eating. So yes, there was more fun coming from the bar. Well, this red-faced, round-shaped man came over to the table and walked up to Chaz and said, "What's up, motherfucker?" Now, everyone knows not to argue with a drunk. But you could tell that this guy meant no harm in his words. Of course, Chaz started laughing. He laughed so hard he squirted drink out of his face. Then the man said, "Take that, motherfucker." And I looked at Dustin and said, "I just found my *Real Housewives* tagline." So the guy joked a few more expletives with Chaz then went back to the bar. Before we left, he asked if Chaz could come over to the bar and have a shot with them, and we said yes. The bar guy made sure it was okay with us. Then when we got ready to leave, the man introduced himself as Danny P. and said that he meant no harm. We knew he didn't. We've met too many people over the years to even begin to think that he was strange.

So we started going to that pizza place more regularly, as Dustin and

Frank liked the pizza. Chaz liked the clientele. And I was there for the family. I couldn't shake off the feeling that I knew this guy from somewhere. Well, during our next visit when he came over to ask "motherfucker" if he wanted to sit at the bar with him and his friends, we said yes. That's when it hit me. "You're Charles's dad." And damn if I wasn't right.

So Danny P. and Chaz became drinking buddies. And Danny P.'s drinking buddies became Chaz's drinking buddies. So now when we go to that pizza place, unless we have a relative visiting from out of town, Chaz sits at the bar with Danny P. and the rest of us sit at a table. Since then, Chaz and Charles have met several times and Danny has become one of Chaz's best friends. And so have the others at the end of the bar.

ROUND, ROUND,
I GET AROUND

When my kids were younger, we were the house that the neighborhood kids flocked to. It might be because I had two daredevils, dogs, and snacks, and we actually talked to the kids when they were here. We'd have kids on bikes, kids on skateboards, and Chaz on his power wheelchair. Over the years, Chaz had accumulated a bunch of mobile equipment.

So if you came down my street—which, after you did it the first time, you didn't dare to it a second time—you'd find a train of kids. There would be Chaz leading in his power wheelchair with someone holding on while sitting in a manual wheelchair then someone holding to that guy on either a skateboard or a bike, and if it was charged, Chaz's old power wheelchair. And sometimes there would be ten or more kids out there doing this.

When the skateboarders and bikers would do tricks, Chaz made sure he wasn't left out, and he would do wheelies in his power wheelchair. And sometimes people, like Dustin, would stand on the back of the wheelchair while he did the wheelie. Chaz would also do donuts. Dustin still does donuts in Chaz's wheelchair. He did one the other day while sitting in the living room.

Chaz has had a few accidents, though. One time Dustin told him not to cut across the church parking lot because they had blocked it off with a chain. Well, Chaz ended up clotheslining himself. It wasn't pretty. But I think he learned to listen a little more.

Another time, Chaz wanted to go fast from one block to another. The city had finally put in accessible curbs. And he was going too fast and everyone told him not to, including Dustin. And he did it anyway. And whoop! He hit that curb going full speed. The base of the wheelchair hit the curb and kind of sat there while the seating system came off of the base and threw Chaz face first onto the concrete. Dustin ran over to him and help him up. He was screaming for people to call us. They were only a few blocks away. But neighbors were coming out of houses to see if they could help. And poor old Dustin was trying to hold Chaz's face and chest off the concrete. Some girl we didn't know called and told us Chaz had an accident. And Frank went flying up there. Well, Chaz was laughing by this point. He was black and blue and scabbed for weeks. His face, neck, arms, and chest were all messed up. But thank God he didn't break anything. At least not on his body. His wheelchair needed some assistance. It actually needed about five figures' worth of repairs. But I guess you could chalk it up to him being out there just being a kid with the rest of them on wheels.

When he first got one of his really fast wheelchairs, he loved to spin in circles. In the house. We warned him that one day he was going to hurt himself. He stayed lucky for months. Then one morning before school, *boom*, broke some toes on my coffee table in the living room. You should have seen us in the emergency room. How did he break his toes? We looked at Chaz like, "Aren't you going to answer?" He only smiled. So we had to tell the doctor about the spinning in circles story.

Oh, and another time we had gone to play tennis, and Chaz and Dustin wanted to take their dogs. Since it was an enclosed court, I didn't mind. Well, the dogs chased the balls. Tennis with dogs became a whole new game. Wouldn't you know it, a ball rolled under Chaz's wheelchair at just the right spot and flipped he went. All I could think was, *Does this happen to other kids in power wheelchairs?*

Well, Dustin started hanging out at the skate park. Bikers hung out there, too. Because they had these things called bowls that you'd ride your bike into and fly out of and flip and turn and stuff. Well, Chaz liked to go and hang out with the people. The skate park also had a beginner's section. The rules did not say wheelchairs were not permitted. So Chaz got him an ID card and guess what? Yep. He was now officially able to ride his wheelchair on the grounds of the skate park. Frank thought I was crazy to let him do it. I figured if he stayed on the beginner's side and went slow, he should be okay. The first few times he did it, I cringed inside. Not outside, though. All of the others would stop so they wouldn't get in his way. And he took turns with the others so he wouldn't have any obstacles or have to stop suddenly because some biker or skateboarder flew up into his way. Well, I'm happy to say that he never had one accident on the grounds of the skate park.

Chaz still likes to do wheelies at times. Not donuts as much. Not because of the danger but because he's nosey. He's too busy watching everything going on around him to drive fast enough to cause any trouble, though he does have trouble stopping quickly. So you might possibly get run over. And for that, I'm sorry. But it's the story of our lives.

CHAZ LIKES TO MOVE
IT, MOVE IT

Chaz may have been required to spend the rest of his life in a power wheelchair, but that didn't stop him from participating in sports. He started off playing tee-ball. A friend of his suggested it. And he was able to have a buddy. Frank and I took turns at first. Then we noticed that siblings were actually doing the buddying. So we let Dustin take over. And he developed his own friendships and his own love of tee-ball.

As he got a little older, he got interested in power wheelchair soccer. And there's two ways to explain this to you. One is to ask you to watch the documentary *Murderball*. The next is to ask you to imagine football mixed with soccer but in metal wheelchairs. The players usually don't use their own wheelchairs for this sport. They usually use sports wheelchairs that are equipped with these buckets around the front to protect the foot and leg area. It's the buckets that you use to "kick" the ball with. And you have a goalie, just like in real soccer. But there is a lot of crashing and smashing of wheelchairs. The first few times you watch this, you're like, "Cool, bumper cars." Then you're like, "That's gotta hurt." Chaz liked it. There was this guy that played. I wish I could remember his name. He had no arms or legs, but he had this sense of humor that kept you in stitches. You could come in there half asleep, in a bad mood, depressed, it didn't matter, he'd cheer you up. He always had a joke or a smart comment. Smart comments were something I could relate to. But it was an expensive sport. Since so few participate in it, you had to travel far and wide to play against other teams, and that cost money. And we didn't have that kind of money.

Chaz also played tennis. This one he did from his manual wheelchair. What I remember most about this one was that this boy had an assistance dog that came with him each week. And his dog looked like Casey. Chaz wanted to show off his Casey, so I asked if I could bring Chaz's Casey one week for show and tell. Well, our two Caseys hit it off. The other thing I remember most is having to run around the tennis court and chase all of those damn balls. Chaz got where he could hit some balls. It was weird watching someone hit left handed. I kept wanting to correct him, even though I was not his instructor. He tried. That's what mattered most.

He also loved wheelchair basketball. This wasn't the contact sport that soccer was. They kept enough distance that they typically never got within reach of one another. Now Chaz and basketball were meant to be. Dribbling, not so much. Shooting, that was his game. We had a basketball set up in our driveway, and we would play whenever possible. We even invented a Chaz-friendly way to play H.O.R.S.E.

As you know, when you play H.O.R.S.E., the first player shoots at the basket from anywhere on the court. If they make the basket, the second player must attempt the same shot. If the first player misses, the second player can shoot from anywhere. And you continue this pattern for the duration of the game.

Okay, in a game of H.O.R.S.E. with Chaz, he can make any shot he wants, at any time. Now if he makes it, then the person behind him has to make the person's shot before them unless Chaz's shot is harder. But if Chaz misses, then the person behind him has to make the shot that they shot previously. Or something to that extent.

Later on, he decided to play bocce. For this one, I got to take my baby with me. It was played outdoors on a Saturday afternoon. There were other sports going on at the same time. And I took my nana with me. Nana was my rescued Australian Shepherd that was a therapy dog. That was her decision, not mine. I say that because her demeanor totally changed when she was around people with disabilities or people in need or in certain settings that required a dog to act like a professional. I took her to all of the necessary classes, and she passed with flying colors, doing things right the first time. When we went to the local hospital for her "test," she passed that, too. For one, we had to walk through the kitchen where they clanked pots and pans. She didn't jump. We rode the elevator, and she didn't shake. We met various people, including patients, and she didn't shy away. My baby was born to be a therapy dog. When not on duty, she was my bestest friend in the whole wide world. So on bocce days, we would go and watch Chaz and people would come up to her and pet her and talk to her. She held many secrets in her time. But, like everything else, Chaz grew bored.

Over the years, he accumulated many trophies, ribbons, medallions, and certificates, so many that I'm not sure I've kept track of them all.

He's participated in various therapeutic recreation activities for almost two decades now. He's done a little bit of everything: karate, arts and crafts, swimming, bowling, movie nights, theater, bar hopping, out to lunch, shopping, day for people with disabilities at the zoo, and the list goes on. Chaz keeps busy, more so than the rest of us. Then again, his dad and I take him to these places and pick him up, so I guess you could say that we stay busy, too.

WASHINGTON, DC, IS LIKE DISNEYWORLD FOR CURIOUS AND ADVENTUROUS KIDS

When we owned our medical equipment company, we actually had money to go on a vacation. Meaning, somewhere that wasn't our parents' house. The fun thing about DC is that the museums are free. You get to see and learn a lot. There's a gift shop at every stop. And you have to eat out every meal. It's a kid's dream. And a parent's, too. Because you can do one museum a day if you want. Or be bold and do two.

The hotels in the area are wonderful. I've never been in a bad one yet. And trust me, we test their patience. I have not just two kids but one with special needs. So I need extra of this. Less of that. Can you get me some of this? Or how about that? I don't usually just ask straight up. I do when I'm inquiring about and making the reservation. But after that, I only ask if they ask first if they can help me. Then I tend to take them up on it. But it wouldn't be just me thanking them, it would be the kids, too. And we believed in tipping everyone.

After the first two trips to DC, we learned to bring about fifty-one dollar bills with us. We had to. Chaz was famous for stopping and talking to every homeless person he came across. And I mean every one of them. So at first we gave him fifty dollars to spend the few days we were there. Then it wasn't long before we bumped it up to one hundred. Because there appeared to be more homeless people and Chaz tended to flock to them and they to him. Sometimes he would carry fifteen- and twenty-minute conversations with them. Sometimes I'd understand what they were saying and other times I wouldn't. His dad and brother and I would walk off to the side and let Chaz do his thing, whatever that was. And whatever it was would end with them smiling and telling Chaz, "God bless you," and them looking to us and saying, "He's special. He's got God in him." This would happen year after year. You'd almost think he was some sort of waking prophet or messiah. I just know each year when I went to the bank teller to tell her why I needed all of the ones, whomever waited on me was fascinated with the story.

Chaz was also the only person that could go to Washington, DC, and actually run into people he knew. It happened all of the time. This didn't happen to the rest of us. He would run into teachers, therapists, paraprofessionals, doctors, all kinds of people.

On our first or second trip to a DC museum, we were looking at one of the exhibits. And I don't know if he got bored or what, but when we turned around, Chaz was gone. Dustin was still right there with us looking at the exhibit. We thought Chaz was. So we looked around and saw no Chaz. I mean, he's kind of hard to miss in a 250-pound power wheelchair. But no luck. So we started asking people if they'd seen him, and they hadn't. So I saw a guard and went off to ask him while Frank went down a corridor to look for Chaz.

When I told the guard that my son with special needs was missing and could he help me find him, he told me that I had to go downstairs. They had an office especially for that. To be honest, I wanted to punch him in the face. "You guys have walkies. You can't announce something?" I asked. He politely said no. So I ran to tell Frank and Dustin where I was going before I went there. They were on the trail: a couple had seen him go down a different corridor a few moments ago. So we started following the people that said they'd seen him. We found him about twenty to thirty minutes later. We hugged him and yelled at him at the same time. And wouldn't you know it, we went to lunch and still stopped by the gift shop.

But back at the hotel, Mommy and Daddy had some daiquiris. Yes, more than two. The kids had their own special daiquiris. We had a few and went to bed. It had been an interesting day, to say the least.

On another trip to DC, Frank took his mom. He said that she was getting up in age, and he wanted to take her. Of course we had to buy a transport wheelchair for her because we knew she couldn't do all of that walking. Well, she grumped and bitched at every bump and crack. But she loved not having to sit and talk to other people from out of town. And she too learned to like daiquiris. And we made it all work in a one-bedroom suite. The kids shared one pull-out sofa and their nanny the other and Frank and I the bed. So at night it was crowded. But we were too tired to care.

On another trip to DC, we took my dad with us. He would only agree if he didn't have to pay for anything. He said it so many times that I finally told him to leave his wallet at home. We did pay for everything. But let me tell you a few things about this trip. One day we went to this gift shop by the hotel. He took the kids through there asking them if they liked this and that and grabbing everything they said yes to. Then he set it all on the counter and came and found me and said, "The kids picked some stuff out, over there, they want to buy." I thought it might be two or three things. It was about ten.

But the next morning, Frank and I woke up and the kids and my dad were gone. We had no idea where they went to. When they finally showed up, we found out that they went for a very long walk before the very long walking we would be doing that day. We thought they were nuts. On another morning, they went to ESPN and played some games. Didn't these people ever sleep in?

I don't think there's a museum or restaurant that we didn't visit during our vacations to DC I miss them, actually. We miss them. I hope we get at least one more in. I know Chaz and Dustin would love to also.

LIFE IN 2020:
WHEN HORROR MOVIES
COME TRUE

I love a good horror movie. Or I guess I should say a good thriller with lots of drama. One that I watched in early 2020 was *Contagion*, which I've watched at least once or twice a year since it came out in 2011.

It's very well written, directed, filmed, and acted upon. If you haven't seen it, let me tell you a little about it. A woman returns from a business trip from Hong Kong and appears to have the flu and dies. Her very young son dies the same day. Her husband appears immune. So at this point, the virus has already begun to spread. Only no one knows it. Well, the doctors and administrators at the U.S. Centers for Disease Control take several days before they realize just how far this infection has reached and how deadly it is. Now they have to try and identify the virus before they can find a way to combat it. And we all know that takes several months to a year or longer. Well, the contagion spreads around the world, chaos erupts, people run out of food, looting begins, societal order begins to break down, and people panic. In a way, it becomes every man for himself.

Now as a movie, this is scary. That's why I classify it as more of a horror movie. Because just the thought of that ever happening is terrifying. And watching that movie gets your adrenaline going, and you want to grab your blankets and pull them tight around you and turn it off knowing that no such thing could ever possibly happen. After all, it's only a movie.

Then a few days later, you turn on CNN and you hear that Wuhan, China, has a virus that is spreading and the United States is one of those areas. Then each week the news gets a little bit more serious. Then they're shutting down the country. No one is coming in or going out. Schools and businesses must close. People and families must stay home. Do not go out unless it's absolutely necessary. Then there's a shortage on cleaning supplies, toilet supplies, paper products, then food, meat has a buying limit. We have to wear mask and stay six feet apart.

And we must quarantine. No more socializing with anyone outside those that live within the wall of our home. And no one knows who has what because there's no test available. And the hospital isn't seeing you unless it's in the emergency room. And here you have a child that, yes, by law is an adult, with special needs, that could have a seizure at any moment. And if he has to go to the hospital—which you pray he doesn't because people there have the coronavirus—you are not allowed to go with him. He's twenty-six years old and has never been to the hospital by himself before and can't answer any of the questions you're going to ask him. But due to the virus, it's too risky to let me, his mom, go with him if he should have to go. And you're telling me not to freak out. Well, guess what? I'm freaking the fuck out! And not just because I can't go with my son with special needs to the hospital, but because there's a virus out there randomly selecting people to kill. And I happen to meet some of the criteria of one of the people it will kill first. So yes, the movie *Contagion* is real, and it's no longer a thriller or a horror movie. It's reality. And it's landed on our doorstep. And we're doing everything we can to keep that doorstep clean.

The hardest part was telling our son and granddaughter that we couldn't see them during the quarantine. That lasted two weeks. Then my daughter-in-law said the baby had to come over. We gave them the third degree and made them wash before they touched us or anything. This was pre-mask.

My son has an attendant, and we left it up to her if she wanted to work or not. She was in the same position as us. She had a child whose health she often worried about. But she was out of school and home with her partner since teachers were out, too. So she was being as protective as we were. Besides, everything was closed and no one was socializing. And we were all doing plenty of hand washing. So she worked her normal hours.

My son works for the shipyard, so they had them on a coronavirus-free lockdown, too. We were all praying we were making the right decisions. Sadly, this meant that all of Chaz's therapeutic recreation center activities were canceled. After all, the city was closed.

So he was missing things like the Sweetheart Ball and the Spring Fling, two dances where they get together and socialize and munch. Then there were the Friday Night Retreats. Those could be anything from movies to seeing a play, which Chaz always loved, and they saw at least one per quarter. He was going to do Top Golf this time, and I couldn't wait to hear all about it. Instead, all of these were canceled. Everything for 2020 has been canceled. And no one knows if or when they'll start back up. That's the problem. It's the *if* part. The city has had to lay off so many people due to a deficit that we might lose our therapeutic recreation center. And then so many people with disabilities will lose their activities, activities like weekly bowling and swimming and so much more. I can't speak for everyone else, but Chaz has been participating for fifteen years. We love the TRC. We pray they will come back. We need them to come back.

So what the TRC decided to do in May was to host a couple of Zoom meetings. This allowed any of the participants that were interested and that had the ability to to sit in and see and check up on each other. It was very emotional. I had planned on making sure Chaz was connected and his camera was in the right direction. But when I saw these people in all of their excitement screaming out names, pointing at screens, smiling ear to ear, I had to sit in. These are people that are used to seeing each other weekly at one event or another. And it brought a tear to my eye.

Chaz happened to be lying in bed for the first call, and I tell you he about jumped out of the bed when he started seeing people pop up on the screen because he was screaming people's names and pointing, too. Especially when he saw the other Chaz. Yes, folks, there are two. And when you get them together, the TRC will tell you that you're in for a treat because they are their very own comedy team.

But the TRC decided to do more Zoom calls. You know Chaz will be in on every one of them. Even though some are starting phase two of the quarantine lift, we are not venturing out there anytime soon. We're going to wait and see how it goes for everyone else.

In the meantime, Chaz will use video messenger and watch WWE without an audience. I don't think having just the other wrestlers there really counts. It's kind of like that WrestleMania t-shirt I bought him this year. You had a choice of one that told you about WrestleMania and then one that told you the truth. It added the words, "I wasn't there." You know which one he got.

REFLECTION

I t's been twenty-seven years this year. Chaz just turned twenty-seven a few short weeks ago. And his attendant and I took a fun day drive to North Carolina to pick up a puppy for him. His dog died last year. And for the past few months, he's been talking about how he missed having a dog.

I said, "Okay. We'll look for one." And his dad and I did. Intermittently. I had rescued my two Aussies a few years before from someone that has his heart in the right place but doesn't know a thing about taking care of dogs. And that experience pained me. We decided to go the rescue route again. So his attendant and I had a nice drive to the outer banks to pick up another Aussie puppy. We had a nice drive. It was like a mini-vacation. For a few hours, we forgot about the horrors of the world. Then we got close, and I got sick. Thank God for Klonopin and open windows. We put on our pleasant faces. Said our hellos. Laughed at his jokes. Grabbed our puppy and away we went. I don't even remember leaving. Hell, I don't even remember getting in the car and driving away. I don't know which way she left there.

All I know is that somewhere on the drive back, I made the comment that he was sleeping. And in my sheer form, I added that I had to pee. I was finally coming out of whatever trance I was in. We agreed that it was still a mini-vacation. A nice drive to North Carolina. Coming back with a sleeping puppy. And in full disclosure, I peed a little on her front seat when I stood to get up. I look at her and said, "I'm sorry. I told you I had to pee two hours ago." Damn coronavirus. No public restrooms are open.

I actually took the puppy for his first puppy visit today. He's healthy as a lark. Whatever that means. That's just something I grew up hearing and saying. And our other two Aussies love him. Especially our crazy Aussie. He even got in the pool with us over Memorial Day.

So, like everything in Chaz's life, in our lives, there's always some shit to go with the diamonds. So you take what life throws at you. You find a way to make it work. And there you have it.

I know that if anyone would have told me that I'd be raising a child with special needs, I would have thought they were insane. Especially a child with physical challenges. Think about it, I had never babysat any child or baby before. And now you were going to give me a child with these kinds of challenges. And you were going to throw seizures, medications, surgeries, botched surgeries, and doctors with God complexes on me. And I was a shy child. An even shier teenager. Now I was expected to be an advocate. I was expected to look a therapist, a nurse, a doctor in the eye and say, "No. Chaz is not going to have that." "No. Chaz does not need that medication." "No. We are not going to put him in that device." And the no's would just keep coming and coming.

I was expected to argue with school personnel. I was expected to look a school principal in the eye and say, "Could you move your car from the handicapped parking spot so I can pull in there to get my son's wheelchair out of the van?" You have no idea how many schools that happened at. I had to argue with school principals and special education directors and such on services and equipment for Chaz. I had to tell them that I don't care where the money comes from. That's not my problem. The IEP calls for it. So you must provide it.

What I didn't know on the day that I gave birth was that I had a voice. And that God expected me to use that voice to advocate for Chaz. And if I didn't feel like the breastfeeding wasn't working and that he wasn't getting enough, then I should have told them all to go to hell and to bring me some formula. I should have told Frank that we were going to formula feed and let God find a way to help us get formula. I should have asked more questions in the hospital. I should have had some more one-on-one time with nurses in the hospital. I should have let Chaz stay in the hospital without me. I should have argued with the nurse over the phone at the pediatrician's office. I should have changed pediatricians immediately when the one I had wouldn't call me back at the hospital.

I should have listened to that gut instinct and followed it wherever it took me. I should have used that new mom voice that I gave birth to that day. Because I didn't just give birth to a son that day; I gave birth to a new me. I became a mom. That meant that I was now expected to take care of this person. And one way to do that was to be vocal about his wants and needs. And I should have done that and said to hell with what everyone else wanted, said, did, or desired. But I didn't.

So when God saved Chaz, he gave Chaz and me a new platform to do that. He used Chaz's near-death experience as a way to save other infants from a horrible fate. He brought attention to a cause that isn't that uncommon. It's more common than you know. It's just no one talks about it. Mothers are ashamed. Hell, if you can't do the one so-called normal, natural thing of breastfeeding your own kid, then you must be a really shitty mother. Right? Wrong! Women can't help when their breasts don't work right. Just like women can't help when they can't have a baby. And we can't help when our thyroid doesn't work right. Or when our eyesight is bad.

In my case, it was a multitude of things. I never produced breastmilk. Chaz was ten pounds four ounces; my body couldn't handle producing even colostrum for him. Chaz had a rough time coming out. They broke his right clavicle. They used suction on him. Then they cut me and gave me fifty-two stitches. The doctor even said later on that maybe they should have pushed him back up the birth canal and given me a C-section. Maybe they should have because then we'd both been able to stay in the hospital for a week and would definitely had been formula feeding.

The thing is it's been twenty-seven very long years, and I'm so tired of beating myself up over not listening to myself. Okay. Lesson learned. Lesson learned in spades.

As for the other people involved, I'm not there yet. I want to be. What is it that they say, you forgive others to make things better for yourself? I want to. Even though not one of them believes they did anything wrong, that I feel quite sure of. I'm not as hardened as I was. Thinking of them causes my head to ache.

And I know that's what everyone wants to hear, that I've made peace with all of this. And in some degree, I have. And in some ways, I have. But I'm just not over it. My child was harmed at the hands of others. That's not something you just get over. Remember, I'm still his mother. I'm still protecting him. I'm still advocating for him.

They say time heals everything. I think I need more time.

I WILL LEAVE YOU WITH ONE THING . . .

It's always been said that Chaz has a contagious smile. People in grocery lines or amusement park lines have complimented Chaz on his smile. They've said that seeing him smile has made their day. It's even been said that he could be a motivational speaker. "Of what?" I've asked. Nothing. He just has to be himself and sit there and smile.

So in case you're having a bad day or I left you feeling not quite satisfied, then here's a smile, just for you. Take one and save it to your phone so when you're having a bad day or you need a little pick me up, remember that through it all, this is how Chaz looks each and every day. So smile.

BELOW ARE RANDOM SMILES FROM CHAZ.

Figure 41: Chaz and his niece Aubrey

The End

AFTERWORD

Few Americans today are aware that, following the development of cow's milk-based infant formulas in the early 20th century, formula feeding of infants became the predominant method of infant feeding in the US throughout the 1940s, '50s, and '60s. During this era, medical training reflected a diminished emphasis on breastfeeding, leaving a generation of health professionals ill-equipped to knowledgeably assess breastfeeding dyads and effectively counsel new breastfeeding mothers. This radical change in infant feeding norms also left nearly an entire generation of grandmothers with no personal breastfeeding experience to enable them to support their breastfeeding daughters and daughters-in-law.

The movement to "return to breastfeeding" began in the mid-1970s, with US breastfeeding rates slowly increasing until 1995, and then climbing markedly thereafter. Despite more mothers choosing to nurse their babies at the time Chaz was born, the lactation education of health professionals lagged far behind the renewed enthusiastic promotion of breastfeeding. To make matters worse, traditional hospital maternity practices did not support the optimal initiation of breastfeeding, and the early follow-up of newborns was not yet routine practice.

Pam Floyd gave birth to Chaz in 1993, during the shameful era of "drive-thru" deliveries, before postpartum length-of-stay laws were enacted to comply with guidelines from the American Academy of Pediatrics (AAP) and American College of Obstetricians and Gynecologists. The enthusiastic promotion of breastfeeding far outpaced essential safety-nets in medical care necessary to ensure optimal newborn outcomes. The "every woman can breastfeed" myth was in vogue, along with its sister myths, "every breastfed newborn will drink the amount of milk she or he needs" and "just one bottle of formula can sabotage breastfeeding." At the time Chaz was born, the first newborn pediatric visit typically occurred at two weeks of age, thus preventing the timely recognition of critically underweight newborns. It wasn't until 1997 that the AAP began recommending that all newborns be seen at an early post-discharge "safety net" visit within 48-72 hours after going home from the birth hospital.

Pam Floyd and I were among the multiple parents and lactation experts who were interviewed by journalist Kevin Helliker for his July 22, 1994, frontpage article in the *Wall Street Journal*, "Dying for Milk: Some Mothers, Trying in Vain to Breast-Feed, Starve Their Infants." In allowing her compelling story and her image—with adorable Chaz on her lap—to be widely disseminated, Pam heroically chose to personalize and publicize the previously taboo topic of "breastfeeding morbidity."

Pam's courageous conviction to share her story and highlight the controversial topic of breastfeeding tragedy has helped to spur many positive changes in hospital maternity care practices, to ensure the early follow-up and assessment of breastfed newborns, and to incorporate essential breastfeeding education in the training of health professionals. Today, we acknowledge that at least 5 percent of US women, for various medical reasons, are unable to produce sufficient milk. We also now recognize that an even larger percentage of newborns may be unable to breastfeed effectively at first, placing them at risk of losing a dangerous amount of weight after birth. Today, however, mothers of at-risk newborns use hospital-grade electric breast pumps to help them establish an abundant milk supply and ensure that their infants remain well-nourished while they are learning to take enough milk by direct breastfeeding. In addition, highly accurate infant scales are now readily available to confirm whether an infant is able to consume sufficient milk during a breastfeeding session.

While additional advances in breastfeeding support are far too numerous to cite here, they include: the presence of lactation care providers in maternity hospitals, obstetric, pediatric, family medicine, and public health settings; the Workplace Accommodations for Nursing Mothers Act; the provision of breast pumps under the Affordable Care Act; Designated Breastfeeding Experts in the USDA WIC Program; Breastfeeding Coalitions in all fifty states; and much, much more. Breastfeeding advocates everywhere owe Pam a debt of gratitude for her bold, tenacious, and enduring campaign to make what happened to Chaz be recognized as a "never ever" medical event. Now, this book will go a step further in ensuring that the paradoxical term, "breastfeeding morbidity," is eliminated from our medical vocabulary!

Finally, I want to emphasize that the central message of Pam's memoir extends far beyond the first six days of Chaz's life, when a senseless tragedy struck the Floyd family. The broader message of Pam's and Chaz's story is that of a mother's unwavering love and a child's unwavering resilience. It is a compelling story of steadfast advocacy, struggle, and endurance, culminating in ultimate acceptance and transformation. Pam's untiring activism on behalf of her own child has helped advance the rights and well-being of countless other persons with intellectual and physical disabilities. What I perceived between the lines in Pam's heartfelt account was: "Parenting this precious child has made me who I am today . . . which is far more courageous, defiant, compassionate, resilient, grateful, and loving than I ever would have been!"

Marianne Neifert, MD, MTS, FAAP
Pediatrician, Academy of Breastfeeding Medicine Co-Founder,
Author, Colorado Women's Hall of Fame 2020 Inductee

ACKNOWLEDGMENTS

I'm grateful that we live where there is a children's hospital. And I'm grateful that the Kluge Center is within driving distance. I want to thank the Muse Writer's Center and those I had classes with that helped me fine-tune this. Your support has meant more to me over the years than I can say.

I want to thank Becky Helliker for helping me edit. I was a reluctant participant, but she finally won me over. I have to thank Joe Coccaro for line editing. Thank you Jessica Meigs for copy editing. Thanks to Kellie Emery and Ariana Abud for my cover. Thank you to Lauren Sheldon for designing the interior of my book. Thank you to John Koehler for taking a chance on me.

Thanks to Michelle Rose for taking my headshots. She had to put up with me on a migraine day, and I'm grateful.

Frank has been with me through everything Chaz has gone through. Not many couples make it through the things we did. And here we are, thirty-one years later. So I have to thank him for hanging in there. And poor Dustin spent most of his young life attending therapies and doctor visits. He was always quiet and well-behaved. More importantly, he always had a positive attitude. I have to thank Chaz for going through everything he has and still finding a way to smile. It's his smile that makes me smile.

I thanked Dr. White earlier. I have to tell you that he was an exceptional child neurologist. He was with Chaz from day six to when he turned twenty-one. Even though he's retired, I still like to run things by him. He became what I like to call "the Chaz Whisperer." I'm not sure how things would have turned out without his support through all of those years. He's the reason Chaz is alive. And for that, I'm eternally grateful.

Like I said earlier, God and I have a complicated relationship. He's there when I need him. He answers my prayers. He also knows that I'm not fond of the fact that I have to ask for his help. But I thank him for guiding the doctors in the right direction so he is still with us and enjoying life twenty-seven years later.

CPSIA information can be obtained
at www.ICGtesting.com
Printed in the USA
LVHW091932210721
693319LV00001B/5